CW00767152

MICK IMLAH
SELECTED PROSE

MICK IMLAH
SELECTED PROSE

Preface by

MARK FORD

Edited by

ANDRÉ NAFFIS-SAHELY
& ROBERT SELBY

Peter Lang Oxford

First published in 2015 by

Peter Lang Ltd
International Academic Publishers
52 St Giles, Oxford
Oxfordshire OX1 3LU
United Kingdom

www.peterlang.com

André Naffis-Sahely & Robert Selby have asserted
their moral right under the Copyright, Designs
and Patents Act of 1988 to be identified as the Editors of this Work.

© Peter Lang Ltd 2015

A catalogue record for this book is available from the British Library

ISBN 978-1-906165-53-6 (print)
ISBN 978-3-0353-0725-2 (eBook)

COVER ILLUSTRATION:

Isabel Fonseca

Every effort has been made to trace copyright holders and to obtain their permission
for the use of copyright material. The publisher apologises for any errors or omissions
and would be grateful for notification of any corrections that should be incorporated
in future reprints or editions of this book.

Printed in the United Kingdom by TJ International Ltd

In Memoriam

Michael Ogilvie Imlah
(1956–2009)

Contents

Preface

In the essay that he wrote for the *Oxford Poetry* issue (XIII, no. 2, Winter 2009) devoted to Mick Imlah's life and work, Alan Hollinghurst praised the 'canny wit' and 'fraternal tenderness' of Mick's discussion of writers, such as Robert Bridges and Laurence Binyon, who were popular enough in their time, but are nowadays not much read. Mick's critical pieces, Hollinghurst continued, 'deserve to be collected, for their own merits, and also as adjuncts to his growth as a poet'. This volume contains all Mick's most significant reviews and literary essays, and does, I believe, fully bear out his friend's assessment. Mick was a shrewd and entertaining critic, whether writing on canonical favourites such as Tennyson, or resuscitating minor figures like S. R. Crockett, or responding to new work by Douglas Dunn or Posy Simmonds; at the same time, the reading that he undertook for these reviews, in conjunction with his co-editing (with Robert Crawford) of *The New Penguin Book of Scottish Verse*, increasingly fed into, even shaped, his poetry. To take the most obvious example, it is unlikely that he would ever have written his brilliant 'B. V.', which deals with the life of the alcoholic Scottish-born poet James Thomson, had he not been sent Tom Leonard's 1993 biography of Thomson to review for the *Independent on Sunday*.

'B. V.' is the middle section of a sequence entitled 'Afterlives of the Poets', which was in many ways the pivotal work of Mick's poetic career. Although the poems of his first volume, *Birthmarks*, were literary to the extent that some were in witty, even cheeky dialogue with poets like Browning and Yeats and Wilfred Owen, very few made specific allusions to other writers or famous people from history; they didn't, in other words, dip much into what Philip Larkin called 'the common myth-kitty', or require ancillary knowledge from further reading to be understood.

After *Birthmarks* appeared in 1988, Mick's poetry stalled for a number of years, and he produced little that satisfied his rigorous notion of what was worth publishing. This impasse was broken by the suggestion that he compose something for the centenary of Tennyson's death for the *Times*

Literary Supplement, whose staff he had just joined. 'In Memoriam Alfred Lord Tennyson', the first section of 'Afterlives of the Poets', occupied the entire back page of the *TLS*'s special Tennyson issue of 2 October 1992; it's a wonderful poem, perhaps his finest, and the composition of it revealed to Mick how stories, true or apocryphal, about literary or historical figures, could serve as vehicles for his own imaginative energies and preoccupations. Mick was a great admirer of Larkin (as a review collected here demonstrates) and indeed commissioned and published in *Poetry Review* his last ever poem, 'Party Politics'; but it was only by embracing, rather than fleeing, as Larkin had counselled, bookishness, that he was able to recover his poetic voice: the result, *The Lost Leader* of 2008, is one of the most original, inventive, various, amusing, moving – I could go on – volumes of poetry so far published this century.

The 'fraternal tenderness' that Hollinghurst identified in Mick's assessments of both the justly and the unjustly forgotten was in part the result of his awareness of the brutal and unpredictable nature of posthumous fame – or rather, since it's far, far more likely, posthumous neglect. All poets write in the teeth of the knowledge that there is not much chance that anyone will be reading their work in a hundred years' time. Mick was drawn to this topic in a spirit that was partly satirical – he always relished the comic gap between pretensions and the reality that invariably punctures them, particularly in his early work – but it also elicited in him a delicate, even uplifting sense of fellow feeling. One is allowed to feel sorry for, as well as to laugh at, the once-great Victorians imagined in 'In Memoriam Alfred Lord Tennyson', slowly realizing, as they watch from above, that oblivion is engulfing their names and achievements (being dead, and therefore expelled from the heaven of the poem, comes from being entirely forgotten on earth):

> And yet, while we keep the old pastimes, we keep the old dread:
> And that, for our sins, is an absolute horror of being dead.
> These days we can hardly get four for bridge; I've seen the departure
> Of Lytton – accepted – but *Manning*, by God, and Macaulay, and *Archer*!

'Afterlives of the Poets' concludes with a much shorter section that is partly a clear-eyed meditation on the random nature of the universe, on the entropy that ends up obliterating nearly all humanity's bids for immortality, but partly also a compassionate commemoration of individual striving, however misguided and misunderstood, in the face of cosmic indifference. The uncanonical – 'rejects', 'busts with broken noses' – are compared to stars that are dead but still visible; yet they also acquire a dignity and a potency through the poem's eloquent acknowledgement of their 'having been'; at the end of the day – to borrow a sporting cliché of the kind that Mick so enjoyed – they cannot be contained or controlled by our systems of value and judgement:

> though nature has done with them, still through the void they hurtle their
> wattage,
> powered with the purpose of having been – being, after all, stars,
> whose measure we may not take, nor know the wealth of their rays.

In their introduction, the editors of this selection illustrate some of the ways that Mick made use of the reading that he undertook for the reviews that are gathered here in particular poems. It is fascinating to compare, say, his review of the Edinburgh University Press edition of various novels by Walter Scott with his verse biography of the Laird of Abbotsford, 'Diehard'. The relaxed, even prosy idiom he allowed himself in the poem blurs the distinction between genres, and invites comparison with the other kinds of biographical and historical narrative on offer in *The Lost Leader* – the razor-sharp Byronic wit of 'Braveheart', the lethal mixture of lyricism and contempt in the book's title poem on the defection of Bonnie Prince Charlie after Culloden, the garrulous blank verse of 'Rosebery'. Mick was seen by some as a traditional, even conservative poet, and it's true that he enjoyed the challenge of complex forms and rhyme; yet almost all his best poems seem to me to be wild, occasionally implausible experiments, journeys into the unknown, like that undertaken by the voyagers of *The Lost Leader*'s opening poem, 'Muck', which describes an oblique and baffling quest that ends in a failure far more startling than any success could have been. The poem illustrates what John Fuller has called Mick's 'vein of penetrating whimsy', a whimsy particularly strong in its concluding address to 'the gay goddess / Astarté'; only in Mick's pantheon is she the 'mother of false starts'.

There is plenty of *faux* – as well as actual – scholarship in Mick's poetry; the convincing-sounding epigraph to 'The Zoologist's Bath', for instance, is entirely fabricated, while his later poems bristle with epigraphs and quotations that remind one that he set the *TLS* competition 'Author,

Author' every week for many years. An element of his wit involved leaving the reader uncertain how to prise apart the real from the fantastical. These essays, on the other hand, exhibit a genuine and respectful scholarly understanding of literary history and context, and of the ideals and compulsions acted out in the lives and embodied in the writings of the authors whom he considers; the knowledge and perceptiveness on display here, combined with his gift for the telling phrase or detail, make them well worth resurrecting from the literary papers and magazines in which they originally appeared.

Mark Ford

Introduction

'Brilliant and unfashionable'

Why write book reviews? For poets, the answer is simple: to hone one's prose, expand one's field of references, and keep one's name before the public – essential activities during the inevitable lulls in between the writing of one poem and the next. Thus, poets tend to devote much of their time to essays and reviews, and for the most part, they tend to be relatively unconcerned with the almost endless notions of what a critic should be, other than that he or she should infuse their critical output with at least as much passion as they devote to their lyrical craft. In his review of W. H. Auden's *The Dyer's Hand*, John Berryman wrote: 'A proper critic is as zealous as a young poet, crawling with ideas he burns to spread and enforce.' Berryman, like Eliot, believed the critic and the creative artist should be one and the same. This was certainly the case with Mick Imlah, who was first and foremost a poet, although the tantalizing – nearly legendary – slowness with which he penned the two collections he produced during his lifetime – *Birthmarks* (1988) and the Forward Prize-winning *The Lost Leader* (2008) – left him plenty of time to focus his provocative brilliance on a slew of other activities. After his demyship at Magdalen College, where he helped to revive *Oxford Poetry*, Imlah spent the next fifteen years juggling various duties – a junior lectureship, editing *Poetry Review* and the poetry list at Chatto and Windus – before becoming the *Times Literary Supplement*'s poetry editor full time in 1995, where he would remain until his untimely death in 2009.

This volume is a testament to the fruits of that provocative brilliance. Although history is likely to remember him as a Scottish poet, Imlah spent almost the entirety of his life south of the Tweed. Born to Aberdonian parents in 1956, he spent his first few years outside of Glasgow, but the family moved to West Wickham, a leafy south London suburb, in 1966. There began for Imlah what he described as the 'years of Southern education' that trimmed his Scottishness to a 'tartan phrase / Brought out on match days and Remembrance Days': he won a scholarship to attend, from 1968, Dulwich College, where he became a star pupil. It was not until the mid-1990s, when Penguin commissioned him and Robert Crawford to edit a new anthology of Scottish poetry, that his Scottishness began a concerted resurgence. Researching and co-compiling *The New Penguin Book of Scottish Verse* (2000), published months after the sitting of the first Scottish parliament in 300 years, had a substantial impact on his poetical preoccupations and ultimately led to what his Oxford contemporary Peter McDonald hailed as 'a compendium of Scottish experience – historical, mythic, cultural and personal – of monumental proportions': *The Lost Leader*.

The steady advance of his cultural patriotism also informed, and was informed by, his reviewing, and not just for the *TLS*. Included in this volume is his 1997 *Guardian* review of *A Dictionary of Scottish Quotations*, edited by Angela Cran and James Robertson. In his review, Imlah alighted on the quotation attributed to the fifteenth-century Archibald Douglas, 5th Earl of Angus, who reportedly told a gathering of his fellow noblemen that 'I am he who will bell the cat' – the cat being Robert Cochrane, Earl of Mar, of whom little is known, save that he was possibly romantically involved with James III, thus explaining why the King even allowed him to mint his own coinage. As Cochrane's power and influence grew, so did the dismay of the Scots, who hated Cochrane all the more for having debased their currency by mixing its silver with copper; the inferior coins are still known as Cochrane's plaks. When the people insisted their plaks be exchanged for proper currency, Cochrane replied: 'The day I am hanged they will be called in, and not before.' History, as it happens, was all too ready to oblige him. Inspired by one of Aesop's fables, 'The Mice in Council', where mice discuss (but never accomplish) the inane task of 'belling a cat' so as to be aware of its whereabouts, Douglas took it upon himself to challenge Cochrane. As Imlah wrote:

A Douglas, with the Douglas wrath
Igniting through his beard of broth,

The red-faced Earl of Angus spat,
'I am he who will bell the cat.'

Three days, and Mar was rodent-fodder
Hung from the packman's bridge at Lauder.

'That single monosyllabic phrase,' Imlah wrote in his review of the *Dictionary*, 'encapsulates the romantic savagery of late medieval Scotland: the same volatile culture that produced verse, in the Scots of William Dunbar, as sophisticated as any in Renaissance Europe.'

In the same review, Imlah also noted the *Dictionary*'s omission of what he called the 'most potent sentence in Scottish history' – the dispersal order given by Bonnie Prince Charlie to his forces after defeat at Culloden: 'Let everyone seek his own safety the best way he can' – and finishes by quoting in full Hugh MacDiarmid's five-line patriotic poem 'The Little White Rose'. Imlah made the fallout from the Bonnie Prince's order the subject of *The Lost Leader*'s titular poem, a poem that serves as a microcosm of the Scottish people's disillusionment with, or sense of betrayal by, its leaders. The *Dictionary* review also hints at the development of 'Flower of Scotland', another poem from *The Lost Leader* – a stern and heartfelt play on the unofficial and popular anthem used during sporting events; the former subverts the jingoism of the latter, giving a pensive and more historically accurate version of Scotland's bloody history. Finally, the conclusion of the *Dictionary* review hints at Imlah's taking up the challenge laid down by Edwin Muir which prefaced *The Lost Leader*: that no poet in Scotland 'could take as his inspiration the folk impulse that created the ballads, the people's songs, and the legends of Mary Stuart and Prince Charlie'.

Imlah's 2005 *TLS* review of new Walter Scott editions published by Edinburgh University Press revealed his partiality for a writer whose novels were 'none of them the highest things in literature' but which were '(no small thing) perfect for the sofa'. His poem 'Diehard' continued this argument, defending Scott's novels against criticism from F. R. Leavis ('who now reads *Revaluation*?') by reminding us that they were written to 'blunt the bills' of debts Scott had honourably taken on. Imlah admits to finding Scott's anachronisms and inventions page-turners:

> The Scott novel's a 'Big Bow-Wow', shaggy,
> Heavy, particular; slow to rouse; but once fixed,
> Will not give up its grip on your reading leg.

Imlah teases Scott for his vanity, but ultimately approves of his project to assert the validity – granted, through the invention of a sanitized Highland culture – of Scottish cultural difference within Britain, for that is what he,

Imlah, was partly attempting too. Imlah portrayed Scott as being treated as a figure of fun by the very people he sought in his writing to immortalize: what will have resonated with Imlah as he struggled to bolster his Scottish credentials from London was that Scott was a considerable contributor to Scottish culture, but isolated to a degree from it.

As a critic, Imlah probed and discussed, but he never forgot to entertain. Of Graham Greene's playful memoir of his night-time psyche, Imlah wrote: 'Anyone else who wants to publish a "dream diary" should be made to play Russian Roulette.' Yet Imlah ultimately balanced his humour with a piercing perceptiveness. His review of Christopher Reid's *In the Echoey Tunnel*, for instance, neatly encapsulates Reid's work:

> Tidy, subtle, faintly surreal poems of a domestic character have established Christopher Reid as a master and advocate of the diminutive; 'little' is his favourite adjective, as in 'our little red Renault'. Like Alan Brownjohn of the preceding generation, he sometimes borrows the manner and materials of children's literature, and the first few pages of this new book are full of innocent perfect spheres: the 'tiddly ball' of a teacher's game, balloons, chubby seals, bubbles blown across a playground. The bubbles are stamped on by a fat boy; and against the implied opposition of braggarts and bullies, Reid has developed an almost provocatively tiddly poetic.

He later concludes: '[Reid's] modesty now seems less of an attractive gimmick, [and] more a genuine discipline from which works of increasing value will emerge.' Imlah's judgement turned out to be rather prophetic, given that Reid's best work was still ahead of him, and his talent later ripened in his 2009 collection, *A Scattering*, which was awarded the Costa Book of the Year.

Most importantly perhaps, Imlah was never conventional, recalling a line from a Richard Wilbur poem: 'If what you want is a "good, grey guardian of art," you've got the wrong person.' Concerning his nineteenth-century favourites, it was clearly the ossified datedness of their idioms that fascinated him, sometimes even the tragic farce of their lives. He had this to say on Samuel Crockett – the B-class J. M. Barrie and Robert Louis Stevenson acolyte: 'Popularity deserted him, with a finality that surprised but would not deter him until he died, in 1914, of a version of Stevenson's lung disease.' Unoriginal even in death – a damning yet illustrative verdict. But what motivated such a fascination with writers like Crockett? The final lines from his piece on Swinburne are perhaps the closest Imlah comes to an acknowledgement of his rather peculiar taste: 'And if the poems appeal only faintly now, as if from underwater, the strange shapes of the life have their own claim on our imagination.'

Supported by lightly carried special knowledge, Imlah passed judgement on a wide array of writers whose stars now shine with varying degrees of brightness: Barrie ('an exceptionally affectable man writing in an affectable age'); Laurence Binyon ('he gives us in several places the sense of what very good poetry sounds like when it is too beautifully refined to be better'); Robert Bridges ('it's unlikely that poetry will ever take him seriously again'); Henry Green ('one of the most forceful personalities in English fiction of the modernist century'); Edwin Muir ('no one would now suggest that our estimate of the poems improves the more of them we read'); Swinburne ('he wrote precociously and by his personal charm earned the baffled respect of his thicker peers'); and so on. A long-standing favourite was Tennyson: 'I've always liked Tennyson more than most people seem to', he told *Oxford Poetry* in 1983. His introduction to a selection he made of Tennyson's verse, published in 2004, revealed the connection he felt with the Victorian Laureate's need to 'put on forms or metaphors' in his poetry 'which would allow him to say his "woe" without dishonour', the woe being his 'unsocial, painful, and shaming' melancholy. These 'forms' included dramatic monologues and narratives, the likes of which characterized much of Imlah's own *oeuvre*.

Imlah also admired Tennyson's 'instinct for the weights and measures of words and lines (a faculty in which the general reader has since lost interest)'. As indicated by the lament in the parenthesis, and demonstrated by his own body of poetry, Imlah was a strong believer in traditional poetic craftsmanship, and in his poem marking the centenary of Tennyson's death, celebrated as his tour de force, he deftly redeployed some of Tennyson's most distinctive forms. He appreciated form in his contemporaries too: he famously defended Michael Hofmann's poetry from accusations of prosaicness with the memorable comment that Hofmann's lines were in fact 'capable of diseased lexical harmonies akin to rhyme', and he called the formalist Douglas Dunn – whose movement towards Scotland as his abiding poetic preoccupation anticipated, and perhaps helped guide, his own – a writer of 'remarkable poems'.

This *Selected Prose* exhibits a dark underside. Almost all the essays included here exhibit a suppressed apprehension of the loss of the poetic gift. In an age when a volume is expected from a poet every few years – to the point where even a decade's gap is considered inordinately long – Imlah's own absence from publisher's catalogues for most of the time he was alive was fairly noticeable, especially for one of his standing. There is a sense in which this comes across in the criticism. Of William Empson he said, 'his career was a falling away from his brilliant beginnings'. This of course comes from someone who knew and understood the pressures of the literary career. In his valuable introduction to Imlah's *Selected Poems* (2011), Alan Hollinghurst wrote: 'It was typical of Imlah not to be troubled by the career pressures which naturally affect most young writers. He had a sensible belief in his own gifts, but he was as indifferent to status as he was to money and to all possessions except books.' Regardless, Imlah's prose demonstrates a profound fascination with those very pressures. Not his, but those of others. He was clearly interested by failures, perhaps because there is more to learn from failure than from success. The latter often stirs either envy or emulation – failure, on the other hand, stirs deeper: it sets the mind to reflection, the heart to sympathy.

*

Although a fixture at literary parties, and a firm part of the London 'establishment', Imlah left few records of his personality in the public domain. His conversation with Nicholas Jenkins, his co-editor at *Oxford Poetry*, was published in 1983, a year after the publication of Imlah's debut pamphlet, *The Zoologist's Bath and Other Adventures*, and is a fine example of his wit. In answer to a rather innocuous question, he says:

> You mean that you find my titles more interesting than my poems? Fair enough. Titles are pure suggestion. I'd like to write a book of them: 'War: A Comic History', 'Love On All Fours', 'Heaven'. I like big, bold titles to go with oblique poems that don't do the discursive work you've been led to expect. I've learned the importance of titles from reading manuscripts at *Poetry Review*: 'Fantasy', 'Waiting For The Bus', 'The Old Man'. Then you get the ones that think they're punchy: 'Socks', 'Sex', 'Implosion', 'Brixton 1981' – or sophisticated: 'Play of Light in New Hampshire (for Harriet)'. You have to read them through, of course, but a poem never recovers from a bad title. Look at 'The Zoologist's Bath.'

This following excerpt, taken from the same interview, is the closest Imlah comes to summing up his *ars poetica*:

> Today's poet is a bit like a Victorian architect; there's no single staple native style available (as, say, the heroic couplet was for Pope) so he has to choose a model for each piece of work: Middle Pointed Gothic, neo-Egyptian, blank verse, this or that kind of stanza, silly one-word lines, whatever. Everyone knows it isn't the real thing, that there's an element of exercise about it, but it's better than rubble. I don't like poems which look like rubble. And I think this self-consciousness and versatility is a good thing in poetry; unlike a town, a book of poems looks better for a mixture of styles.

We are delighted to be able to offer admirers of Imlah's poetry the opportunity to read his criticism too. This *Selected Prose* provides a range of insights into a poet both 'brilliant and unfashionable', as he was hailed in one obituary; a poet who was mourned by writers of all kinds – and inspired numerous elegies – when he succumbed to motor neurone disease at the height of his success.

Yet this is not to say this collection is fit only for the specialist. The section entitled 'Digressions' features an odd but beautifully chiselled gem which Imlah wrote for the *Independent on Sunday* in 1996: 'The Legend of Iron Joss'. Its subject is Joss Naylor, a farmer and fell-runner from Cumbria, who, on his sixtieth birthday, climbed sixty of the highest peaks in the Lake District in just thirty-six hours. In this piece, Imlah wrote: 'Naylor is famous because for a period of nearly twenty years he could absorb his suffering at a pace and for a duration that no one else could match; and because in the course of this supremacy he performed new acts of resilience that demanded more than local astonishment.' He could have been writing about himself.

ON WRITERS

Blind Harry and Robert Baston

A Burel Broth

The Wallace by Blind Harry
Edited by Anne McKim, Canongate

Metrum De Praelio Apud Bannockburn by Robert Baston
With a translation by Edwin Morgan, Scottish Poetry Library

Born within three years and thirty miles of each other, Sir William Wallace and Robert the Bruce led the successive phases of Scotland's ultimately victorious uprising against the occupation of Edward I. But these two great champions were not natural allies: and beyond their shared hatred of the English, they might even be taken to illustrate the internal division of their country and its psyche. Though he was born the son of a knight in Renfrewshire, Wallace has turned into an emblem of the Highlands and the 'People', sentimental, gallant, scenic, doomed; Bruce was an aristocrat of Norman descent and a politician, who took up the cause of independence only when it grew identical with his own interest, and then pursued it with the kind of calculation and self-belief that would characterize the type of the Lowland Scot.

There is a misleading symmetry, too, about the literature that rose to commemorate them. The original twelve-book poem of Blind Harry's *The Wallace*, in rugged couplets, nearly 12,000 lines in length, was composed between 1460 and 1470, nearly a century after its model and companion epic, John Barbour's *The Bruce*, which it now joins in Canongate's series of Scottish classics. The text of Anne McKim's edition is substantially that of the late Matthew P. McDiarmid for the Scottish Text Society (two volumes, 1968–9), itself prepared from the sole surviving manuscript written in 1488 by the same scribe, John Ramsay, who a year later copied the two extant manuscripts of *The Bruce*.

But while Barbour wrote his poem within the national memory of Robert's exploits, Blind Harry's was dished up from a broth of tradition and folk-tale that had been bubbling for 160 years. Harry refers to an eye-witness account of Wallace's campaigns, written in Latin by his chaplain, John Blair, but his narrative enjoys the latitude of romance, embracing, as one eighteenth-century commentator observed, 'the actions which Wallace did not perform, as well as those which he did'. Hence, our hero marches on St Albans; hence, he wins a notable victory at the imaginary Battle of Biggar; hence (though he was thirty-four when he was put to death), he fights the English from his sixteenth year to his forty-fifth, with a similarly enlarged capacity for the slaughter of 'Southeroun' men.

Not much is known about Harry. According to the historian John Mair, he was blind from birth, and made his living as a wandering min-strel. His name last appears in contemporary accounts in 1492; sixteen years later, he has joined the ranks of Scots makars lamented in William Dunbar's 'I that in Heill Wes ...': 'He has Blind Hary and Sandy Traill / Slane with his schour of mortall haill'. His own poem's conclusion famously defines Harry as 'burel' – simple, rustic, barely educated. This has been read as false modesty by apologists keen to show how he had certainly read Latin, absorbed the conventions of romance writing, etc. Yet the most 'sophisticated' (and incredible) episode in the whole poem, the interview in Book Eight between Wallace and the Queen of England, seems to be imported from a foreign idiom, and works to confirm our suspicion of fair language – in this instance, of the soft words of the Queen, likened (in one of the poem's few diminutive figures) to a catcher whistling 'byrdis' towards the snare, 'With the small pype, for it most fresche will call'. And much the greater part of *The Wallace*, even compared with Barbour, is plain stuff, 'baran of eloquens', as it declares, and not without purpose: its defects commend it to a popular audience. (In the eighteenth century, the poem became a fixture in literate Scottish households: only, how-ever, as rendered by William Hamilton of Gilbertfield into low-pitched English couplets: 'Here while they tarried Wallace took a bee / Into his head, that maiden for to see, / Of whom we spoke before'. The Edinburgh firm of Luath offered the public a new edition of this in the wake of the 1998 movie, *Braveheart*, where Mel Gibson makes a fetish of Wallace's verbal reserve.)

In other words, *The Wallace* is one of those poems which can be said to be 'against' poetry. It is not paradoxical that its few flights, like those of *The Bruce*, hover over the daunting display of English arms in the field ('Thai playntyt thar field with tentis and pailyonis / Quha claryouns blew full mony mychty sonis') – against which the Scots line up as the 'few folk of a simple land'. For England's strength is fatally undermined by the baser nature of her individuals. In Book Seven, for instance, before a group of them is burned to death in the Barns of Ayr, they are caught drinking like pigs: 'Of ayle and wyne yneuch chosyne haiff thai, / As bestly folk tuk of thaim self no keip. / In thar brawnys sone slaid the sleuthfull sleip / Throuch full gluttre in swarff swappyt lik swyn; / Thar chyftane than was gret Bachus of wyn'. Anne McKim's editing displays the odd qualm of morality, and she feels obliged to append a footnote to this passage: 'Goldstein … cites this as an example of Blind Harry's "racist discourse"'. Edward I – *Malleus Scottorum* – used to joke of killing Scots that 'Bon besoigne fait qy de merde se delivrer'. But this was all a long time ago.

It is a pity, too, to find fault with Canongate's production. But to make room for an extensive English gloss in the right-hand margin, the text has been set too narrowly. As a result, any number of unexceptional lines – 'The Sotheroun men maid gret defens again', 'The Scottis slew all was thar of that nacioun', 'And slew all men of Sotheroun was thar foun' – are run over, which gives the effect of paragraphing where none exists, obscures it where it does exist, and generally melts the body of the poem into porridge. Neither does it help the readability of the whole that no summary of the action or indication of its contents is appended.

Much that is best about the poem can be found in Book Eleven: because it uniquely has defeat to deal with (Wallace's at Falkirk in 1298), and because it involves the greater complexity of the character of the Bruce. The single most potent scene is the exchange between the defeated Wallace and the confused Robert, who has just fought with the English against his own countrymen, and feels the lash of Wallace's insult, yelled at him across the River Carron: 'Thou renygat devorar of thi blud!' If the end of Wallace is near, the poem conveys, this is the proper beginning of the Bruce.

After Falkirk, Wallace was driven into hiding, until he was betrayed in the summer of 1305. Executed at Smithfield, his parts were 'dispersyt', his head impaled on London Bridge and an instructive quarter sent to each of Newcastle, Berwick, Perth and Aberdeen. Bruce declared himself king and fled with his life. Nearly a decade later, on the field of Bannockburn, he contested the sovereignty of Scotland with Edward's unfortunate son.

Travelling north in 1314 with the English army was Robert Baston – according to the chronicler Walter Bower, 'the most famous poet in England' at the time – whose mission was to write official verses, in his customary Latin, to celebrate its inevitable success. But as the English script unravelled on the battlefield, Baston was taken prisoner and turned, like captured artillery, against his own; for the ransom mockingly set on his head was to produce the opposite poem, in praise of England's defeat. The result, first collected in Bower's edition of the *Scotichronicon* (c.1440), was the 174-line *Metrum de Praelio apud Bannockburn*, a rank oddity among commissioned poems: cheerless, as we would expect, but also surprisingly modern in tone, squeezed as it is by the stresses of its composition into an objective protest at the nightmare waste of war: an even handed lament for 'gentes submerse fabricantes prelia per se' ('Whole peoples sunk in the fen, still fighting').

This curiosity is now made available by the Scottish Poetry Library, alongside a tremendously resourceful new English translation by Edwin Morgan, in a trim pamphlet edition to mark Morgan's appointment as the first official 'Scots Makar' or national laureate. Morgan has given us the full value of Baston's percussive internal rhyme scheme, which can have a doomy, rapping effect in the English equivalent he finds for it: 'Spears are at hand, the Saxon satraps look grand, / But things are at a stand, clear strategy seems banned'. The poem culminates, though it has had to blame the Saxon once more for spending the eve of a battle 'cum Bacho', in a tender lament for the noblest of the 10,000 English dead, imaginatively closer to Morgan's own spirit in these matters than Harry's gloating over their innards:

> Clare comes, venerande fornes, Glovernice cultor,
> heu! moreris, sub strage peris. Sic fit Deus ultor,
> Nobilis Argenten, pugil inclite, dulcis Egidi,
> vix scieram mentem cum te succumbere vidi.

> (Clare of Gloucester, fosterer of courage, earl and landlord,
> Ah, you are out among the dead, by God's avenging word ….
> Noble Argentan, great gentleman, sweet Giles,
> I would fain have fainted when I saw you in those falling files.)

Walter Scott

This Right Hand

The Heart of Mid-Lothian
Edited by David Hewitt and Alison Lumsden

The Fortunes of Nigel
Edited by Frank Jordan

Reliquiae Trotcosienses
Edited by Gerard Carruthers and Alison Lumsden
Edinburgh University Press

The leading article of the *Times Literary Supplement* of June 6, 1918 proposed a toast, in the departing spirit of those days, to Walter Scott's *The Heart of Mid-Lothian*, published a hundred years ago that week: 'In spite of the presence to-day in England of a drilled regiment … who brag of turning the cold shoulder to the Wizard of the North, there are still, thank Heaven! a mob of gentlemen who read Scott with ease'. (The author of the unsigned article was Thomas Seccombe.)

The phrase 'a mob of gentlemen' to describe Scott's readers might just as easily have been coined by a detractor: by either, in particular, of Thomas Carlyle and E. M. Forster. Forster devoted several pages in one of the lectures making up *Aspects of the Novel* (1927) to a comic synopsis of the action of *The Antiquary* (1816), Scott's own favourite among his novels, to show how ludicrous and poorly contrived it is. This was humorously done, as it might have been to almost any novel of his choosing. It was not, however, as funny as the best of *The Antiquary*: say, the thirty-first chapter, written (as Scott's admirers might have claimed) in the time it took Forster to deliver his lecture.

Carlyle's more sustained challenge came in a long essay, 'The Amoral Scott' (1838), written as a review of Lockhart's worshipful *Life* of his father-in-law. Carlyle begins by granting his fellow-Borderer qualities such as 'a sunny current of true humour and humanity', declaring him, with sly irrelevance, 'a most robust, healthy man!' Next, the wrong superlatives are applied to the novels, 'faster written and better paid for than any other books in the world', and made to gratify that very mob of 'indolent languid men' whose cry is 'Be mine to lie on this sofa, and read everlasting Novels of Walter Scott!' Soon the critic is fairly launched on his stern Lowland mode, half minister, half dominie.

For Carlyle, the fate of Scott as a writer is bound up with his ruling and demeaning obsession: the building and appointing of the Gothic house of Abbotsford, on the bank of the Tweed between Melrose and Galashiels. Hence the appalling spectacle of 'a Walter Scott writing daily with the ardour of a steam-engine, that he might make £15,000 a-year, and buy upholstery with it': hence the 'deplorable correspondence' about 'curtain and the trimmings of curtains, orange-coloured or fawn-coloured'; hence 'one of the gifted of the world ... must kill himself that he may be a country gentleman, the founder of a race of Scottish lairds'.

But Scott's motivation, and his practical preference for an 'impromptu' method of composition, is not quite so simple or so low. As he seldom attempted to write slowly, we might suppose that hurry became a necessary condition of what he did; indeed he would claim that 'the works and passages in which I have succeeded have uniformly been written with the greatest rapidity'. A letter written by Henry Cockburn from Edinburgh, retailing literary gossip, seems to anticipate Carlyle's lament at Scott's self-destructive regime: 'Walter Scott still keeps the printer's devil chasing him for sheets, like a fool. I know no poet who has committed such suicide as Watty'. But this was written (the 'poet' gives it away) in March 1810, before the bard of *Marmion* had bought the plot for Abbotsford: before he had written a word of *Waverley* (1814), *Guy Mannering* (1815), *Old Mortality* (1816), *Rob Roy* (1818), *Heart of Mid-Lothian* (1818), *The Bride of Lammermoor* (1819), *Ivanhoe* (1820), *Redgauntlet* (1824), *The Talisman* (1825), or any of the other romances that steamed from his deplorable workshop. If this was suicide, Scott seems to have been born to it.

Scott would express his detachment from critics in general by quoting the nursery proverb, 'The children in Holland take pleasure in making / What the children in England take pleasure in breaking'. And it is that slightly feeble term 'pleasure', along with the charge of immaturity, that his partisans have had to get used to as their own. Scott needs to be read briskly and broadly, in his own spirit of hit and miss; the reader, like the writer, will have his 'favourite' novels, scenes and characters: none of them the highest things in literature, nothing for Carlyle, who didn't care for novels, or Forster, who cared only for The Novel; but (no small thing) perfect for the sofa.

With the publication of the latest volumes, *The Heart of Mid-Lothian* and *The Fortunes of Nigel*, the monumental Edinburgh Edition of the Waverley Novels is now more than two-thirds complete. (All Scott's novels were published anonymously, most 'by the author of Waverley', others in a series called 'Tales of My Landlord'; but after authorship was owned in 1825 they were known and published together as the 'Waverley Novels'.) A part of our immediate response to these exemplary volumes is to feel the discrepancy between Scott's slapdash, hearty, headlong method of composition and the painstaking toil of his editors, directed by David Hewitt. *The Fortunes of Nigel*, for instance, has a substantial historical note, a fifty-page essay on the text, fifty pages of textual emendations, 100 pages of explanatory notes, an impressively comprehensive glossary of terms both Scots and English, and such *de luxe* features as a list of hard hyphens obscured by line endings. Most intervening editions of the novels have been happy to take as their copy-text the so-called Magnum Opus edition of 1829–33, which Scott supervised; the Edinburgh editors have reverted to the first editions, but have also combed the manuscripts for missed readings and lost materials: some of the latter, such as the portraits of Edinburgh literati in *Guy Mannering*, are substantial discoveries.

The Heart of Mid-Lothian (1818) is one of those books that seemed, a little while ago, to have been taught to death. Though Scott has been generally thought of as a boys' author – and it remains the only novel to have given its name to a football team – this piece, with a female protagonist, a female 'cause' and a portable moral, was the fodder chosen through much of the past century for the schoolgirls of Scotland and England (my sister, moving at fourteen from one to the other, had to study it twice). The title refers to the nickname of the old Tolbooth or prison that formerly stood in the middle of Edinburgh by the Parliament and St Giles. (In 1818, the Tolbooth had recently been demolished, and Scott had succeeded in picking up as a souvenir the great door that slams through the early pages.) But there is also allusion to the local form of female pluck.

The novel opens with its set-piece triumph, an electrifying narrative of the Porteous Riots in Edinburgh in 1736. At the hanging of a convicted robber, Captain Porteous of the City Guard has his troops fire on the assembled crowd, killing several. Porteous is himself condemned to death; but then reprieved. At this, an angry mob, led by the robber's associate George Robertson, breaks into the Tolbooth, seizes Porteous and hangs him. On to this authentic history Scott grafted his main tale. The farmer's daughter Effie Deans, who has been seduced by Robertson (in reality George Staunton, a debauched English aristocrat), is accused of child-murder, on the grounds that she concealed her pregnancy and her son cannot be found. Her half-sister Jeanie Deans refuses to give false evidence to secure her acquittal; instead she tramps to London to meet the Queen and get a pardon there.

To lay the burden of the novel on Jeanie's shoulders was a gamble. Gentlemen had been accustomed to let their heads loll back on the sofa when Scott's heroines came centre-stage: from *Waverley*'s Dresden pair of lovely Rose Brawardine and passionate Flora McIvor onwards. But Jeanie is presented with none of the advantages her predecessors had by right, neither beauty nor wit nor breeding: she is short, stout and a bit smug. Scott was much taken by his own creation: 'the lass kept tugging me by the bean-strings'; and half of contemporary Europe seemed to follow. But Jeanie's male foils are less successful; in particular, the remorseful seducer Staunton, who announces himself with a Byronic bark – 'I am the devil!' – and finds no route back to sympathy. Applying the usual euphemism of 'dissipation', Scott means him to be understood as a habitual drunkard; but because he is 'quality', his vices, like the child he spawned, are withheld from view. In one passage, they are even attributed to the influence of his base-born wet-nurse: 'the source from which I derived food, when an infant, must have communicated to me the wretched – the fated – propensity to vices that were strangers in my own family'. (We can contrast the plain distress, the honest alcoholism, as we would call it, of Nanty Ewart, the doomed ship's captain of *Redgauntlet*.)

The Waverley Novels generally filled three volumes: only *The Heart of Mid-Lothian* is stretched to four, Scott being paid in advance for that number. The third volume, and the story proper, ends with the successful conclusion of Jeanie's interview with Queen Caroline:

'… O, my Leddy, then it isna what we hae dune for oursells, but what we hae dune for others, that we think on maist pleasantly. And the thoughts that ye hae intervened to spare the puir thing's life will be sweeter in that hour, come when it may, than if a word of your could hang the haill Porteous mob at the tail of ae tow.'

… 'This is eloquence,' said her Majesty …

What is not eloquence is the desultory hauling-in of the plot that follows, conducted at times in something not much better than note form: 'This retrospect, so far as the placid loves of Jeanie Deans and Reuben Butler are concerned, forms a full explanation of the preceding narrative up to their meeting on the island as already mentioned'. The island in question is Roseneath, in the Firth of Clyde, where all parties are conducted by Scott's fairy godmother for the mellowest, most Protestant of happy endings. It is less odd of Scott than it would be of other writers, that while *The Heart of Mid-Lothian* is still accepted as his 'greatest' work, none of his admirers have a good word to say about this particular one-fourth of it.

In pursuit of an effect like that of a perfected first edition, the EEWN declines to reproduce the lengthy and sometimes revealing or entertaining introductions (as well as the historical notes) that Scott prepared for the 'Magnum Opus' edition. These are scheduled to be collected in two future volumes: for the moment, their omission seems a little austere. The introduction to *The Heart of Mid-Lothian* gave the text of the letter sent to Scott by Mrs Goldie of Irongray, with her account of her meeting with Helen Walker, the 'original' of Jeanie Deans: instructive as proof that this sort of virtue really did take to the roads in mid-eighteenth-century Scotland. However, the more valuable prefatory matter to *Nigel* is reproduced here: the 'Introductory Epistle' purportedly signed by 'Captain Clutterbuck', the latest of Scott's fictitious intermediaries. This features an interview with the phantom 'Author of Waverley', and is the closest thing Scott offers to an apologia, made of witty disclaimers and good-humoured shrugging. The Author cannot work to a stricter pattern, he says, because 'there is a demon who seats himself on the feather of my pen when I begin to write, and leads it astray from the purpose … the story lingers, while the materials increase: my regular mansion turns out a Gothic anomaly'.

The Fortunes of Nigel (1822) is one of Scott's fustiest titles, and the Laird of Glevarnoch one of the palest of all his titled heroes. What are his fortunes? – we forget them as soon as we lay down the book. Instead we remember odd bits of Gothic detail, the life in the margins, not all of it strictly related to the novel's structural mass. The torrential soliloquy of the Greenwich barber has sometimes been instanced: the watchmaker's speech at the start of the second chapter is something similar – much repaired, in this meticulous edition, from earlier garbling:

> The ancient gentleman bustled about his shop, in pettish displeasure at being summoned hither so hastily, to the interruption of his more abstract studies: and, unwilling to renounce the train of calculation which he had put in progress, he mingled whimsically with the fragments of the arithmetical operation, his oratory to the passengers, and angry reflections on his idle apprentices. 'What d'ye lack, sir? Madam, what d'ye lack – clocks for hail or table – night-watches – day watches? – *Locking wheel being* 48 – *the pinion of report*, 8 – *the striking pins* are 13 – What d'ye lack, honoured sir? – *the quotient* – *the multiplicand* – that the knaves should have gone out this blessed minute! – *the acceleration being at the rate of 5 minutes, 55 seconds, 53 thirds, 59 fourths*, – I will switch them both when they come back – I will, by the bones of the immortal Napier!'

This is vaguely reminiscent of the presentation of Miss Bates's scattered delivery in the late Jane Austen's *Emma* (1816): '– Candles everywhere. – I was telling you of your grandmamma, Jane'. But Scott diverges from the subtler writer in signposting the experiment; in distinguishing the strands of thought that mingle in the speech, and marking one of them off in italics. And where Miss Bates's chatter has a real function in *Emma*, exposing the heroine's impatience, this single speech has the value only of its novelty. Neither does Scott much resemble Sterne, though he is obviously charmed by *Tristram Shandy* and imitates its flourish in places ('Shall this be a long or a short chapter?'). There are more showy episodes of this sort in Scott than are normally counted. But the analogues brought to mind in a novel like *Nigel* are as frequently theatrical (it is set in Jacobean London) or pictorial as literary. The author seems unsure which of his materials will settle to become novelistic convention; his manner, meanwhile, is that of a host exhibiting a new collection of miscellaneous furnishings.

The group of editors responsible for the EEWN is simultaneously doing valuable curating work on a number of unpublished works by Scott, specifically projects from the last two years of life that were abandoned as ill health progressively disabled him. The latest of these to appear in print is the *Reliquiae Trotcosiensis*.

As everyone once knew, the collapse of the Edinburgh publisher Archibald Constable in 1826 entailed the ruin of the fifty-four-year-old Scott, who found himself responsible not only for his considerable private debts, but for those of the printing business of James Ballantyne, in which he was a partner, and for the bank advances to Constable which had been guaranteed by that company. The total sum was £120,000. Yet, in the manner of Carlyle's image of him as Border reiver born out of time, with a quill for a spear, Scott surveyed the softer solutions that offered themselves; then turned towards his study, as the myth has it, with a firm 'No! This right hand shall work it all off!' His creditors, in their turn, declined to sequester his property, and agreed to the establishment of a trust, to which he committed all his future literary earnings and which eventually (though not in his lifetime) repaid the lot.

At least this arrangement preserved Abbotsford and its contents. But it tied Scott to a volume of production – of Napoleons, demonologies, Scottish histories, formula novels – that defeated even his prodigious energies. The first stroke came in February 1830. Even so he made yet further, private commitments, to maintain a Baronial standard of living. He was meant to support himself with income from his legal duties: but now he sought out a deal with the publisher Richard Cadell for certain minor projects, not subject to the claims of his creditors, that would bring him a bit on the side. The contract for *Reliquiae Trotcosiensis* was signed in September 1830; Scott received payment of £750 in exchange for the right to print 5,000 copies. The book was half-finished at the time of his death in September 1832, but both he and Cadell had given the work up by then. To ready the fragmentary text for publication now, David Hewitt and Alison Lumsden have had to confront and amend manuscript evidence of Scott's physical incapacity and dwindling coherence.

Reliquiae Trotcosiensis, or The Gabions of the Late Jonathan Oldbuck Esq of Monkbarns is a description of the rooms of Abbotsford and its collections, passed through a fictional mediation (at once muddling and relentless) involving Jonathan Oldbuck, the titular collector of *The Antiquary* (1816) – the exuberant comic novel to which it is a melancholy

pendant. In the novel, Oldbuck is memorably twitted by the beggar Edie
Ochiltree for identifying a mound on his land as the 'Praetorian Gate' of
a Roman camp supposed to have been situated there: 'Praetorian here,
Praetorian there', says Ochiltree: 'I mind the bigging [building] o'it'. In
an attempted reprise of this spirit, the *Reliquiae* mocks the antiquarian
instinct while duly recording the anecdotal significance of each 'gabion'
or 'auld nicknack' in the author's possession. These items were to fill the
display-cases of today's Scott Museum; at the time of writing Scott could
have expected their dissolution. (A *gabion*, according to the *Dictionary
of the Older Scottish Tongue*, is 'a wicker basket filled with earth used
in fortification' – which encourages Hewitt, in his exact and interest-
ing introduction, to characterize Scott's *Reliquiae* as 'fragments shored
against his ruin'.) If the gambit sadly misfires now, it is partly because
Scott's own case is worse than the ailments he imagines: 'I think it was
Lucian – but I suffer far too much under the rheumatism to reach the
book from the shelf – ...'

Alfred, Lord Tennyson

Selective Affections

Alfred, Lord Tennyson
Faber and Faber

Sunset and evening star,
And one clear call for me!
And let there be no moaning of the bar
When I put out to sea …

Tennyson wrote the hymn-like 'Crossing the Bar' in twenty minutes, on a drizzly afternoon in October 1889, aboard a boat carrying him across the Solent from Portsmouth towards his home on the Isle of Wight (the 'bar' is the extending limb of a harbour). He was eighty years old, and had barely recovered from a serious illness. When he shared the poem that evening with his loyal son Hallam, he was told, 'That is one of the most beautiful poems ever written.' (Hallam refined his remark for posterity, when compiling his *Memoir*, to 'That is the crown of your life's work.')

The poem has since been bracketed with other poems of the period which vaunt their faith in the face of death or adversity: especially Browning's 'Epilogue' to *Asolando*, which was published on the same day in December 1889 as Tennyson's *Demeter*, containing 'Crossing the Bar' – the same day, moreover, on which Browning died:

What had I on earth to do
With the slothful, with the mawkish, the unmanly? …
No, at noonday in the bustle of man's work-time
Greet the unseen with a cheer!

Yet 'slothful', 'mawkish' and 'unmanly' are all epithets which can be found in contemporary reviews of Tennyson's early poems. And the passenger of 'Crossing the Bar' – who is yet, in the euphemism, to 'put out to sea' – shares his situation, brave though he is in the face, with the classic Tennysonian character of the stranded mariner, who recurs time and again through a long career, from 'The Lotos-Eaters' (1830) and 'Ulysses' (1833), to 'Enoch Arden' (1864) and the men on 'The Voyage of Maeldune' (1880), to name only the most literal. Readers of the lines 'When that which drew from out the boundless deep / Turns again home' would cross over from Tennyson's own coming voyage to remember the reference to the *De Profundis* at the climax of Tennyson's Arthurian epic – 'From the great deep to the great deep he goes' ('The Passing of Arthur'). 'Mind you put my Crossing the Bar at the end of all editions of my poems,' insisted the old man, like one arranging his funeral, or stage-managing his carriage to Avalon. At the last, succeeding to the properties of his own legendary gentleman, Tennyson has outworn the trouble of being alive. What had been up with him was almost over.

Alfred Tennyson was born in 1809 at Somersby, Lincolnshire, the fourth son of the rector there. The Tennyson family history had been blighted by madness, alcoholism and opium addiction; the rector himself, in thrall to drink, had been passed over in favour of a ruthless second son. What Alfred called the 'black blood' of his kin showed itself in his own case as 'a hereditary tenderness of nerves': he was afraid of epilepsy, and susceptible to trance-like states, of the kind he was to describe in *The Princess*:

> On a sudden, in the midst of men and day,
> And while l walked and talked as heretofore,
> I seem'd to move among a world of ghosts,
> And feel myself the shadow of a dream

And so, while his childhood introduced him to grand houses and perfect lawns, and though at the age of thirty he still had £3,000 to throw away on a business venture, he felt himself unfortunate: as a suitor, he could claim to be thwarted by 'marriage-hindering Mammon'; and instability of several kinds seemed to be the sum of his inheritance.

Poetry, too, was in his veins. Two of his brothers, Charles (later Tennyson-Turner) and Frederick, each wrote his share of good verse.

But Alfred was pulled out of Louth Grammar School at eleven, so it was only at home, by a miserable, bleary father, that his special talent was marked. And somewhere the juvenile eagerness and freedom of the mock-Jacobean drama, 'The Devil and the Lady', that he wrote when he was fourteen, with its carefree casting off to sea –

> Thereat my shallop lightly I unbound,
> Spread my white sail and rode exulting on
> The placid murmurings of each feathery wave

– thins into the feyness and anaemia and stagnation of his earliest published poems. Unfavourable reviews of Tennyson's first two books (1830 and 1832) mocked in particular that part of them which was a metrical scrapbook of girls' names: 'Claribel', 'Lilian', 'Isabel', 'Madeline', 'Marion', 'Lisette', 'Eleanore', 'My Rosalind', 'faintly smiling Adeline', 'rare pale Margaret', etc. Though these had memorable older cousins in the towered-up Lady of Shalott and the morbidly frustrated Mariana 'by the moated grange', there was no future in a poet of either sex for a style so guardedly feminine.

In 1832, Tennyson's temperament seemed inimical to his promise. The exemplary poet of that day, and incidentally Poet Laureate, was Wordsworth, whose radical innovations had been autobiography and the plain style. Tennyson's problem in presenting poems to the public was that his deepest experience was unsocial, painful, and shaming to a degree; this was no ordinary reticence. And how he might have sounded then without the dress of artifice is to be heard in an unpublished fragment of the period:

> Pierced through with knotted thorns of barren pain,
>   Deep in forethought of dark calamities,
>   Sick of the coming time and the coming woe,
> As one that tramples some volcanic plain
>   And through the yawning rifts and chasms hears
>   The scummy sulphur seething far below
> And dares not to advance or to retire
> E'en so I lay upon my bed at night:
>   All my delight was gone: my hope was fresh
>   No longer: and I lay with sobbing breath,

Walled round, shut up, imbarred, moaning for light,
A carcase in the coffin of this flesh,
Pierced through with loathly worms of utter death.

That 'coming woe' is always large on Tennyson's horizon. He was daunted by society and sex, by life as well as death; and his poems had to put on forms or metaphors which would allow him to say his 'woe' without dishonour. One valuable resource was the dramatic monologue: a speech of fictional self-disclosure, normally in Shakespearean blank verse, which he developed independently from, and rather in advance of, its more thoroughgoing exponent, Robert Browning. The difference between them was that while Browning wrote such poems to explore the dilemmas of other characters, Tennyson wrote them to mythologize his own, choosing figures from classical and other legend in 'Ulysses', 'Tithon' (remade as 'Tithonus'), and 'St Simeon Stylites': three of his very best poems of middle length, all written in 1833. But as the situation of these personae was essentially the same, marooned in helpless or perverse inactivity, they could not, as Browning's might, meet or multiply. 'Me only cruel immortality / Consumes . . .': the further development of Tennyson's poetry depended on traffic with the world, and it might yet have perished by withdrawal, had there not been an accident of grief.

Tennyson had gone up to Trinity College, Cambridge in November 1827. As an undergraduate there he won the Chancellor's Gold Medal for Poetry. But he was to leave Cambridge without taking a degree; and the real benefit of the University for him was the friendship and love of Arthur Hugh Hallam, the son of an eminent historian and himself the golden boy of his Trinity generation. Tennyson and Hallam walked the Pyrenees together in 1830: the following year, Hallam published an essay in the *Englishman's Magazine* in extravagant praise of his friend's poems. He also fell in love with Alfred's sister; and their engagement seemed providentially to absorb and dispel the private doom of the whole family. In the autumn of 1833, news came from Vienna that Hallam was dead, of a brain haemorrhage, at twenty-two.

For fifteen years to follow, the loss of Arthur Hallam, and the hope embodied in Hallam, blended with Tennyson's constitutional depression to produce extended attacks of paralysis and complementary agitation. The exact nature of his illness – the poet himself looked back on it serenely as 'hypochondria' – is obscured by the loyalty of his friends and family. In 1840,

Edward FitzGerald found him in the latest contraction of the Tennyson family home, this one at Tunbridge Wells, 'really ill in a nervous way'; in 1843, he had treatment in a hydropathic hospital near Cheltenham; friends were shocked anew at his 'pitiful' condition in 1847. But at least his sorrows were feeding now on something more substantial than self-pity. Some have marvelled at the anguish Tennyson expended on the loss of an undergraduate friendship, and inferred a homoerotic attachment; alternatively, we can read the Hallam poems (and 'Hallam' was what he called his son) as the meeting of a morbid strain with a dearly needed occasion. And in due course, the warmer reception given to the *Poems* of 1842, the award of a Civil List Pension in 1845, and the secret, intermittent development of the series of elegies for his friend, began to prepare his fortunes for a decisive turn.

There can be few better examples of the biographical phenomenon of *annus mirabilis* than Tennyson's 1850 – the midpoint of his own span, as well as of the century to which it belonged. First, in May, came the anonymous publication of, and boundless acclaim for, *In Memoriam A. H. H.*, the long poem, in lyric form, which airs and wilfully resolves the twin despairs of grief and religious doubt. The poem's success led to his being offered the title in November, after Wordsworth's death in April, of Poet Laureate. Most radical of all was his marriage in June to Emily Sellwood: a wife who had known him for twenty years, who doted on him, and rather scolded his demons (she called the black-blooded one 'Ally'). Though he had already written perhaps three quarters of the poetry on which his reputation would come to rest, he was now to enjoy four decades of a worldlier sort of success, the very heights of the stardom his age could confer.

Tennyson liked the Troubadour description of poetry as a 'gay science'; and his peers would say that English verse since Milton had known no better technician, none with so refined an instinct for the weights and measures of words and lines (a faculty in which the general reader has since lost interest). His 'ear' was commonly celebrated as a marvellous instrument, and its individual felicities collected and quoted. These included the mouthful of lines from 'Come down, O maid' –

> every sound is sweet;
> Myriads of rivulets hurrying through the lawn,
> The moan of doves in immemorial elms,
> And murmuring of innumerable bees.

– and the bathtime hullabaloo of a line from one of the ldylls, 'Oilily bubbled up the mere', which embodies the sound and sight of what is being described, but also communicates the relish of its writing.

And Tennyson was certainly pleased with his virtuosity. His friend Edward FitzGerald remembered a boating expedition on which the poet rolled out the lines from 'Morte d'Arthur' (later incorporated in 'The Passing of Arthur') on the sub-marine manufacture of Excalibur: 'Nine Years she wrought it, sitting in the deeps/ Upon the hidden bases of the hills', breaking off to suggest, 'Not bad that, Fitz, is it?' His private readings, which Tennyson enjoyed at least as much as his audience, were occasions for showing off. FitzGerald again, on the ascetical monologue 'St Simeon Stylites': 'This is one of the Poems A. T. would read with grotesque Grimness, especially at such passages as 'Coughs, Aches, Stitches, etc', laughing aloud at times.'

When Tennyson's poetry is at its best, these lavish gifts are in balance with the prompting of his wounds and fears; but in the calm of his maturity their display could seem like facility. FitzGerald saw this as early as *In Memoriam*, observing that the poem, while 'full of finest things', had 'that air of being evolved by a Poetical Machine of the highest order'. We get more of what the Victorians called 'Parnassian' – poetry produced by the ream under low pressure and generalized outlook – as Tennyson began to shape a career.

This meant, first, a broadening of his subject-matter, which met with some reward. He produced poems in the Lincolnshire dialect, like 'The Northern Farmer' pieces, increasingly valued for their novelty, their regional cachet and relaxed naturalism. There are poems of friendship, mostly in letter form, all finely decorous and graced with feeling, of which several examples are included in this selection. And there are the identifiably 'Laureate' poems, the most successful ever written in that discredited genre: paeans to heroes of English history and prehistory, responses, like 'The Charge of the Light Brigade', to the day's events, but also the more demanding and (in the execution) aptly ceremonial 'Ode on the Death of the Duke of Wellington'.

The Poet Laureate of the foremost national power of the day was famously short-sighted (one reason why his landscapes were so often 'glimmering'), and that might be said to apply also to his sympathies. He felt with England rather than mankind; if he especially deplored the 'red fool-fury' of the French, even the Greater Britain, incorporating 'the blind hysterics of the Celt', could provoke his conservative distaste. In comparison with his Romantic predecessors, he shunned the forward look, and if he favoured 'liberty' it was by gradations, in a land 'Where Freedom slowly broadens down / From precedent to precedent'. The best remedy he can come up with for the corruption of the capitalist system, as discovered by the manic narrator of *Maud*, is war.

Yet within his limits, which did not extend to conditions in the mill towns, Tennyson had always busied himself to look in touch with the present day. His self-consciousness on this front produces curious effects in the poems he grouped under the title 'English Idyls' ('Edwin Morris' is included here), where fragments of the contemporary, in particular the new geology, are presented like museum pieces. In 'Audley Court', picnickers enjoy a 'pasty costly-made! Where quail and pigeon, lark and leveret lay! Like fossils of the rock'; in 'The Golden Year', an old Welshman ponders the seasons: 'He spoke; and high above, I heard them blast! The steep slate-quarry'. Again, the fashionable side of Tennyson devised modern frames for legendary narratives, things like the apologies with which later poets dress their wares at readings: 'The Epic', a 'prelude of disparagement' which provides an amiable fireside context for the Homeric 'Morte d'Arthur'; or the preamble to a poem about Lady Godiva, beginning, like Philip Larkin at his flattest, 'I waited for the train at Coventry ...' Still, the old-style poems are the point; not the insinuating prologues.

These shuffles of address are one sign of Tennyson knowing exactly what he was good at, and how this differed from what he might like to write. He told a friend, James Knowles,

> I soon found that if I meant to make any mark at all it must be by shortness, for all the men before me had been so diffuse [he was thinking of Wordsworth], and all the big things had been done. To get the workmanship as nearly perfect as possible is the best chance for going down the stream of time. A small vessel on fine lines is likely to float further than a great raft.

The choice of the small vessel was not quite so strategic: if T. S. Eliot's verdict that 'For narrative Tennyson had no gift at all' is an exaggeration, Tennyson knew that his genius was for stillness, not for action. Yet the poet coveted the major status that could only be conferred by larger structures. Hence, each of the four 'big things' of his maturity hazards, with conscious and sometimes laborious originality, a new combination of forms; and each of them registers a total word count that belies the local scale of its most memorable effects.

The first of these, *The Princess* (1847), while still striking every reader as too long, deliberately sheds the responsibilities of the long poem, in all manner of disclaimers that begin with the protective modesty of its subtitle, 'A Medley'. In the poem's conclusion, the narrator wonders afresh what kind of poem (were he to make it into a poem!) would suit the material he has just put before us: should it be burlesque or epic? Should he aim to satisfy 'the mockers' in his audience, or the realists?

> And I, betwixt them both, to please them both,
> And yet to give the story as it rose,
> I moved as in a strange diagonal,
> And maybe neither pleased myself nor them.

Indeed, the poem's chief distinction by far are its ten interpolated lyrics or arias, 'Tears, idle tears ...', 'Now sleeps the crimson petal ...' and the others, whose place is dismissively contrived – 'And let the ladies sing us, if they will, / From time to time, some ballad or a song' – and whose millions of readers have generally met them relieved of their context. These beautiful luxuries are inset like gems in a narrative – about a women's university, incidentally – that is speculative, whimsical, rambling, unsure of its trajectory or success.

Succeeding ventures were no less a matter, formally speaking, of seeking out the 'strange diagonal'. *In Memoriam* (1850) is made up of as many as 132 sections, each of several quatrains in the same simple stanza form and humble diction: to the connoisseur of these things, it is not least an album of the changes that can be rung out of a single lyric idea. But the poem repeatedly questions whether the physical flimsiness of its parts, 'Short swallow-flights of song, that dip / Their wings in tears, and skim away', are up to the philosophical labour, the engagement with death and the Universe, that it sets out to accomplish. By contrast, the book-length poem *Maud* (1855) unleashes a whole range of different lyric forms, intended to simulate the fluctuating and contending moods of the narrator, an unnamed madman. In *Maud*, the story is shadowed rather than told: since the action occurs between the 'scenes', and is erratically reported, the puzzle is what really happens – a murder, we suppose. A contemporary reviewer, Ralph Mann, coined the genre 'monodrama' to define the poem; Tennyson immediately adopted the suggestion as a subtitle, and nothing else has been called a 'monodrama' since.

Then there was *Idylls of the King*: the project, developed over forty years, that Tennyson considered (especially before he had finished it) his magnum opus: here the battle between the big scheme and the little vessel is enacted in the title. Tennyson's own choice of title, both for the four-book volume published in 1859 and for the final scheme of 1885 that evolved around it, posits a blend of the matter and proportions of epic with the local techniques of the miniature. The *Idylls* of 1885 appeared 'In Twelve Books', in blank verse, with Homeric formulae, a distinct moral design, and an allegorical drift; on the other hand, Tennyson explicitly rejected the term 'epic' as a 'misnomer', and wrote pedantically of his alternative definition, 'I spelt my Idylls with two *l*s mainly to divide them from the ordinary pastoral idyls usually spelt with one *l*'. Moreover, these are not *The Idylls*, as if they were exhaustive, but *Idylls*, a selection of the possible. The work is at once one poem, and twelve, or neither; both vastly ambitious and sweet with the pathos of inadequacy.

The *Idylls* will never again be read for its (or their) wooden dialogue, for its moral design or the tentative gimmicks of its narrative – if it ever was. 'I can only read it for the sake of the next lollipop', complained one contemporary, 'but the lollipops when they come are delicious'. The pick of those treats are the moments, still, of trance: whether they strike Arthur, or Guinevere, or Lancelot ('Round whose sick head all night, like birds of prey, / The words of Arthur flying shrieked'), or Merlin:

> So dark a forethought rolled about his brain,
> As on a dull day in an ocean cave
> The blind wave feeling round his long sea-hall
> In silence ...

For these are not illuminations of a particular character: the reader's experience in every case is of the same single mind reeling in its isolation. The lines of Tennyson's longer poems, like the mass of his shorter ones, can be separated almost categorically into the live (for this is how it strikes the reader) and the manufactured. And the essential energy, whatever fabulous guise it assumes, whatever the landscape it echoes in, is privately generated; it is the poet's sadness.

In consequence of such things, the word 'from', indicating an extract, is unusually prevalent on the contents page of this volume. But no one says of Tennyson that you need to read the whole to appreciate the parts. Just as the *Idylls* is a pageant whose longueurs justify its sudden depths, *Maud* a contrivance for the venting of buried steam, and *The Princess* an elaborate cabinet setting for its sublime lyrics, the whole of Tennyson's long career is a shelter for the sensational revelation of his melancholy. The 'life's work' of which 'Crossing the Bar' may be called the 'crown' is the practice – covert at times – of a lyric vocation. Tennyson stands as he intended, as a great poet of proven range and formidable stamina: but one who is none the less ideally read in selection.

Anthony Trollope

'An Ample Living by his Pen'

Dr Wortle's School
Penguin Classics

Dr Wortle's School is a 'late' work, the fortieth, in order of publication, of Anthony Trollope's forty-seven novels; he wrote it in April 1879, the month of his sixty-fourth birthday, fewer than four years before his death. At 85,000 words, it is not the shortest of his books, but it was certainly (though Trollope was always amazingly fluent) the most rapidly composed. Trollope began it on 8 April and finished it on the 29th, filling exactly twelve manuscript pages for each of twenty-two days. The book's first claim on our curiosity may therefore be as the fastest-written of all novels of lasting worth.

One benefit of the book's almost instantaneous composition – especially when set against the longwindedness of other novels of Trollope's last years – is its effect of concentration. (Compare *John Caldigate*, published in the year *Dr Wortle* was written, which the *Times* reviewer fairly called 'a good novel expanded into a dull one'.) There is one rather perfunctory subplot: the romance between Mary Wortle and Lord Carstairs, appealing – so the author calculated – to his army of young lady readers; this is carried off with much avuncular winking, and is so thoroughly conventional as to culminate in the moment at which Mary becomes 'the happiest young lady in the *diocese*' (my italics). Otherwise, the novelist sticks fast to his central issue, which would have seemed less conventional: the question whether the moral principles on which his society is built may not, in certain situations, be found unjust. His test case is one of bigamy.

The theme of bigamy had been broached in two of the novel's recent predecessors, *Is He Popenjoy?* (1878) and *John Caldigate* (1879). But in *Dr Wortle's School* the offence is indeed committed, and prolonged, though in circumstances so extenuating that the novel's central intelligence is unable to condemn it outright. The grounds of the bigamy precede the action of the novel. Mr Peacocke, a Classical scholar from England and an evidently decent man, is 'vice-president' of a university in St Louis, Missouri. There he falls in love with Ella Lefroy (née Beaufort), whose degenerate husband has deserted her to try his luck on the frontier. The would-be lovers dutifully suppress their feelings, until rumours reach Peacocke that the husband – Ferdinand, one of two brothers, both called 'Colonel Lefroy' – has been killed in a mélée on the Mexican border. Peacocke heads off to Texas to investigate these rumours; on hearing their confirmation from the other brother, Robert, he returns to marry the 'widow'.

But whether or not Robert Lefroy has been consciously lying, Ferdinand is still alive. He materializes one day – a 'horrible apparition' – in his wife's (and Peacocke's wife's) drawing-room, and exposes their unwitting bigamy. Dismayed and desperate, 'the Peacockes' migrate to England, where they hope to pass as man and wife, and come to live in Dr Jeffrey Wortle's school at Bowick, in the imaginary Midlands county of Broughtonshire; he as assistant teacher of Classics, she as school matron. But doubts creep in over Mr Peacocke's conscientious reluctance to act as curate in the parish church (where Wortle is Rector); and his confession to Dr Wortle is hastened by the sudden appearance at the school of the blackmailing Robert Lefroy. (Lefroy comes, like the retributive figure of Raffles out of Bulstrode's shady past in George Eliot's *Middlemarch* [1872], the worse for alcohol.) Dr Wortle, disinclined to judge his unfortunate new friends, finds that in their case 'the common rules of life seem to be insufficient for guidance' (Chapter XIX), and holds out against the world's view – the malicious gossip of Mrs Stantiloup, his Bishop's concern for respectabilities, the impeccable but unforgiving logic of Mr Puddicombe, the timidity of his own wife – until, as the scandal heightens, the future of his school is put in jeopardy. The crisis is only resolved, somewhat fortuitously, by twin actions of American depravity: for a fee of a thousand dollars, the blackmailer Robert Lefroy conducts Peacocke once more through the Western states to the place where Ferdinand Lefroy has drunk himself to his second death. This time, the evidence is allowed to be sound. The Peacockes are absolved, and the school prospers anew.

The matter of the novel gave some disquiet to William Blackwood, proprietor of the magazine which bore his name and in which *Dr Wortle's School* had its serial publication between May and December 1880. Blackwood wrote to Trollope on 7 April of that year:

> I was rather alarmed about the story when I read that Mr & Mrs Peacocke were not man & wife but your explanation of the mystery speedily dispels any disagreeable feeling about the tone of the story that might startle sensitive readers and I am sure that the plot in your hands will not take any unpleasant turn.

It is to head off such unpleasantness that Trollope plants the explanation of the novel's 'mystery' so early in his narrative (in Chapter III, within the first serial instalment). As he makes the revelation, he acknowledges that this is to sacrifice potential 'interest'. But the loss will not have seemed so much to Trollope. In the same chapter he distinguishes his own brand of fiction from the type of the novel of action, as patented by Sir Walter Scott. What stimulates his own 'interest' here, as ever, is the psychological drama activated by events, rather than the course of events themselves.

This emphasis on the subjective and character-revealing view of a moral question is reminiscent of some of the dramatic monologues written in the 1850s and 1860s by Trollope's friend Robert Browning. In the early 1860s, Browning offered Trollope the use of a collection of documents he had found on a Florentine stall relating to an Italian murder trial of the seventeenth century. Trollope declined the gift; and Browning turned the materials instead into his masterpiece, *The Ring and the Book* (1868–9). Here, a number of speakers contribute different and sometimes contradictory fragments towards a complex 'truth' – and pose therefore a philosophic challenge to the idea of an absolute morality. The review of *Dr Wortle's School* in New York's *Critic* magazine in February 1881 makes it sound like a miniature experiment on similar lines:

> There is originality as well as ingenuity in the idea of developing all the characters of the story simply by their relation to a single event not in itself important to any but the chief actors. By their approval or disapproval of Mr Peacocke's course, we gain a complete photograph of the mental and moral qualities of all the persons in the story.

But if this was Trollope's original plan, its traces are obscured in the execution. The reader of the novel does not feel the equality of characterization this review suggests. Though the early chapters display half-a-dozen viewpoints on the bigamy, it is Jeffrey Wortle's attitude that predominates, until those who disagree with him become so many adversaries for him to overcome. Wortle's 'victory' converts what might have been a more communal scheme into something with the self-justifying atmosphere of the earlier model of Browning monologue. (Wortle, moreover, has the bristling, exclamatory temper of many of Browning's 'speakers'.) It registers as much, perhaps, that Trollope changed his title in the course of composition from 'Mr and Mrs Peacocke' through 'Bowick School' to *Dr Wortle's School.*

But there is a further dimension to the priority of Dr Wortle within his novel, and that is the extent to which he resembles his creator. Trollope's first biographer, T. H. S. Escott, noted that 'Dr Wortle has the same reputation as Trollope himself for blustering amiability, an imperious manner and a good heart'; Trollope's son Henry, writing to Michael Sadleir in 1923, remembered being 'struck in reading *Dr Wortle's School* with a likeness, not on all fours, between the Doctor and my father'.

This would give *Dr Wortle's School* a special place in Trollope's *oeuvre.* There is nothing much like self-portraiture in all the fiction that had gone before. Some have seen a reflection of Trollope's marriage in a pair of characters in 'Mrs General Talboys', a story of 1860 with overtones of sexual licence judged 'ill-natured' by Trollope's wife Rose. The American 'literary lion' Conrad Mackinnon is 'a big burly man, near to fifty' (Trollope was forty-five when he wrote the story), 'somewhat awkward in his gait, and somewhat loud in his laugh', proud, as Trollope was, of earning 'an ample living by his pen', and something of a flirt: he 'liked to be smiled on by pretty women, and liked, as some said, to be flattered by them also'. Of Mrs Mackinnon, by contrast, 'no one did make much … always in good humour, never stupid … yet she was generally in the background. She would seldom come forward of her own free will, but was contented to sit behind her teapot and hear Mackinnon do his roaring.' Mrs Mackinnon thus anticipates Mrs Wortle, who 'went nowhere without the Doctor, and wherever he went she enjoyed her share of the respect which was always shown to him'.

But Mrs Wortle has also, for a while, a more active complacency about her which connects her to Rose Trollope. Rose refused to have

Anthony's friends 'George Eliot' and George Lewes in her home (Lewes was married to another woman); and Trollope may have heard from his own wife the stubborn orthodoxy ascribed to Mrs Wortle, that a 'woman should not live with a man unless she be his wife', pronounced with all 'the comfort, the beauty, the perfect sense of her own position', and he may have struggled, like the Doctor, not to find this 'hard' (Chapter IX). Mrs Wortle's softening – from this fixity, through a baffled, mouselike clinging to convention, to the womanly sympathy of Chapter XIX – is less a moral maturing than a growth of her compliance: in the end, had she been in Ella Peacocke's shoes, 'she certainly would have done whatever Dr Wortle had told her'.

What makes these marital correspondences more intriguing is the presence of an American beauty as a catalyst. Through the two decades of his life preceding the writing of *Dr Wortle's School*, Trollope was sentimentally attached to a beautiful, vivacious and outspoken young woman from Boston, Kate Field. They had met first in the autumn of 1860, at the Villino Trollope, the home in Florence of Anthony's elder brother Tom, when he was forty-five and she twenty-two. (In the novel, Wortle is in his mid-fifties, Mrs Peacocke 'something over thirty'.) Though there is no evidence, and little likelihood, of actual impropriety, there was certainly unaccustomed sweetness for Trollope in the intimacy; and many a scene, to judge from his surviving letters to Kate Field, like the one in *Dr Wortle's School*, Chapter XIII, where 'Then, and not till then, he dropped her hand.'

The nearest approach in Trollope's fiction to a portrait of Kate Field is the story 'Miss Ophelia Gledd' (1863), whose heroine, 'the belle of Boston', makes a surprising choice of suitor, accepting an English 'literary man of some mark' fifteen years her senior. The story, narrated by a figure on the margin of events, ends with an obscure question-mark over the perceived morality of American girls, anticipating the ground between snobbery and moral uncertainty that is braved by Dr Wortle: '... will she or will she not be received in London as a lady, – as such a lady as my friend Pryor might have been expected to take for his wife?' Kate Field never married. Such questions and situations offer imaginary playgrounds for Trollope's feelings for her.

According to the most recent biographer, 'Rose knew about her husband's infatuation, and was upset.' But Trollope was neither furtive in, nor ashamed of his affection. He writes of it in *An Autobiography* – in 1876, though the book was only to be published posthumously; more bluffly, perhaps, than if the passage were to be read when he was alive, but with no sense that the admission might be at all scandalous:

> There is an American woman, of whom not to speak in a work purporting to be a memoir of my own life would be to omit all allusion to one of the chief pleasures which has graced my later years. In the last fifteen years she has been, out of my family, my most chosen friend. She is a ray of light to me, from which I can always strike a spark by thinking of her. I do not know that I should please her or do any good by naming her. But not to allude to her in these pages would amount almost to a falsehood.

Editing the *Autobiography* for its first publication, in 1883, after his father's death, Henry Trollope omitted the word 'American', apparently feeling the need for more discretion than his father had shown. In fact, the passage falls within a discussion of the various strengths and weaknesses of Americans in general; and by taking away its context, Henry made it seem a stranger and more pointed confessional.

Part of Trollope's complex relationship with America was inherited. When he was a boy at school in England, his mother, Frances Trollope, lived for two miserable years in Cincinnati, Ohio, where she owned a 'bazaar'; on her return to England she wrote her celebrated *Domestic Manners of the North Americans* (1832). The gist of the book is expressed in its closing chapter: 'I do not like them. I do not like their principles, I do not like their manners, I do not like their opinions.' The book was a phenomenal success. In England, it was influential in forming the English idea of American behaviour for some time; 'trollopize' became a recognized verb, meaning 'to abuse the American nation'. Across the Atlantic the book caused an immediate frenzy and lasting soreness.

But the son's view of America was altogether more even-handed. He made five trips in all to the States, which made him something of a connoisseur of the country among English writers of his day; and he found much there, beside Kate Field, to admire. On the second of his trips, in 1861–2, during the Civil War, he visited Washington College, St Louis, Missouri, where in *Dr Wortle's School* Mr Peacocke is a professor (Trollope's host there was T. S. Eliot's grandfather). His observations on that trip are recorded rather shapelessly in his two-volume *North America* (1862), which he later judged 'tedious and confused … not a good book'.

There are over thirty American characters in Trollope's fiction, and few of them are stereotypes as plain as the Lefroy brothers of *Dr Wortle's School*. Three short stories – 'The Courtship of Susan Bell' (1860), 'Miss Ophelia Gledd' and 'The Two Generals' (both 1863) – are set in America; but *Dr Wortle's School* is the only one of the novels to have American scenes. (The eponymous American Senator of 1877, Elias Gotobed, is used exclusively to give an outside perspective on English matters.)

The American scenes of *Dr Wortle's School* were said, by a contemporary New York reviewer, to have 'an antique flavour which carries one back to the days of Martin Chuzzlewit' (*Nation*, 10 March 1881). A recent critic (James R. Kincaid) has repeated the charge that they 'simply reiterate … the America of *Martin Chuzzlewit* [1843–4]', the land of 'nothing but revolvers and bowie-knives', in Mark Tapley's summation. But it should be borne in mind that these scenes depict a journey into and through the lawless West, in the company of an embittered dipsomaniac from the defeated South. If Trollope – at odds with the opinion prevailing in England – was unsympathetic towards the South, he had an active dislike for the life he had encountered in the West. The tone of *North America* turns sour with Western motion. Trollope finds the people of St Louis, which was still then considered a 'Western' city, lacking in culture, discipline and grace; he hates in particular the behaviour of the men in bars, standing to drink or 'loafing' over newspapers and cigars (the vice is extended in *Dr Wortle's School* to the men of Chicago): 'In the West I found the men gloomy and silent – I might almost say sullen … They are essentially a dirty people.' Trollope revisited the West in 1872, on his way back to England from Australia, and found the place rife with commercial speculation, greed and dishonesty. The worst of the several speculators in *The Way We Live Now* (1875), which he started to write on his return to London, is described as having 'sprung out of some California gully'.

These perceptions of America are relevant to the whispers against Mr Peacocke that blow through the cloisters and drawing-rooms of Broughtonshire. Peacocke's decision to take a post there seems, to provincial England, like a defection from his natural place:

He had been well known to a large Oxford circle, but he had suddenly disappeared from that world, and it had reached the ears of only a few of his more intimate friends that he had undertaken the duties of vice-president of a classical college at Saint Louis in the State of Missouri ... after five years Mr Peacocke appeared again at Oxford, with a beautiful American wife, and the necessity of earning an income by his erudition. (Chapter II)

Further, and even to his advocate, the choice of St Louis involves a necessary element of 'backsliding'. For, while his motive may have been simply financial (though distasteful enough for that reason to privileged opinion), he has chosen, after all, to make his career in a place, like the Australia of *John Caldigate*, where the usual conventions of marriage may not apply. (In *The Way We Live Now*, Winifred Hurtle has survived shadowy but stormy marital experiences in America; it is suggested that she may have used a pistol on her husband.) In allowing Peacocke to be judged so by association, Trollope is conflating a prejudice against America in general, which he does not share (though his mother was partly responsible for creating it), with his own local grudge against the West.

Neither is it in Peacocke's favour, if the respectability of his character is under scrutiny, that on his return from America he should have sought employment as a schoolmaster. To have a school – like Dr Wortle – is one thing; to be any sort of assistant master is much less; and to be a plain 'usher', like Peacocke, is something lower still. (Trollope himself was an usher in a private school in Brussels, for a few humiliating weeks, when he was nineteen, and his bankrupt father had fled with the family to Belgium.) In *An Autobiography*, Trollope honours the distinction regretfully when chronicling the misfortunes of a doomed friend, 'W. A.': 'He then became a schoolmaster, – or perhaps I had better say usher.' In the opening scene of *The Claverings* (1867), Julia Brabazon slights Harry Clavering, in the course of rejecting his suit, by calling him an 'usher', a charge against which he vigorously defends himself: 'No, madam, I am not an usher at a school ... I am a schoolmaster.' The distinction is reinforced at the beginning of the second chapter of that novel:

> Harry Clavering might not be an usher, but ... who can say where the usher ends and the schoolmaster begins? He, perhaps, may properly be called an usher, who is hired by a private schoolmaster to assist him in his private occupation, whereas Harry Clavering had been selected by a public body out of a hundred candidates ... He was certainly not an usher, as he was paid three hundred a year for his work ...

Usher or not, the jilted Harry Clavering announces on the same page his intention to become a civil engineer.

The prejudice against any rank of the teaching profession beneath that of headmaster was not peculiar to Trollope or his novels. A witness before a Royal Commission of 1877 (two years before *Dr Wortle's School* was written) refers to 'women ... and the second- and third-rate men who ... become schoolmasters' as those for whom English was a suitable subject for study at university. Otherwise, the profession was the resort of those with third-class or pass degrees, giving them a meagre annual salary of around £80 or £90. Vincent Van Gogh, teaching at a private school in Isleworth in 1876, received no salary at all. A gentleman could hardly consign himself to a less prestigious position; or one less honourably represented in fiction.

The first issue of the *Preparatory Schools Review* in 1895 carried an article by W. T. Sutthery entitled 'The Assistant Master, Past, Present and Future':

> The world is waiting for one of two things: either for a novelist who will give us a portrait of one of the many gentlemen ... who become preparatory school-masters ... or for a race of schoolmasters who will so inspire novelists ... there will be a rush to make them the heroes of fiction.

Trollope is not that novelist, and Peacocke is not his hero; the novel is less concerned with Peacocke's dilemma than with Dr Wortle's reaction to it. That said, the physically vigorous and sexually unambiguous Peacocke fares better than most of his fellow-teachers in serious fiction before and since. The figure of Richard Phillotson in Hardy's *Jude the Obscure* (1895) – published a few months after Sutthery's article – is typically pinched and bloodless:

> A chastened and disappointed man ... a spare and thoughtful personage of five and forty, with a thin lipped, somewhat relined mouth, a slightly stoop-ing habit, and a frock coat, which from continuous frictions shone a little at the elbows ... An unhealthy looking old-fashioned face ... His greying hair curly and radiated from a point in the middle of his crown. There were lines across his forehead, and he wore spectacles when reading at night.

If the stereotype of sexual incapacity and social isolation has persisted in our century, in figures like Andrew Crocker-Harris, 'shrivelled inside like a nut' in Terence Rattigan's play *The Browning Version* (1948), it was already well established when Trollope chose to submit Peacock to its associations. Charles Lamb had written of 'The Old and the New Schoolmaster' in an essay of 1821:

> Why are we never at ease in the presence of a schoolmaster? – because we are conscious that he is not quite at his ease in ours. He is awkward, and out of place, in the society of his equals. He comes like Gulliver from among little people, and he cannot fit the stature of his understanding to yours. He cannot meet you on the square. He wants a point given him like an indifferent whist-player ... the jests of a schoolmaster are poor or thin, they do not tell out of school ... He is forlorn among his co-evals; his juniors cannot be his friends.

It is this common perception to which W. T. Sutthery, the preparatory school master who would be a hero, forlornly objects in his article of 1895: 'The fact is, we fear, that a false estimate of our profession is abroad which considers a gentleman in an absurd position if he teaches or looks after little boys.'

The teaching staff of *Dr Wortle's School* – with their 'absurd' positions – are enumerated in a single sentence: 'There was a French master, a German master, a master for arithmetic and mathematics with the adjacent sciences, besides Mr Peacocke, as assistant classical master' (Chapter IV). Only one of these other ushers is subsequently named, and they do not appear as persons in the narrative; even in a novel named after the school they serve, they are beneath notice. They are 'out of place' in adult society, with the dangers this implies for Peacocke's case. He comes to his crisis thus doubly diminished, by his 'escapade' in America and by the lowliness of his occupation.

Peacocke has to be a blameless man for Wortle (with Trollope's backing) to risk his moral reputation as well as his livelihood in his usher's cause. His essential virtue is therefore established as early as Chapter II, by having him rescue little Jack De Lawle from the danger of drowning. But just as his 'small and wiry' person seems overshadowed by Wortle's, so his character remains remote, even insipid next to the Doctor's expressive 'manliness'. Neither Trollope nor Wortle extend themselves to make him likeable; he is indeed allowed to be annoying: 'This the usher [the pejorative term again] said with a tone of self-assertion which grated a little on the Doctor's ear' (Chapter IV). Wortle's allegiance is revealingly confused. We are told (in Chapter II) that 'Mr Peacocke had some power about him which was potent over the Doctor's spirit': but the first words of the next sentence tell us what that power is – 'Mrs Peacocke …' Trollope plays a variant of this trick later in the novel: 'As he thought of it all he began to be almost tired of Mr Peacocke. Nevertheless, on the Saturday morning, before he started, he called on Mrs Peacocke …' (Chapter XV).

The effacement of Mr Peacocke is part of the novel's love-affair with Mrs Peacocke; and so is the rough treatment meted out to 'poor' Mrs Wortle. The most clearly positive remark about the Doctor's wife – that 'in her day she had been the beauty of Windsor and those parts' – is almost boorishly faint praise; as if we were to say of a woman today that 'in the mid-1970s she had been thought the best-looking girl in Slough'. By contrast, the living 'loveliness' of Mrs Peacocke is not only felt but acted on; it cannot be separated from the rest of the Doctor's motivation: 'It would perhaps be unfair to raise a question whether he would have done as much, been so willing to sacrifice himself for a plain woman' (Chapter XIII).

Wortle is libeled. The London satirical weekly *Everybody's Business* runs a light-hearted piece suggesting that this rural clergyman, having sent the second husband to America to deal with, or be dealt with by, the first, is meanwhile enjoying the company of their wife. In Chapter XV, the Doctor finds himself repeating aloud the most wounding phrase of the article: '"Amo" in the cool of the evening!' And yet the phrase resonates through the novel in unsuspected ways.

It is not only that the phrase suggests (in a less coarse fashion than he pretends) how Wortle's middle age has been warmed by the chance to act gallantly on behalf of beauty in distress; or that we can match this pleasant feeling with our knowledge of the way the last third of Trollope's life was touched by Kate Field's 'ray of light'. Trollope pitched his fiction consciously beneath the level achieved by the highest literary art; his is a sociable gift. One consequence of this is the narrowed and particular sense we get of the reader he seems to be addressing. The reader of *Dr Wortle's School* may feel like an intelligent young woman, recipient of the experience and affection of an older gentleman who can flirt without foolishness; one in whom, 'at the end of the day', wisdom and tenderness are instructively combined.

Matthew Arnold

A Poet Aged Before His Time

A Gift Imprisoned: The Poetic Life of Matthew Arnold
Ian Hamilton, Bloomsbury

At several points in Ian Hamilton's recent collection of essays, *The Trouble with Money* (1997), the lives of literary men are seen to break in two. Reviewing a book about Louis MacNeice, Hamilton records that 'when (MacNeice) joined the BBC in 1940, at the age of thirty-three, he spoke of his past life as 'dead'. Something comparable happened in 1915, when 'Ford Madox Hueffer became Ford Madox Ford – by deed poll. Around the same time, at the age of forty-one, he enlisted for active service in the British Army.' A third piece, on Salman Rushdie, is prefaced: 'When I first discussed with him the idea of a biographical essay, he said that he would co-operate, provided that I did not pursue my researches beyond what was for him the final day of his first life: Valentine's Day, 1989' (the day after the passing of the Iranian fatwa, when, like the expiring 'Hueffer', Rushdie was forty-one). The essay is called 'The First Life of Salman Rushdie'. Beside these modern instances, the 'double life' of Matthew Arnold (1822–c.58; c.1858–88) is an established classic of the genre. The given line is that, at some point in his mid-thirties, Arnold the poet perished, and a prose Arnold (in Hamilton's unenthusiastic phrase, a 'cultural physician') arose to take his place.

In his review for the *TLS* of Nicholas Murray's full-scale biography (June 14, 1996), Nicholas Shrimpton protested at the durability of this simplistic 'binary picture'; he noted, for instance, that while Arnold's most celebrated single poem, 'Dover Beach', has been routinely linked to the poet's honeymoon in 1851, there is no external evidence for the piece having been composed at any stage before its first publication in 1867, deep into the purportedly 'dead' years. Yet it is precisely the discontinuity in Arnold's story that has appealed to Hamilton; and in his stylish short study of the 'poetic' or 'first' life, which takes its title from W. H. Auden's Freudian reading ('He thrust his gift in prison till it died'), Arnold is divided as never before. 'I soon enough abandoned plans for a cradle-to-grave Life', Hamilton's preface tells us, as if the latter were a mountainous aim rather than the ordinary shape of such things; as if the two lives were so distinct that one would naturally write a book about one and pass over the other. That his time on earth should include a metaphorical death – the short bloom and irreversible withering of his poetry-writing accords with Arnold's acute, even exaggerated awareness of ageing and personal mortality. The latter he got from his father.

Matthew and his brothers and sisters grew up under the kindly but demanding influence of 'the most earnest man in England'; the eldest son's reaction, as a young man, was to strike the foppish pose of a 'scented wit' (which, being put on, annoyed as many as it charmed). But while Matthew was still an undergraduate at Balliol College, Oxford, Dr Arnold, recently installed as Regius Professor of Modern History at the University, collapsed and died of heart disease, like his own father before him, at the age of only forty-six. Hereafter Matthew, who had inherited the family abnormality, was aware that he in his turn could die at any minute. His first substantial poem, 'Mycerinus' (begun around 1843, when he was twenty), tells of a young Egyptian ruler who learns from an oracle that he must die before his time. Meanwhile, Arnold had to make a living. He had neither yet taken a job, nor written anything of note, when, in 1845, he was cursing the lot of the poet forced into uncongenial employment, quoting, in a letter, from Goethe's *Wilhelm Meister*:

> And thus the poet is at once a teacher, a prophet, a friend of gods and men. How! thou wouldst have him descend from his height to some paltry occupation? He who is fashioned like the bird to hover round the world, to nestle on the lofty summits, to feed on buds and fruits, exchanging gaily one bough for another, he ought also to work at the plough like an ox; like a dog to train himself to the harness and draught; or perhaps, tied up in a chain, to guard a farmyard by his barking?

In fact, Arnold's first appointment was in all respects advantageous. In 1847, through family connections, he was installed as Private Secretary to

Lord Lansdowne, then President of the Council and a considerable private patron of the arts: a stimulating and socially enhancing position, with a salary of £300 a year, and one which was ideally suited for the trying-out of poetry as a vocation. Measured by the output of verses, these were prolific years. What brought them to an end was a compulsion, suddenly overwhelming other considerations, towards marriage.

Hamilton has little to add to the baseless heap of speculation on the identity of 'Marguerite', the blue-eyed muse Arnold encountered in Switzerland in September 1848, and with whom he suffered an embittering reunion twelve months later. But he notes suggestively how soon after Arnold's rebound from the Alps he is determinedly pursuing his bride-to-be – so soon, indeed, that her eyes blend with Marguerite's in a composite love poem – 'eyes too expressive to be blue / Too lovely to be grey' ('On the Rhine'). 'Flu' Wightman, the daughter of a pious, High Anglican and Tory judge, had grey eyes and parental expectations beyond £300 a year. Arnold married her in June 1851. By October, he was at work as an Inspector of Schools, on a salary of £700. As Hamilton puts it, this was to exchange a life of friendships, parties, grand houses, art and leisure for hard slog, 'shabbily provincial stop-offs' and well-mannered weekends at the Wightmans' house in Eaton Place. Of course, grind is relative, and Arnold's new lot permitted him – less than eighteen months into the job and the marriage – to make a 'solemn vow' with his wife 'to spend at least seven weeks abroad next year'. But Arnold's habitual moaning suddenly had a focus, and his anxieties about poetry were submerged beneath an 'avalanche' of 'paperwork' and concrete excuses. His marriage was soon favoured with children, who turned his home into a 'howling wilderness'. If Arnold could observe, before he was thirty years old, that 'a great career (in literature) is barely possible any longer', he had made certain choices that suggest an unconscious desire to be delivered from the possibility.

But the central thesis of *A Gift Imprisoned* is that Arnold's best qualities as a poet are those he valued least, so that his principles fought an intermittent fruitless battle against his practice. He diagnosed the age as needing the kind of poems he couldn't really write; by the same token, in Hamilton's words, he was driven to 'repudiate … those elements which urged him towards poetry in the first place'. He strained (and much of his verse shows the strain) against the accusation of self-absorption, 'against the modern English habit (too much encouraged by Wordsworth) of using

poetry as a channel for thinking aloud, instead of making anything'; in
'Resignation' (finished in 1847) we are told that the poet 'does not say I am
alone', but sees 'That general life, which does not cease'. Hence the unsuit-
able device of the first person plural in subsequent poems: 'We mortal
millions live alone' ('To Marguerite – Continued'). His first collection, *The
Strayed Reveller and Other Poems* (1847), is a casebook of authorial anxi-
eties, and the volume's lukewarm reception only left him more defiantly
at odds with himself: '(Campbell) Shairp urges me to speak more from
myself: which I less and less have the inclination to do …' He was in no
less of a muddle by 1852, when he published *Empedocles on Etna and Other
Poems*, only to withdraw it six months later on the grounds that it was
'monotonous'. A further reshaping of the *oeuvre*, *Poems* (1853), published
when Arnold was thirty, was intended to project a purposeful new image
of the poet. The intense, subjective poems of youth were excluded. The
book was centred on the heroic narrative 'Sohrab and Rustum' (slighted
here as 'Homer for beginners' and an 'adventure in maturity') and intro-
duced by the neo-classical prescriptions of the famous 'Preface' – a 'wan
prospectus', in Hamilton's enjoyable phrase.

Poems (1853) was reviewed in the *Daily News* by Arnold's friend and
admirer Harriet Martineau. This is the review for which Hamilton's nar-
rative has been waiting, the implied answer to his question, 'Was he,
so to speak, a natural?': He was not born a poet, and therefore never
can be one. Many claim the rank; few show claims as plausible as his,
because of the superiority of his general talents and culture; but his
claims also want the genuine stamp. Hamilton's own estimate of the
poetry is lower than the reader of his book might have expected. He
likes 'Dover Beach', 'The Buried Life', 'Empedocles on Etna', 'The Scholar
Gipsy' and some of the 'Marguerite' poems; not that he trumpets their
qualities here, but he spares them from the gentle cynicism with which
in general he approaches the verse. He is economically sharp about
the 'Greek drapery' of Merope, the mock-Hellenic verse play on which
Arnold laboured in the mid-1850s – 'so diligent, so well-intentioned
and so wrong' – and catches in a phrase the 'chin-forward, missionary
striving' of later poems like 'Obermann Once More'. But his treatment
of *Balder Dead* (1855), a stiff piece of Norse Homeric, points out how –
in a half-dozen similes which seem to have intruded from eighteenth-
century English pastoral – a native poetry could poke through the frigid
designs of Arnold's 'maturity':

And as a spray of honeysuckle flowers
Brushes across a tired traveller's face
Who shuffles through the deep dew-moistened dust,
On a May evening, in the darkened lanes,
And starts him, that he thinks a ghost went by
So Hoder brushed by Hermod's side …

Ironically, Hamilton considers 'Growing Old' (1867) to be one of the few later poems to recapture the 'distressed and unaffected eloquence' of the best early poetry:

It is – last stage of all –
When we are frozen up within, and quite
The phantom of ourselves,
To hear the world applaud the hollow ghost
Which blamed the living man.

'Growing Old' recalls those strange letters, written in the cool late phase of their friendship, to Arthur Hugh Clough, in which the young Arnold had lamented lost youth; one, written in 1852, when he was newly married and about to become a father for the first time: 'How life rushes away – and youth. One has dawdled and scrupled and fiddle-faddled – and it is all over'; and another, a few months later, to the same recipient: 'I am past thirty and three parts iced over.'

Hamilton's study culminates in 1858, when, in an unhappy and opaque letter to his sister Jane, Arnold seems to announce his resignation from poetry: 'to attain or approach perfection in the region of thought and feeling, and to write with this perfection of form, demands … an actual tearing of oneself to pieces, which one does not readily consent to … unless one can devote one's whole life to poetry.' The few remaining pages of *A Gift Imprisoned* assemble further full stops and funereal reflections. Arnold at forty considers how:

The twenty years from 20 to 40 seemed all life to me then – the very heart of one's time here, the period within which all that was interesting and successful and decisive in one's life was to fall. And now, at 40, how undecided and unfinished and immature everything seems still – and will seem so, I suppose, to the end.

Amold's 'Second Life' ('so to call it'), his prose incarnation, was to last more than two decades, until his fatal heart attack in 1888. But, for Hamilton, 'the poetic life' ends with the Athenaeum's 'obituary notice', its review of the two-volume *Collected Poems* of 1869: 'The poet is dead; we have lost a poet ... aged before his time.' This was printed when Arnold was forty-six – the age at which his father had died. This father-and-son symmetry is insisted on with untypical emphasis in the last two paragraphs of the book.

Here, as occasionally elsewhere, there seems to be a private resonance for this partial biographer in Arnold's story. It may be relevant that Hamilton's own 'poetic life' has not proved as full as once seemed likely. His first book, *The Visit* (1970), formed the core of *Fifty Poems*, eighteen years on; the pamphlet *Steps* is the only verse he has published since. His energies have been directed instead into biography and literary journalism. But the company of those in whom the poet has died before the man has many distinguished members. Their patron saint is S. T. Coleridge. Having 'given up' poetry once already, in 1800, 'being convinced that I never had the essentials of poetic Genius, and that I mistook a strong desire for original power', Coleridge embarked on a journey to Malta in the spring of 1804, at the age of thirty-two, in the hope of resuscitating his poetic self. In transit, he completed the beautiful prose gloss to *The Ancient Mariner*; but he disembarked with the knowledge that his vocation had escaped him, and was resigned from that day to remaking himself in prose. He liked subsequently to quote these words from the *Epistles* of Petrarch:

> With age all things are gradually consumed, and in living we die and are snatched away while we are still here. In that passing I shall not seem myself: another brow, other habits, a new form of mind, another voice sounding.

James Thomson ('B. V.')

Sad Days in the City of Dreadful Night

Places of the Mind: The Life and Work of James Thomson ('B. V.')
Tom Leonard, Jonathan Cape

The mid-Victorian imagination built dream cities on either side of the religious divide. Prophesying that the New Jerusalem would be established in the year 1867, the millennialist John Cumming spoke with an architect's passion of its revolutionary lighting: 'Darkness shall flee away ... no night shall draw its sable curtains over head.' When this failed to materialize, the poet and free-thinker James Thomson constructed its opposite, 'The City of Dreadful Night', where 'none can pierce the vast black veil uncertain / Because there is no light behind the curtain.'

Finished in 1873, this is the most resolutely pessimistic long poem of its time, anticipating by 50 years the setting (urban) and mood (dismal) of *The Waste Land*. Drawing on Shelleyan diction and Spenserian rhythm, and importing its central image (the figure of 'Melencolia') from an engraving by Durer, it may not have the essential originality of great poetry, but that it should stand so far above the rest of Thomson's verses says something about the power of a great title.

It is a miserable poem all right, but its miseries are generalized and philosophical. The verse gives no clue to the particular horror of the poet's life, the degrading alcoholism which aggravated his personal and vocational solitude. Though he knew William Rossetti and George Meredith (who innocently commended 'The City ...' for its 'utmost sobriety'), Thomson's exclusion from the supportive network of Victorian letters is suggested by J. A. Symonds, who found him 'too far from the average Englishman (e.g., from the ordinary public schoolboy, Oxonian and litterateur such as I am) to be approached familiarly'.

For a start, he was a Scotsman, from Port Glasgow, though all but the first six years of his life were spent in London. After an unprivileged but apparently happy education in an Islington 'asylum' for the children of dead or disabled Scottish soldiers and seamen, he worked as an army schoolmaster until 'discharged with disgrace' in 1862. Though the reason for his expulsion remains obscure, it seems likely that his binges had begun, the violent exeats which are marked in his later diaries by clusters of black days.

Thereafter he lived alone as a lodger in various single rooms, depending on the secularist Charles Bradlaugh for employment (it was for his contributions to Bradlaugh's *Investigator* that he coined the pseudonym 'B. V.' – Bysshe Vanolis – in honour of Shelley and the German poet Novalis). When he blew this arrangement in his habitual way, he got what money he could freelancing for magazines like *Cope's Tobacco Plant*, but was constantly in debt. Against the grain of his decline, he had books of verse published in 1880 and 1881. But in 1882, aged forty-seven, he died, in a stupor, from a broken blood vessel in his bowel (the bowel was found to be 'nearly non-existent', which suggests cancer, but since his last months were smeared over with alcohol the standard account is that drink killed him).

Short, dingy, crapulous, solitary lives in bedsits need their biographies, too, but they generate fewer sources than others. And Thomson made his biographer's task all the harder by destroying his private papers as he approached his thirty-fifth birthday. Anyway, Tom Leonard has found a conventional 'life' beyond or beneath his ambitions, and has created instead what he describes as 'a shape, containing a biography, made slowly in response to the shape of the art of another'. Extracts from Thomson's surviving notebooks are suspended without commentary in the midst of a narrative that is queerly reticent on matters of real importance to the subject, such as whether or not he had sex, or cancer.

There are some unrewarding flourishes of experiment. Observing that Thomson's diary entries usually begin with a note on the weather, Leonard supplies two pages of examples: 'Cold, dull, dry', 'Dull, cold, dry' and so on. Then there is an exercise called 'Stone on Stone', a random selection, made by computer, of 100 entries from four years of diaries, with chronology cast to the winds and seventy-nine blanks stripped in for good measure; rather than responding to any 'shape' in Thomson's art, and contrary to the usual aim of biography, this turns an untidy life into total chaos.

The book works best when the sources dictate the shaping, as they do for the tragi-comedy of Thomson's last few weeks. These are vividly documented – not by the poet – in ten pages of letters and reminiscence more interesting than anything that has come before. In February 1882, Thomson, staying with friends in the Leicestershire countryside and writing good, cheerless poetry again, squanders his chance of rehabilitation by disappearing to drink himself sick in a local pub. Returning to the city he embarks, broken-nosed and black-eyed, on a last long dreadful debauch ('on the warpath', as one letter has it, 'in very full paint'), to the exasperation of his long-suffering landlord, the characterful Gibson, who makes the mistake of demanding the rent:

> It appears that about 5 in the morng. G[ibson] awoke with a distinct idea of fire hovering about, so he descended & found the rubbish well alight & our hero calmly surveying the scene from his arm-chair, refusing any word of explanation.

Summarily evicted, with nowhere to go, Thomson's life-force makes its last groggy protest:

> This morng. Gibson was saying how relieved he felt at being rid of such a nightmare, & crowing that, if ever B. V. did turn up there again tight, he'd get a warm reception. Now listen, the whole time G. was thus yarning, B. V. was upstairs in one of his unlet rooms!! […] he had slipped in upstairs while they were at breakfast. About 10 he was bundled out again – he had left *his mark* in the room – saying he should go & see some friends in the Park, & since then no one seems to have seen him.

So perished the one Victorian poet for whom life really was (in Matthew Arnold's phrase) a 'long disease'. These riveting pages apart, the effect of Tom Leonard's study is to suppress that distinction. Scholars will appreciate Leonard's quirky, patient reconstruction of the background to the work; but the general reader, the social drinker, would be dismayed at how little curiosity is shown about the nature of the disease.

A. C. Swinburne

Swallowed by the Sea

A. C. Swinburne: A Poet's Life
Rikky Rooksby, Scolar Press

He was 'hardly a normal person' (Turgenev), 'not quite a human being' (Edmund Gosse), 'virtually supernatural' (Guy de Maupassant), or 'a very spoilt child' (many an unimpressed dinner guest). Those who met Algernon Charles Swinburne did not compare him to other men. The oddness of his appearance, which so endeared him to the cartoonists, was part of it: his agitated little body was hardly broader than his big, beaky head, an effect accentuated by a lavish outgrowth of curly red hair. Gosse's first impression of 'some orange-crested bird' is elaborated in Henry Adams's well-known conceit of a tropical bird, high-crested, long-beaked, quick-moving, with rapid utterances and screams of humour, quite unlike any English lark or nightingale. One could hardly call him a crimson macaw among owls, and yet no ordinary contrast availed. But Swinburne was more than physically freakish. Meeting him when both were in their mid-twenties, Adams also found him 'astonishingly gifted, and convulsively droll', with 'a wonderful sense of farce' that was to Adams more marvellous than the strange new ballads he recited. That sense of farce is amply indulged in Swinburne's brilliant letters (edited in two volumes by Cecil Y. Lang, 1959); on the other hand, it is detectable nowhere, beyond the set-piece parodies of his 'Heptalogia', in the 2,000 pages of his published verse. The discrepancy makes him seem, as well as the most exotic, the most perverse of the principal writers of the Victorian age.

Rikky Rooksby's new biography is the first to propose a clinical cause for Swinburne's singular appearance, and perhaps also for some of the

eccentricities of his behaviour. Throughout his life he suffered from trem-
ors and fits, attributed by his family doctor to 'an excess of electric vital-
ity'. These are consistent, in the recent opinion of an American physician,
with minor brain damage, or arrested hydrocephaly, sustained at birth.
When Swinburne came into his privileged place in the world – on the
Isle of Wight, in 1837, the first child of a marriage between two ancient,
inbred families – he was, in his own words, 'all but dead, and certainly not
expected to live an hour'. But he survived to wear what Rooksby tells us was
'the largest hat in Eton', where he wrote precociously and by his personal
charm earned the baffled respect of his thicker peers. His immaturity
only seems to have begun at Oxford; 'dear little Carrots' was taken up by
the Pre-Raphaelites like a mascot, and he left without taking a degree.

Swinburne never married. But he did not, as a young man, believe
himself doomed to a solitary life; and the poems and letters allude qui-
etly to a lost love. This, as Cecil Lang first revealed in the 1950s, was
Swinburne's cousin Mary Gordon, with whom he had ridden and played
as a teenager. Mary later insisted that the relationship had always been
brother-and-sisterly, as if it were ludicrous to surmise otherwise – with
someone so like a little boy or bird. Perhaps he only became aware of
the depth of his own feelings when, in 1864, she announced her engage-
ment to Robert Disney Leith, a giant one-armed hero of the Indian wars,
a man twenty years his senior and effectively of another species. In the
semi-autobiographical novel *Lesbia Brandon*, Herbert Seyton has his
suit refused: 'he sat and felt a breakage inside him of all that made up the
hopefullest part of his life'. That winter, aged twenty-seven, Swinburne
wrote 'The Triumph of Time':

> Before our lives divide for ever ...
> I will say no word that a man might say
> Whose whole life's love goes down in a day;
> For this could never have been; and never,
> Though the gods and the years relent, shall be.

– a poem which grew sadder and stronger as the years fulfilled its rheto-
ric. In the meantime, the little virgin's name became a byword for sexual
licence. *Poems and Ballads* (1866) was a literary sensation and a public
scandal. Progressive readers were spellbound by its new rhythms and
melodies. (At one recitation of the poems, John Ruskin cried out, 'How

beautiful! How divinely beautiful!') But pieces such as 'Anactoria' (featuring sadistic lesbianism), 'The Leper' (necrophilia) and 'Dolores' (addressed to 'Our Lady of Pain') excited the reprobation of England's chaster critics. The publisher withdrew the book. Before long, authorship was confused with practice, and tales about England's 'libidinous laureate' spread abroad. 'Absolutely anything', marvelled Turgenev, 'could be expected of Swinburne'; including, one rumour had it, eating the monkey that had been his mistress. Rooksby declines to repeat these stories, as if they had been invented to discredit his man. In fact, Swinburne revelled in his unearned reputation: 'I have a character to keep up', he wrote to the man of the world Richard Burton, '– at least in my writings.' Oscar Wilde saw through the publicity that Swinburne was 'a braggart in matters of vice, who had done everything he could to convince his fellow citizens of his homosexuality and bestiality, without being in the slightest degree a homosexual or a bestializer'.

A taste for flagellation had been swished into him at Eton; and a number of grown-up letters (to a surprising number and variety of correspondents, including women) get adolescently worked up on the subject. In 1866, he began visiting 'Verbena Lodge', a high-class flogging establishment in St John's Wood. Dismayed at this development, D. G. Rossetti hoped to cure the habit by introducing his friend to some woman who might 'make a man of him'. Rossetti's choice, the five-times-married American circus performer, Adah Mencken, took to Swinburne, but had to report back that 'she hadn't been able to get him up to the scratch, and couldn't make him understand that biting's no use'. The experiment seems not to have been repeated, and the 'copulatory' passages of Swinburne's poems remained curiously indistinct: 'and all his heart / filled hers ...'

It was drink, rather, that became his defining vice. He was introduced to brandy in 1862 by Richard Burton – who after their sessions would tuck the unconscious Swinburne under one arm and carry him out to a cab. The 1860s furnish innumerable accounts of Swinburne's disgraceful behaviour, snatching at bottles 'like a mongoose', 'belching out blasphemy and bawdry and prostrated by drink'; in the 1870s, as his health gave way, his letters are full of 'prostration', 'influenza' and 'seediness', but he was incapable of admitting the cause, blaming one bout of sickness outrageously on the 'perfume of Indian lilies in a close bedroom'. As he made himself impossible to live with, so he had to live on his own, which increased his vulnerability and deepened his melancholy. In a letter of

1875, Swinburne congratulates his friend Edmund Gosse on his marriage; though the happy event must bring to his own mind 'the reverse experience which left my young manhood "a barren stock" – if I may cite that phrase without seeming to liken myself to a male queen Elizabeth'. Swinburne's phenomenal energies were at last subdued by his alcoholism, and Gosse's tender account of the poet's subsequent visits to his home and baby includes the most plainly human image we have of him:

> ... he was waiting for me when I came back from the office. The maid had seen him into the study, brightened the fire and raised the lamp, but ... I found him mournfully wandering, like a lost thing, on the staircase ... When he and I were alone, he closed up to the fire, his great head bowed, his knees held tight together, and his finger-tips pressed to his chest, in what I call his 'penitential' attitude, and he began a long tale, plaintive and rather vague, about his loneliness, the sadness of his life, the suffering he experiences from the slanders of others ... (He) said that a little while ago he found his intellectual energy succumbing under a morbid distress at his isolation, and that he had been obliged steadily to review before his conscience his imaginative life in order to prevent himself from sinking into despair. This is only a mood, to be sure; but if there be any people who think so ill of him, I only wish they could see him at these recuperative intervals. Whatever he may be elsewhere, in our household not a kinder, simpler, or more affectionate creature could be desired as a visitor.

By the summer of 1879, these 'recuperative intervals' were too rare to save him, and his family and most of his friends had privately given him up. As an emergency measure, he was taken by Theodore Watts, a kindly lawyer with literary aspirations, to stay for a few days with him and his sister in Putney (then a village suburb); the arrangement was to last thirty years, until the poet's death at seventy-two. It was once usual to make fun of the motherly Watts, even to be suspicious of him: Rooksby, leaving open every option for loyalty to Swinburne, hints darkly, 'I think it possible that further research may yet uncover some ugly tales of life at The Pines.' But Watts's intervention and his subsequent dedication certainly saved the poet's life. According to Coulson Kernahan in *Swinburne As I Knew Him* (1919), he managed to wean the poet off strong drink in stages over a period of a few months: from brandy to port, because port was Tennyson's drink; from port to burgundy, the drink of the Three

Musketeers; from burgundy to claret, 'the proper drink for gentlemen'; and finally to 'Shakespeare's brown October, our own glorious and incomparable beer', which was all the poet took in the regime to which he now consented. He would leave the house at eleven each morning to walk across Wimbledon Common, pausing to admire babies in their prams along the way, dropping into the Rose and Crown, and returning for lunch (and his single bottle of Bass) at one-thirty. He would read aloud before dinner, usually from Dickens, and afterwards work late into the night. As he grew increasingly deaf, he saw few visitors.

This was the sort of cosy pattern that Swinburne could never have devised for himself, and his biography peters out in it. Rooksby can spin no more than fifty pages out of the last thirty years, despite his determination to disprove the notion that the poet in Swinburne 'died' when he moved to Putney. (Having things both ways, though, he believes that Swinburne would enjoy major-poet status today if someone had shot him when he was thirty-two, before, that is, he could obscure his better poems with so many worse.) In fact, it is not clear that his dwindling band of readers separate the old and the young Swinburne in their heads, or the good and the bad, as they do with Wordsworth or Browning. Though their quality may vary, the poems seem imaginatively of a piece, resembling one another through a common lack. The critic Edmund Wilson commented that Swinburne 'can never surprise or delight by a colloquial turn of phrase, a sharply observed detail, a magical touch of colour'. But Swinburne's art is founded precisely on the banishment of these tricks, 'such beauties', as he called them, 'as strike you and startle and go out … sharp-edged prettinesses, shining surprises and striking accidents that are anything but casual … intrusive and singular and exceptional beauties which break up and distract the simple charm of general and single beauty, the large and musical unity of things'. A letter about what he considered his masterwork, the Wagnerian narrative *Tristram of Lyonesse* (1882), shows this self-censorship in action. Quoting one sequence, 'And the sweet shining signs of women's names … / Flame from Queen Helen to Queen Guenevere', the letter continues, '(I instantly added in my own mind' – as if the more solemn verse were the product of someone else's – 'this couplet – While toothless mouths of cuckolds in the dark / Grin from King Menelaus to King Mark).' This Byronic devilry has no place in Swinburne's project of monotony, the creation of featureless verbal landscapes or seascapes that read as if they could go on forever:

> Miles, and miles, and miles of desolation!
> Leagues on leagues on leagues without a change!
>
> ('By the North Sea')

Swinburne's poems return again and again to the North Sea's 'limitless floating fields of wan green water', in which, as a boy, he had bathed off the Northumbrian coast. Nearly 1,000 single lines, and over thirty poems, end with 'the sea'. It is the last word of his Tristram, as, after 150 pages of couplets as rolling and repetitive as the waves, the verse rouses itself to bring the lovers to the same submarine entombment he once imagined he might share with Mary Gordon:

>   And the king
> Built for their tomb a chapel bright like spring
> With flower-soft wealth of branching tracery made ....
> There slept they wedded under moon and sun
> And change of stars: and through the casements came
> Midnight and noon girt round with shadowy flame
> To illume their grave or veil it: till at last
> On these things too was doom as darkness cast:
> For the strong sea hath swallowed wall and tower,
> And where their limbs were laid in woful hour
> For many a fathom gleams and moves and moans
> The tide that sweeps above their coffined bones
> In the wrecked chancel by the shivered shrine:
> Nor where they sleep shall moon or sunlight shine
> Nor man look down for ever: none shall say,
> Here once, or here, Tristram and Iseult lay:
> But peace they have that none may gain who live,
> And rest about them that no love can give,
> And over them, while death and life shall be,
> The light and sound and darkness of the sea.

Harold Nicolson prefaced his own brief study of Swinburne (1926) with gratitude that the poet had been fortunate in his biographers: 'for it would indeed have been regrettable if the life-story of one who, although surpassingly strange, was yet so exquisite a gentleman, had been marred from the outset by any ungentle handling'. Rikky Rooksby's biography – the eighth, by his calculation, but the first for two decades – represents the return of kid gloves. He has set himself against 'those who wish to substitute ridicule for intelligent appraisal', even though his subject is revealed as one of the richest and most tireless ridiculers in the business. Rooksby's criticism is not adventurous, and he overrates Swinburne's social and political influence ('His very name became a watchword against oppression and humbug'). *A. C. Swinburne: A poet's life* has been rather meanly produced, and is poorly edited. It may therefore not be a biography on the scale or of the quality that Rooksby thinks Swinburne deserves. But it is generous, even loving, in spirit. And if the poems appeal only faintly now, as if from underwater, the strange shapes of the life have their own claim on our imagination.

Robert Bridges

You are Old, Doctor Bridges

Robert Bridges
Catherine Phillips, Oxford University Press

No writer's reputation can ever have plunged more steeply than that of the poet Robert Bridges, whose decline has been mirrored and mocked by the rise of his friend and contemporary Gerard Hopkins. Bridges would hardly have believed it. It was he who first prepared Hopkins' poems for publication, but not until the author had been dead for thirty years, and even then in the certainty that they would be ridiculed. His support was qualified, not only by his distaste for the flavour of Hopkins' religion (of 'The Wreck of the Deutschland' he wished 'that those nuns had stayed at home'), but by a fellow-craftsman's queasiness at the strains and extravagances we have come to admire. He seems never to have mentioned his dead protégé without apologies for the 'very difficult and unpopular' nature of the work; and couldn't have guessed that a future generation would prize that very quality. Today the Jesuit's contortions are on the national curriculum, while smooth, lucid, Anglican Bridges – whose *Testament of Beauty* sold more than 65,000 copies – goes, with a vengeance, unread.

Bridges didn't want his biography to be written, and destroyed documents to obstruct it; but the surprise, in 1992, is that anyone should want to write one. It's not only that Bridges' artistic programme – to combine 'the Greek attainment (technical excellence) with the Christian ideal' – seems so fusty and alien; also that the life was an untroubled marriage of privilege (Eton, etc) and virtue (he is said, not excitingly, to have personified 'wisdom and temperance'). The last word of the book is 'religious', but, unlike Hopkins, Bridges' faith had no place for human suffering, and certainly involved him in none of his own.

Still, Catherine Phillips, herself first a Hopkins scholar, has laid out her unpromising materials with impeccable scholarship and the sort of good manners that Bridges would have approved. The highlight, as you would expect, is her subject's only significant intercourse with the world at large, his spell as a physician in St Barts casualty ward, which gives a vivid picture of the hospital before antiseptic practices became the norm. Bridges describes one surgeon of the old school in prose that is typically fluent and fascinated:

> So short-sighted was he (no doubt he saw more accurately for that) that he seemed to be working as much with his face as with his hands – like a dog at a rabbit hole – all that he did seemed to be a confused groping – and when he had done there was no more attempt at cleanliness than what seemed a casual mopping up with odds and ends of sponges, before the walls were stitched together.

Alas for his biographer, the exhausted Bridges – for whom to see 150 patients in two hours at Barts was 'not unusual' – gave up his career in 1882, before he was forty, and thereafter his life was spent in the libraries of his various homes near Oxford, devoted, not exactly to poetry, more to the science of versification. All Phillips can do is to render this latter vocation straight, though even the specialist reader will find heavy going in the realm of enclitics and scazons ('Milton's extra syllables are always elidable into disyllabic units; anyone writing accentual trisyllabic feet, he said, would use unelidable monosyllables as well'). Given Bridges' careful protection (as in the poems) of his private life, and the absence of sig-nificant event, the charm of the poet's personality becomes the theme of the second half of the book. This can hardly be said to have come under much strain, expressing itself as it did in thank-you notes for presents of clavichords ('The gift is one that above anything else I should like to have, but if I had had to choose I should never have thought of'). None the less, Phillips' account manages to convey why almost all who met him – even Ezra Pound – were favourably impressed. But he was 'class-bound', and he was old (for a long time), and his friends had eventually to defend him against snipers and iconoclasts (E. M. Forster, for instance, to Stephen Spender: 'Events moved too quickly for him, yes: now they move far quicker, and if in 20 years there is such a thing as an old man, he'll be infinitely more on the shelf').

The kiss of death was to have been made Poet Laureate in 1912, a Grand Old Man when there were a lot of them about. (Bridges was himself exasperated at the composition of Edward Gosse's geriatric 'Academic Committee of English Letters': 'I should be content if we could get two or three young men amongst us …') The poems he tried to write at the outbreak of the war were hostages to his detractors, coining the sort of slogan – 'To Beauty through Blood' – that the beautiful bleeders came to resent. The First World War can now be seen to have killed off Bridges' kind of poetry, and indeed he seemed unable to function as a writer while it continued – 'as if', as a contemporary put it, 'his words had hibernated during the war'. But Bridges was lucky, at least in life, and the words came back. His last four years – his mid-eighties, no less – were spent on his most ambitious single work, though *The Testament of Beauty* (1929) has shed most of the interest it might once have had. Even more remarkable, perhaps, is the spurt of 1921, which produced a dozen or so pieces – 'Melancholy', 'Poor Poll', 'Kate's Mother', 'Low Barometer' (a tremendous war poem in disguise), the weird but delightful sonnet 'To Francis Jammes', the glorious opening of 'Come Se Quando' and others, each surprising and rewarding in a different way – with claims to be among the best unknown poems of the century.

What they suggest is that Bridges, for all his archaisms, for all his age, and above these his constant lack of worthwhile subject matter, had mastered supple new metres that really might have influenced the course of English verse – had it not by then already changed so violently in another direction. Now it's unlikely that poetry will ever take him seriously again.

S. R. Crockett

The Grey Galloway Land

Where the Whaups Are Crying: A Dumfries and Galloway Anthology
Edited by Innes Macleod, Birlinn Ltd

'About half a century ago … I went to school in Warwickshire. The other boys asked me what county I came from, "Wigtownshire," said I. "Wigtownshire," asked they, "and where is that?" "In Galloway," said I. "In Galilee!" they cried – (laughter) – and I ran a narrow shave of being kicked out as a Jew. (Laughter.)' This was the local landowner and MP, Sir Herbert Maxwell, as recorded in the *Galloway Gazette* of September 1906, speaking after a dinner at Dalbeattie, Kirkcudbright in honour of the writer S. R. Crockett. Not every schoolboy knows, even today, that Galloway is the long-standing name for the south-west corner of Scotland, divided for most of its administrative history between the old Shire of Wigtown and the Stewartry of Kirkcudbright. With a coastline of smugglers' caves, saltmarshes and mudflats fringing the Solway Firth, a wilderness of moors and mountains to the north, and pleasant farmland and pretty valleys in between, it is one of the most lightly populated and thinly visited bits of mainland Britain. Only one of its towns, the ferry port of Stranraer, approaches medium size, and in its traffic with Northern Ireland maintains the region's reputation for outlaws and illicit cargoes: recently, paramilitaries on drugs business, and Slavic refugees.

The Industrial Revolution and tartan tourism both bypassed Galloway; and literature might seem to have overlooked it too. Connections with Robert Burns surround the region – Alloway and Kirkoswald, Ayr and Mauchline to the north, Dumfries to the east – but make few inroads. Scott set *Guy Mannering* (1815) in a 'Galloway' of fictional place names, and Meg Menilies, the novel's formidable Gypsy queen, is a Galloway type. In 1818, on his way to the Burn's belt, John Keats stayed 'in Meg Menilies' county', at a Kirkcudbright inn whose barefoot landlady confirmed that 'very few Southerners passed these ways'. Indeed, *The Scottish Tourist*, a guide-book published in Edinburgh in 1825 at the height of enthusiasm wrought by the Waverley novels, manages to avoid any allusion to the province; the map of 'Scotland' accompanying the fourth edition is bounded to the south by a line running from Ayr to Edinburgh. In John Buchan's *The Thirty-Nine Steps* (1915), the fugitive Richard Hannay, seeking a remote place to lose himself, 'fixed on Galloway ... the nearest wild part of Scotland' for the necessary chapters. Its want of a familiar native literature made Wigtown, the handsome little county town on the green Machars peninsula, a surprise choice as Scotland's official 'Book Town' in 1998.

Wigtown's annual Literary Festival, launched in September of the following year, has evolved to suit the scale and temper of the place: no bunting or suits or name-badges here, no theatrically exhausted organizer. This year, the presence of Pete McCarthy was the one concession to national celebrity – though as he was topping the bill at Knutsford five days later this was no special coup. The first recognizable sign of the festival was a horse-drawn Carol Ann Duffy, taking her family on a six-minute buggy tour of the town courtesy of Ming Books. Bookshops are the year-round business of a Book Town. Wigtown has a dozen or so; but not even the biggest of them, dominantly called 'The Bookshop', can manage much of a show of local produce. You might buy a copy of *A Galloway Childhood* (1967) by 'Ian Niall' (the *Country Life* pseudonym of John McNeillie, who before the war had written harsher political novels like *The Wigtown Ploughman* under his own name, and whose son, Andrew, has contributed poems to the *TLS*), and an excellent anthology of the modern entity 'Dumfries and Galloway', *Where the Whaups Are Crying*, edited by Innes Macleod.

The poet Alastair Reid, now resident in New York, was raised in the village of Whithorn, a few miles down the peninsula, and is an honoured friend of the festival; but you can't find his books in The Bookshop. In the 'Second-Hand: Scottish' section, however, are some small provincial curiosities: particularly, on a shelf marked S. R. CROCKETT, no fewer than six copies, all first editions, all from separate sources, all long-term unsold, of a novel of 1894, *The Lilac Sunbonnet*. These days, aside from such second-hand traces in Wigtown, you would most likely have come across the name of S. R. Crockett in the title of a despondent late poem by Robert Louis Stevenson. Written in 1894, the last year of his life, when Stevenson knew he would never see Scotland again, 'Home Thoughts from Samoa' was first called 'To S. R. Crockett (on Receiving a Dedication)'. The poem begins (the 'whaups' are the curlews of Galloway, the 'martyrs' its Covenanting dead),

> Blows the wind today, and the sun and the rain are flying
> Blows the wind on the moors today and now,
> Where about the graves of the martyrs the whaups are crying,
> My heart remembers how!

The background to these lines is the sort of awkward, imbalanced relationship that may sometimes get refined out of literary biography: here, the trade between a great writer and a talented but helplessly ambitious disciple.

Samuel Crockett was born at Little Duchrae Farm, Balmaghie, Kirkcudbright, in September 1860, the same year as J. M. Barrie. (He added the 'Rutherford' in his twenties in allusion to a local hero, Samuel Rutherford, 1600–61, minister of Anwoth near Gatehouse-of-Fleet and 'Saint of the Covenant'.) He was the illegitimate grandson of the stern Cameronian couple (followers of the Covenanter Richard Cameron) who farmed there and who were not minded to press his mother into an unhappy marriage. After school at nearby Castle Douglas, he qualified from Edinburgh University as a minister of the Free Kirk. As a student, he had written bits of journalism for pocket money; and he began to consolidate his practice as he settled into the ministry at Penicuik, ten miles from Edinburgh, in 1886 – the year the world got *Kidnapped*. 'SRC' (as he presented himself for a while) was proud of his correspondence with RLS, and exaggerated its extent. His hapless, overawed biographer of 1907, M. MacLaren Harper, a Galloway scribbler who had known Crockett since their schooldays, was somehow convinced that Stevenson 'frequently visited at Bank House, Penicuik' (just as John Ruskin, in the morbid delirium of his final years, 'frequently invited the author to Coniston'). In fact, the earliest attempt at contact between them was a speculative package sent by Crockett (when Stevenson was already embarked on the voyage that was to end in Samoa), containing a copy of his first book, a volume of poems called *Dulce Cor*, published in 1887 under the dashing pseudonym 'Ford Bereton'. Crockett was always a ready borrower, conscious and otherwise. The reviewers' choice from *Dulce Cor* was 'Idyll of the Hayfield', with its unruly echoes of Cory's 'Eton Boating Song' (1866):

> Hey for the haymaking weather!
> Hey for the meadows green!
> Scythemen all swinging together,
> Swish of the blades so keen.

'Keen' as he was himself, and hearing nothing back, Crockett wrote again to Stevenson, in September 1887, enquiring after his gift. Stevenson replied from New York, in his own time, on April 10, 1888, as to a stranger, addressing the 'Dear Minister of the Free Kirk at Penicuik, – for O, man, I cannae read your name! – that I have been so long in answering your delightful letter sits on my conscience badly …' *Dulce Cor* has got lost, guesses Stevenson, without anxiety, on its way across the Atlantic. By return of post, Crockett fires off another copy. The poems did not stimulate the exchange for which the importunate young minister had hoped. But he persevered, for in May 1893 RLS is recorded as writing coldly to 'Mr Crockett' that 'I do not owe you two letters, nor yet merely one sir!', and protesting that it was 'ungrateful' of SRC to have published in the *Bookman* an article, entitled 'The Apprenticeship of Robert Louis Stevenson', which quoted passages from his first, implicitly private letter. Stevenson takes issue with Crockett on other matters; then dismisses, with impatience (the worst of it suppressed), the latter's stagey pessimism about the chances of his forthcoming volume of prose pieces: as it appears in Ernest Mehew's edition of Stevenson's *Letters*, 'Why should you suppose your book will be slated, because you have no friends?… (Six or seven words heavily deleted, apparently by RLS)… A new writer, if he is any good, will be acclaimed generally with more noise than he deserves.' *The Stickit Minister and Some Common Men* (1893) was a typical product of what was already known, in the dismissive phrase of an Edinburgh critic, as the 'Kail Yard' (or Cabbage-Patch) school of fiction. In the early years of the decade, popular taste in Britain and émigré North America had somehow got fixated on innocent, sentimental tales of daily life in the small towns of Scotland.

Strangely enough, most of the writers and editors who catered to this demand were connected with, if not actively ministers of, the Free

Kirk. Their spiritual head was William Robertson Nicholl (1851–1923), a former minister who had migrated to London to edit the *British Weekly*. A regular feature of the British was a story, sketch, or 'idyll' drawn from the Free Kirk manse; among the authors enlisted by Robertson Nicholl for the column were the young J. M. Barrie (whose Gavin Dishart is minister at 'Thrums', based on his home town, Kirriemuir in Angus) and John Wilson, minister at Logiealmond, Perthshire, whose *Beside the Bonnie Brier Bush* (1894), written as 'Ian Maclaren', is the quintessential Kailyard text, honoured with the acronym BBBB by borrowers from Mudie's Library. Crockett claimed independence from the school in so far as he contributed his sketches to a different nonconformist periodical, *The Christian Leader*. These were the pieces collected in *The Stickit Minister*, whose title unashamedly shadows that of Barrie's *The Little Minister* (1891). The volume's dedication reads:

> To Robert Louis Stevenson of Scotland and Samoa, I dedicate these stories of that grey Galloway land, where, about the graves of the martyrs, the whaups are crying – his heart has not forgotten how.

This time, receiving his copy of Crockett's book, Stevenson wrote back from Samoa: frail and homesick, and as imaginatively fond of Galloway and its scattered memorials as of anywhere in Scotland, he had been moved by the dedication. Its last three lines were incorporated in 'Home Thoughts from Samoa', and he paid Crockett the further respect of an honest appraisal: 'while some of your tales are a trifle light and one at least seems too slender and fantastic … the whole book breathes admirably of the soil'. He finds Crockett's outdoorsy minister 'complementary' to his studious counterpart in Barrie's 'Thrums', and even manages a kindly, conspiratorial dig ('Might I just breathe in your lug, that Angus is rather a dreary pairt of the country?') at Barrie – a close friend, a regular correspondent and, in Stevenson's early and exact judgement, 'a genius'. Alongside the dedication to Stevenson, *The Stickit Minister* carried a preface in which Crockett referred to his Master's generosity to him in correspondence. It continued, perhaps remembering also his Master's disapproval,

> It goes to my heart not to quote from, for they are in some wise the poor patent of my nobility. But, perhaps with more wisdom, I keep them by me, to hearten myself withal when the days of darkness grow too many and too dark.

The 'wisdom' was short-lived. Crockett's publisher, T. Fisher Unwin of Paternoster Square by St Paul's, printed an extract from Stevenson's innocent letter of thanks as an advertisement at the front of Crockett's next book, *The Raiders*, a historical novel of Galloway, which came out in March 1894. Stevenson was exasperated, and said as much; but he had other things to worry about. When W. E. Henley, on his old friend's behalf, roughed up *The Raiders* in a review – largely on the grounds of the publisher's lapse in quoting private correspondence as advertisement – RLS, his equanimity restored, wrote to him in mock protest: 'What ails you at poor Crockett? He seems to me not without parts from what I have seen of him. But you know I was always inclined to be a merciful and hopeful critic.' No one opening *The Raiders* then, or now, in John Burns's new paperback edition (Canongate), would need advance notice of Crockett's debt to Stevenson. The bridle-reins that jingle in the first sentence echo all the way from *Treasure Island* (1883), and the relationship of its hero, the bold but priggish young Patrick Heron, to the mysterious, savoury, providential figure of 'Silver Sand' is pure Balfour and Breck (though 'Silver' Sand, of the deformed arms, has a family connection also with Long John). The story describes the passage of Heron, the orphaned Laird of Isle Rathan on the Solway coast, through the menace of pirates and cattle-thieves and kidnappers of women, through a pack of sinister place-names – the Dungeon o'Buchan, the Wolfs Slock, the 'Murder Hole' – to achieve his marriage and majority. The first and more adventurous half of the novel follows him into solitude, heroic discomfort and outright danger; here the excitement is bound up with the weather, the epic events of storm and ice, and with the ever-freshening language of foul weather, its 'stonespouts' and numbed extremities, 'dazed and stupid by the tempest'. In the second half (just as *Kidnapped* had been succeeded by the rather insipid *Catriona*), the spirit of 'Silver Sand' is eased out by Patrick's beloved May Maxwell (or 'May Mischief', in her schoolma'amish nickname) – 'that randy lass … standing with her hands on her sides and her elbows crooked out', like a pantomime Peter Pan before her time – who has been kidnapped by Gypsies and rescued (for the story's sake) too abruptly.

The novel is unembarrassed by its own failings. 'Silver Sand' is gradually revealed to be the 'good' Cameronian Gypsy Johnny Faa, by royal decree 'Lord of Egypt' and leader of these broken clans and Gypsy bands – who has to vanish whenever his protégé shoots at his kin; and the generalized villains of the piece, the 'Marshalls, Macatericks and Millers', never quite emerge from the plural trappings of their terrible surnames. The love story is concluded, all bar the nuptials, by half-way, and Patrick's motivation is accordingly depleted; the vacuum is filled by the Sentimental. Besides the kidnapped May, there is the subplot of a missing little girl, Marion Tamson (Crockett's own first-born, Maisie, was five or six when the novel was published); not one of them, but both May and Marion happen to be imprisoned in the moorland cottage where Patrick fetches up in a blinding storm. The triumph of Sentiment is complete when 'Silver' and Patrick are depicted sobbing together over the legend of the Covenanting widow who lost her last and youngest son or 'lamb' in the 'Killing Times'.

But the strengths of *The Raiders* are no less conspicuous. Most of them derive from its place of origin. The handling of local dialect is not always comfortable, least of all at the start, when the 'English' of some words is disconcertingly given in brackets within speeches – 'deevin (deafening)', 'heuchs (cliffs)', 'gellecks (little beetles like earwigs)'. At other times, its display of the dialect is too clearly the whole purpose of a speech: 'Ye'll hae to get berried and scartit, whammelt and riven, till ye learn as I hae learn'd'. But the Galloway tongue reveals itself as a moral force or indicator, the guarantee of certain 'common' values, even when spoken by Patrick's ferocious captors: 'The dialect reassured me amazingly. No one could speak good Galloway Scots and be a complete blackguard.' And the novel may in general be said to assert the superiority of the provincial to the mobile or the metropolitan or the cosmopolitan beyond. The assertion is proved, as it were, by Crockett's evident and intimate powers of local description:

> If a Galloway cow lagged and threatened to keep back the troop, she received a sharp lash across the nose and was driven into the darkness. Sometimes, however, after a drink at the wayside burn, the terrors of loneliness so pressed upon her that she would come racing after the company, bellowing as loud as she could, and so rejoin the herd.

(It is worth noting of this passage that the epithet 'Galloway' could be replaced in any one of four or five points to much the same partisan effect.) There are satisfying set pieces too, inseparable from the ground that stages them: especially the twentieth chapter's spectacular bridge-head skirmish, told for immediacy and with rare success in the present tense. In this episode, a band of cattle-thieves, penned in by Heron and angry Gallovidians, scatter pots of 'Greek fire' (made from shepherds' pitch and oil) over the cattle to stampede them through their assailants: a scene which tellingly gains strength from the superior realism and more interesting emotions of temporary defeat. The month after publication of *The Raiders*, Stevenson wrote to Mrs Sitwell in April 1894 that 'I shall never do a better book than Catriona, that is my high-water mark'; which reminds us again that the taste of the fin de siècle was not our taste, nor always what we otherwise take it to be. And S. R. Crockett shared the market's appetite for sentimental romance, or, at any rate, was able to profit by it. His second novel, already lodged with the printer, was *The Lilac Sunbonnet*, whose title fairly evokes its whimsical, feminine, garden charm. Within a few months, Crockett had his second smash-hit, and Stevenson was dead.

The success of *The Raiders* and *The Lilac Sunbonnet* persuaded Crockett to give up the ministry and live by his writing. His next productions, scrambled into print to capitalize in the later months of 1894, were the wayward *Mad Sir Uchtred of the Hills* and the spiritless *The Play Actress*, neither of which had more success than they deserved. *Men of the Moss Hags* (1895) and *The Grey Man* (1896), however, kept up the earlier momentum. In these two historical novels, Crockett intuitively stuck to his own ground. *The Moss Hags* is a Covenanters' novel set around Wigtown, where a memorial still stands to the two women martyred by drowning in the Bay; in *The Grey Man*, he pushes north into the region known as Carrick, once the earldom of Robert the Bruce, and equivalent to what is now South Ayrshire. *The Grey Man* deals with the murderous disputes in the seventeenth century between contending tribes of Kennedys, and with the black career of Sawney Bean, the cannibal cave-dweller of Bennane Head near Ballantrae. The opening action of that novel, the firing of Ardstinchar Castle, suggests again how easy it was for Crockett to write excitingly in the adventure mode; and makes one wonder how his *oeuvre* might have looked, had he written less, had he borrowed more selectively, had he known patience and his own limitations.

Elliot Dickson was another Galloway storyteller of the time. Dickson's narrator in *My Bagdad* (1896) – the title refers to Gatehouse of Fleet – is a shepherd and amateur critic, Michael McTear, who sees the case shrewdly: Crockett, he reckons, 'had done some guid work, but naething to what he'll dae if he tak's time – but only if he tak's time'. Instead, in twenty years, Crockett produced fifty-one novels and four collections of short stories. He moved on the crest of his success to Torwood House near Peebles, south of Edinburgh, where he built himself a library with room for 50,000 volumes. His compass broadened: there are glimpses of a social-issue novelist in *Cleg Kelly Arab of the City* (1896); and historical novels of France and Spain, the lesser Samoas where he began to spend his winters. At stages, he makes appeals to his original constituency, in what we might call sequels, *The Stickit Minister's Wooing* (1900), or *Raiderland* (1904) – but without fresh inspiration.

Popularity deserted him, with a finality that surprised but would not deter him until he died, in 1914, of a version of Stevenson's lung disease. There are now over 100 titles in the Canongate Classics series, a project which has valuably enlarged the resources available to casual devotees of Scottish literature. The Raiders may not be one of its superior productions: it features a diffident introduction by John Burns, but no map or footnotes; the cover illustration is a nineteenth-century painting of King Lear in a storm. The novel was already available in what might be called a tourist edition from 'Alloway Publishers'; Canongate's 'Classic' may not be much more than a cut above that; but S. R. Crockett would have loved them for it.

J. M. Barrie

The Curse of Sentimentality

Farewell Miss Julie Logan: A J. M. Barrie Omnibus
Edited with an introduction by Andrew Nash, Canongate

Thomas Hardy's verse sketch, written at a rehearsal of J. M. Barrie's *Mary Rose* in 1920, is a fond glimpse of an established fellow in the company of famous writers:

> If any day a promised play
> Should be in preparation,
> You never see friend J. M. B.
> Depressed or in elation,
> But with a stick, rough, crooked and thick,
> You may sometimes discern him,
> Standing as though a mummery show
> Did not at all concern him.

But if Barrie seemed to Hardy steadiness or serenity personified – the Barrie of Kensington – his biographers have revealed an undertow of violent suffering, traceable to his origins in Kirriemuir. And if his place in the pantheon then seemed secure, the most celebrated playwright (Shaw notwithstanding) of Edwardian Britain soon fell off stage and out of print. Robert Louis Stevenson considered him his superior, a master, a 'genius', and there is about his work a force and peculiarity that makes that term appropriate. Yet, these days, the institution of Peter Pan apart, you are as likely to see a play about the man – Andrew Birkin's television play *The Lost Boys*, for instance – as one by him. Curiosity about his personality has displaced whatever interest lingered around the old ocean liner of his collected works; and knowing what we do about him helps confirm a prejudice against those works as being immature and obsolete, an art of butlers, maids, hats and gloves, ghostly children, fairies and desert islands.

Barrie was born in Kirriemuir, Angus, on the northern edge of the Scottish Lowlands, in 1860, the son of a weaver. After the death of his elder brother David, aged thirteen – the first of several in his life who would not grow up – the boy Barrie grafted close to his mother, Margaret Ogilvy, the subject of a hagiographical book-length portrait published after her death in 1896. Literary success came early with his definitively 'couthy' tales about life in the railyards of Kirrie – fictionalized as 'Thrums', after the bunches of thread that hang above a hand-loom – largely based on his mother's reminiscences. Moving to London, he began to write for the theatre, and in 1894 married the actress Mary Ansell. The marriage was physically a non-starter – the 'fault' it seems, of what a wag called 'the boy who couldn't go up, J. M. Barren' – though divorce did not come until fifteen years later. Meanwhile, Barrie transferred his affections to two little boys he found in Kensington Gardens: the eldest of five brothers, sons of Arthur Llewelyn Davies and Sylvia du Maurier. He proceeded to impose himself on this family to the point of appropriation, encouraged by the mother and nobly tolerated by the father. When both parents died in turn of cancer, Barrie became the boys' indulgent guardian.

Of his two favourites, the eldest, George, was killed in Flanders, and the beautiful and beloved Michael drowned while a student at Oxford. His grief in each case was spectacular. Barrie's emotional make-up was singular. If the tender, terrified letters he wrote to George at the Front seem strangely unselfconscious in their scrambling of gender and relationship – '… I do seem to be sadder to-day than ever, and more and more wishing you were a girl of 21 instead of a boy, so that I could say the things to you that are now always in my heart' – it is because Barrie was not shy of such things. He was just another Great War mother: 'I shall have many anxious days and nights too, but I only fall into line with so many mothers.' The letters to Michael are apparently stronger still; a surviving brother destroyed them in the 1950s on the grounds that they were 'too much'. And yet they may not have seemed quite that at the time. Barrie was an exceptionally affectable man writing in an affectable age.

The two great authors for children of their time, both Kipling (his junior by four years) and Barrie were short ('The things I could have said to them (ladies) if my legs had been longer …'), smokers, energetic, melancholy and ill (Barrie had a permanent cough from an early bout of pleurisy and pneumonia); and they enjoyed a similar fertility of narrative invention. Both of them 'lost boys' in the Great War. But if it doesn't seem fanciful to say so (since the Anglo-Indian Kipling was temperamentally more like a Scottish than an English writer), they represent the separate tendencies of the Scottish mind, the practical and the sentimental. Kipling was devoted to the real, to the workings of man and other machines, to the spoken voice in all its accents, and the boy he lost was his son. Literature, to Barrie, was play, as in the opposite of earnest, and it happened in Never Land, or Never-Never Land (a more winkingly ambiguous formula), in the Might-Have-Been, in the world as it isn't. And the boys he lost were someone else's.

Andrew Nash's attractive omnibus aims to restore Barrie's credibility as a writer for adults, even, in its selection, to make him seem potentially fashionable. Three genres are represented. The prose fable *The Little White Bird* is the first (1902) and most original exploration of the Peter Pan material, where the fantasy is set in the context of a middle-aged narrator's engagement with creativity and childlessness; 'Captain W—' invents a son for himself, 'Timothy', while playing with another family. (There followed the play Peter Pan in 1904, two prose treatments, *Peter Pan in Kensington Gardens* and *Peter and Wendy* in 1906 and 1911 respectively, and a printed version of the play in 1912.) There is a one-act play of proto-feminist satire, *The Twelve Pound Look* (£12 being the price of a typewriter, and so of a woman's independence). The sampler is completed by *Farewell Miss Julie Logan* (1932), a late return to the wintry Scottish settings of Barrie's first fictions, an uncanny tale in diary form, where the sexual repression of a village minister flares into 'love' and madness. There are other contenders for inclusion in such a compilation. The one-act play *Shall We Join The Ladies?*, for instance, is as brilliant (in its uncharacteristically objective manner) as anything Barrie wrote. But any reassessment of Barrie's achievement requires us to look at the core of his writing life; another editor might have gathered together the best of his twenty-six plays: say, *The Admirable Crichton* (1902), *Dear Brutus* (1917) and *Mary Rose* (1920).

Barrie's plays are neither particularly original nor much like any other sort of literature. The printed texts have a great volume of matter which has no relation to an experience in the theatre. *The Admirable Crichton,* for instance, begins before it begins: 'A moment before the curtain rises, the Hon. Ernest Woolley drives up to the door of Loam House in Mayfair.' Later in the Act, another character (The Earl of Loam) is excessively rendered before he has yet spoken: 'He takes in all the weightiest monthly reviews, and prefers those that are uncut, because he perhaps never looks better than when cutting them; but he does not read them, and save for the cutting it would suit him merely to take in the covers.' Elsewhere, the italicized 'stage directions' are a vehicle for little ballets of whimsy: ('He means every word of it, though the flowers would here, if they dared, burst into ironical applause.'); or ('... Perhaps these are smiles that she has left lying about.') These are a part of Barrie's very measured scrambling of the actual and the fantastic. The opening of Peter Pan, for instance, asserts the unreal nature of the setting while applying the appearance of reality: 'The night nursery of the Darling family, which is the scene of our opening Act, is at the top of a rather depressed street in Bloomsbury. We have a right to place it where we will ...' The same play harangues us to believe in fairies, and it is not just Tinker Bell's 'existence' that hangs by our response. Barrie knew sentimentality to be his besetting weakness ('that leering, distorted thing' as he called it in his self-deprecating novel, *Sentimental Tommy*). In some plays, the corruption starts with the title – in *Alice Sits By The Fire* (1905), for example, or in *A Kiss for Cinderella* (1916) – but little of what he wrote is quite free of it. Barrie's secretary, Cynthia Asquith, suggested that most of the embarrassing bits were transferred from Barrie's own experience, in many cases the reported speech of a child, with a private resonance for Barrie that is lost on his audience or reader. Watching an early performance of *Peter Pan*, Anthony Hope found the sight of the Beautiful Mothers adopting the Lost Boys too much to stomach, and groaned aloud, 'Oh, for an hour of Herod!'

But what may redeem parts of Barrie for a modern readership is the streak of cruelty which contends with the fey in his plays, as it did in his psyche. Captain Hook, after all, is exactly a defeated Herod: 'A holocaust of children, there is something grand in the ideal', Hook muses, and whether or not this is pantomime, Barrie would have felt the strength of the phrase. And the strongest impression one gets from reading Barrie – far from Hardy's image of his unconcern – is his active presence in every scene, sometimes in more than one character, and sometimes, given his infantile or distorted view of human relationships, to uncomfortable effect. In *Dear Brutus*, written when Barrie was fifty-seven, an inscrutable, ancient impresario figure called Lob, 'rather like what Puck might have grown into if he had forgotten to die', has invited a group of people to stay in his house on Midsummer's eve. ('LOB is very small, and probably no one has ever looked so old except some newborn child.') In the Second Act, the party enters a magical wood, where they experience an hour of what they might have been. Most simply confirm their set strengths and weaknesses, and learn that 'There is more in it … than taking the wrong turning; you would always take the wrong turning.' The painful exception is a man called Dearth, a once-talented artist who has declined into an alcoholic 'waster'. In the First Act, Dearth laments, 'Three things they say come not back to men nor women – the spoken word, the past life, and the neglected opportunity.' His lot in the wood is vigorous health, a stream of paintings and Margaret, the daughter he never had, a rich source of what Cynthia Asquith deplored: 'To be very gay, dearest dear, is so near to being very sad', she says, and 'How awful it would be, Daddy, to wake up and find one wasn't alive', and 'I think men need daughters …', and, finally, 'Daddy, come back; I don't want to be a might-have-been.' The Third Act brings everyone back to their senses, but Barrie's focus is unmistakably on Dearth in the agony of his renewed barrenness. He says only, 'Lob, I thank thee for that hour' – and then '(The seedy-looking fellow passes from the scene)'.

W. B. Yeats

A Genius, A Fool

W. B. Yeats. A Life. Volume One: The Apprentice Mage 1865–1914
R. F. Foster, Oxford University Press

'If you have revisited the town, thin Shade, /... to look upon your monument /... Let these content you and begone again' ('To a Shade'). Though useful shorter lives, by Joseph Hone (1942) and A. Norman Jeffares (1949; revised, 1988), appeared soon after the death of W. B. Yeats, it has sometimes looked since as though posterity would fail to deliver a biography appropriate to his giant stature as a poet or to the fearsome complexities of his public life. The critic Denis Donoghue approached the task in the 1960s and withdrew. The historian F. S. L. Lyons assembled his materials, but died in 1983 before he could write them up. But their successor R. F. Foster, who in his *Modern Ireland: 1600–1972* had already smoothly accomplished one labour of Hercules, is not to be jinxed. *The Apprentice Mage 1865–1914* is the first of two volumes, and plots Yeats's multiple careers as far as his fiftieth year. What Yeats was to achieve thereafter will not fit into the decorous chapter or two that would serve for the growing-old of most poets. But this first instalment alone, over 300,000 words of it, is the fullest biography of a writer in English since Michael Holroyd's four-volume life of Shaw (1988–92). With annotation that upholds the standards set by John Kelly in his ongoing edition of Yeats's letters, and a capacity for detail that is matched and marshalled by formidable powers of organization, it triumphantly fulfils one of the most ambitious biographical undertakings of the century. 'Most biographical studies of WBY are principally about what he wrote; this one is principally about what he did.'

This approach may be particularly suited to these 'early' years, when lyric poetry often seems peripheral to Yeats's activities in other fields. But Foster's distinction also suggests how his enterprise complements the more readerly achievement of Richard Ellmann's *Yeats: The Man and the Masks* (1949) and *The Identity of Yeats* (1954). Foster gives us Yeats in the coolest, neutral, chronological, prose, confining his own intervention to the slight push of an adverb, a charged 'as usual' or an ambiguous 'superbly'; outrageous remarks about the base-born are said to be 'breezily' or 'jauntily' delivered. Where Ellmann figures the younger Yeats as 'a man in a frenzy, beating on every door in the hotel to find his own room', Foster marks the end of the same phase in the poetry with a much more subdued metaphor, 'the poet's ruthless search for a theme ended in himself'. What Foster provides additionally are the hundred facts which make such statements true.

Yeats's parents personify the decline, in the mid-Victorian period, of Ireland's Protestant Ascendancy. His father was a renowned wit but an improvident artist who could never finish a picture; his mother, of the mystical and morbid mill-owning Pollexfens, was to be crippled by depression. Susan Yeats's account of their honeymoon at the Railway Hotel, Galway, passed down through their daughter Lily, is like something out of *Dubliners*; quoted at length by Foster, it exemplifies how the luxurious proportions of his biography allow apparently marginal details their unexpected resonance:

> Mama had never stayed in an hotel, and Papa got ill, and she tried to light a fire and failed, and Papa got cross ... then she went out for help and stood on the landing and looked down the great well to the hall, and heard some children on the top floor saying their prayers, and she felt homesick ... Papa had to go to bed. She sat alone for dinner and they brought her a shoulder of mutton. She cut it once, and then, aghast at the way it opened out, looking as if she had eaten quite a pound of meat, she had not the courage to cut off even one slice, and so took just the vegetables. Next day Papa sent for his mother, who came and took him to Dublin in an invalid carriage, and his illness proved to be Diphtheria!

The marriage improved sufficiently for 'Willie' to be born in Dublin in 1865; when he was two, the family moved to London, where he developed into a remote, unbiddable, only eccentrically gifted schoolboy. He pursued his private curriculum with 'high style' – his sister recalled how he 'decided to eat his way through the animal kingdom – but couldn't get beyond the sea gull' – read unusual books, and had precocious literary ambitions. But in one class, of thirteen, he came thirteenth in Maths and English. (Foster has preserved the bad spelling that accompanied Yeats through adulthood: he could even, at the height of his infatuation, anticipating the pun of later poems, mis-spell 'Miss Gone'.) His poor schoolwork denied him the traditional Protestant welcome at Trinity College, Dublin; he went to art school instead. The peculiar division of his intellect was already apparent. Edward Dowden – the Professor of English at Trinity, and a friend of Yeats's father – judged the young Yeats to hang 'in the balance between genius & (to speak rudely) fool'. Young men are traditionally a bit foolish, but Dowden's verdict is echoed twenty years later by a nationalist journalist: 'When you are on the point of convicting him of being a tuneful trifler and a melodious ninny-hammer, he will suddenly change his mind and talk with amazing brilliance on the most elevated of themes ...'

Just as the sublimity of Yeats's mind has its counterweight of absurdities, the charm of his person was compromised by infuriating and unpleasant qualities – his vanity, his snobbery, his studied absent-mindedness; so that all Foster's witnesses, excluding only the graciously long-suffering Augusta Gregory and the humourless Maud Gonne, contribute to the undercurrent of satiric protest. 'His' actors at the Abbey Theatre saw the worst of him; when one of them was driven by his appalling rudeness to threaten to knock him out, it was another who observed venomously how 'W. B. drifted off the stage moaning for Lady Gregory who waddled along and led him by the hand to have a cup of coffee'. For others, it was his esoteric and spiritual preoccupations that made a 'fool' of Yeats. Ezra Pound complained in 1913 that when 'some question of ghosts or occultism comes up, then he is subject to a curious excitement ... his ... usual quality of mind goes'.

Foster does not attempt to dignify Yeats's long involvement with the Order of the Golden Dawn – his was the seventy-eighth name on the membership roll of the Isis-Urania Temple. His motto, and sobriquet, was 'Demon Est Deus Inversus'; indeed, he quotes this piece of correspondence for its tickling silliness:

with reference to the Fire Wand enclosing a magnetized rod, our G. H. Frater Non Omnis Moriar, usually keeps a stock here .... At the present moment

we are out of them …. When they come in, I will send you one if you wish
it, but if you prefer it, you can, of course, have one made yourself. The usual
size is about six inches.

But Yeats's ceaseless interrogation of the spirit world through mediums –
though his family found it a 'worrying obsession' – is a different matter;
not only because, with whatever success, it was probing what he reasonably
deemed 'the most important problem in the world', but also because it fed
directly into some of his best poems. In the latter years of his apprentice-
ship, through the teenaged Elizabeth Redcliffe, Yeats trafficked with the
likes of Leo Africanus, a productive alter ego from the sixteenth century,
and – to his alarm – with Maud Gonne in sexual transport. Foster traces
direct dividends from these sessions in the great lyric 'The Cold Heaven',
which fuses the lacerating memory of his failure with Maud Gonne and
an initiate's dread of the exposed afterlife:

> Ah! When the ghost begins to quicken,
> Confusion of the death-bed over, is it sent
> Out naked on the roads, as the books say, and stricken
> By the injustice of the skies for punishment?

Until he married in his fifties, Yeats's sexual career was one of almost
uninterrupted frustration. Four affairs are confirmed; none was physical
for long. He shook off his virginity at twenty-nine with Olivia Shakespear.
Like many of his peers, he had an affair with the free-thinking actress
Florence Farr; she concluded it in her brisk fashion – 'I can do this for
myself'. In 1908, he sparred with a well-bred 'medical gymnast', Mabel
Dickinson, who saw him off (if that was her intention) with a claim, not
borne out, that she was pregnant. But Maud Gonne ('the troubling of my
life') made each of these entanglements, as he wrote in his diary, 'but as the
phoenix nest, where she is reborn in all her power to torture or delight'.

Not everyone saw Gonne through a Homeric glaze; one gentle Trinity
don recoiled from 'a great red-haired Yahoo of a woman'. But Yeats was
at her mercy from their first meeting in 1889, and she hardly spared him.
She declared persistently to this suitor a 'horror and terror of physical
love'; but on the day they met, she was five months pregnant by the mar-
ried Boulangist politician Lucien Millevoye, a liaison she kept from Yeats
for ten years, while urging him to celebrate their own spiritual union.

When, in 1903, she staggered him by proclaiming her engagement to the alcoholic nationalist John MacBride, she could write airily to her sister, 'As for Willie Yeats I love him dearly as a friend but I could not for one minute imagine marrying him.' (The marriage collapsed within eighteen months; MacBride had seduced Gonne's seventeen-year-old half-sister and molested her daughter Iseult, then aged eleven. Nothing ennobles Yeats's 'Easter 1916' so much as his granting MacBride an equal 'transformation' with the other casualties of the rising.) In December 1908, Yeats and Gonne finally (as Ellmann had previously established) became lovers. But Foster quotes the letter sent by Gonne the day after the event:

> I have prayed so hard to have all earthly desire taken from my love for you & dearest, loving you as I do, I have prayed & I am praying still that your bodily desire for me may be taken from you too.

Withdrawing now for good, her immediate restoration of occult sweet-talk – 'I have had a partial initiation of the sword, but feel it is not complete' – is thrillingly insensitive. For a time – notably in the staging of *Cathleen Ní Houlihan* (1902) – Gonne's Irish nationalism (she was English) gave Yeats's politics a colouring they did not organically possess. He was voluble in favour of Home Rule; but as a Protestant who spoke no Irish and whose home (as far as he had one) was in London, his own 'nationalism' was necessarily above religion, and even above politics: an assertion of Irish modes and myths against English ones; the creation, when it comes down to it, of a culture which would honour an Anglophone poetry on Irish themes. Increasingly, however, his allegiances were less national than social. His summers in the master-bedroom at Coole deepened his contempt for the Catholic middle class and blurred his own origins (gawped George Russell, 'W. B. Y. believes he is the Duke of Ormond'). One wonders what Gonne would have made of his remark to J. M. Synge, 'The country towns of Ireland are mainly animal, but can sometimes be intoxicated into a state of humanity by some religious or political propagandist body, the only kind of intellectual excitement they have got used to.' His scornfulness looks better when it is deployed in culture's name against commercial or clerical small-mindedness: in his long campaign against the Dublin Corporation's refusal to fund a building to house Hugh Lane's collection of paintings; or in the controversy over the Abbey's production of *The Playboy of the Western World*.

Yeats's work for the theatre, from the formation of the Irish Literary Theatre in 1898, through the founding of the Abbey Theatre in 1904, is really the core of Foster's first volume; it involves the biographer in much patient dissection of internal politics and exhumation of forgotten plays (at least three of which, by various hands, are called *Deirdre*). Yeats saw his mission as putting 'an end to democracy in the theatre', and many of his associates will have felt what that meant. His own plays, pitched to be unpopular, did their bit. In a production of his *Diarmuid and Grania* in 1901, one line of Diarmuid's – 'The fools are laughing at us' – brought the house down. The project of the Abbey was built on his vision, energy, ambition and name, no less than on the money of Miss Horniman, who adored him. But it could have fared better with less of his high-handed and blundering administration. George Russell – a former friend, appearing in this biography as a constant thorn in Yeats's ego – expressed the general exasperation: 'If I was autocrat of Ireland, I would give him twenty thousand a year if at the end of a year he had written two hundred lines of poetry – if he opened his (mouth) on business or tried to run any society, I would have him locked up as dangerous to public peace.'

But as Russell's tone suggests, the critical consensus, as Yeats approached middle age, was that he had finished his important literary work, and would serve Irish Literature in the future rather as a 'schoolmaster' to others; the poet himself noted gloomily in 1912 that he was still best known for the 'sedative' verse he had written before he was thirty – 'The Lake Isle of Innisfree' and other fairy flights. Of course, no one could have predicted, since it has been true of no other poet, that of the (say) fifty poems by which his greatness as an artist would finally be reckoned, all but two or three were conceived after his fiftieth birthday. *The Apprentice Mage* closes in 1914. The onset of war has curtailed the movement towards Home Rule by constitutional means. Yeats has just published *Responsibilities*, the volume of lean public verse which announces his casting-off of mythology and enacts a belated assumption of 'masculinity' in verse, with its moving but self-confident apology to his 'fathers':

> Pardon that for a barren passion's sake,
> Although I have come close on forty-nine,
> I have no child, I have nothing but a book,
> Nothing but that to prove your blood and mine.

Responsibilities looks forward; *Reveries*, a prose memoir of childhood completed in the same year, looks back. Indeed, its melancholy conclusion is one of the few failures of Yeats's capacity, noted by his future wife, to foresee 'how things would look to people afterwards': 'all life weighed in the scales of my own life seems to me a preparation for something that never happens'. Did he not know what he would do?

Laurence Binyon

In his Master's Moonlight

Laurence Binyon: Poet Scholar of East and West
John Hatcher, Clarendon Press

'For the Fallen' – at least, one stanza of it, the fourth of seven – is one of the best-known poems in the language, inscribed on thousands of war memorials and intoned at Armistice Day services around the English-speaking world:

> They shall grow not old, as we that are left grow old:
> Age shall not weary them, nor the years condemn.
> At the going down of the sun, and in the morning
> We will remember them.

This is poetry aspiring to the diction, function and, especially, the ano-nymity of the Prayer Book; its secondary prophecy is that the unheroic, amongst whom the poet is calmly included, should go unsung. And indeed, while few enough could have identified the author as Laurence Binyon, fewer still will have known much more about him; until the arrival of John Hatcher's richly detailed and softly spoken biography. What this gives us is the gentle imprint of a man for whom effacement was not a fate but a creed; to whom 'losing himself' was a term for the profoundest human experience; whose diffidence was immortalized in his friend Henry Newbolt's jingle – 'Mr Binyon / Reserved his opinion'.

Born in Lancaster in 1869, the son of a clergyman, Laurence Binyon won a scholarship to St Paul's, and witnessed the school's removal from the crowdedness and animation of the cathedral precincts to its new

site in what he called 'Hammersmith and Prose'. His most important
adolescent friendship was with an Indian boy, Mamnohan Ghose, who
introduced him at this early age to oriental thought, but who reacted, as
their friendship waned, against the element of priggishness in Binyon's
precocious reserve: 'you are too perfect, too reasonable, too sinless, and
on that account in danger of being a little cold …. Be true to your real
self' – an injunction which already seems misplaced. After Oxford, where
he gained a reputation for deep rather than quick thinking, Binyon set-
tled on the fringes of the literary and artistic set of Fitzrovia, an appren-
tice poet. But he needed to work for a living, and applied to the British
Museum, settling in the Department of Prints and Drawings, where, in
time, he began to specialize in oriental art.

Indeed, as Hatcher's properly balanced account demonstrates, Binyon's
work with Eastern art, over nearly forty years as cataloguist and critic,
was as considerable as anything he achieved in poetry. Although he was
unable to visit the East until he sailed for Japan on his sixtieth birthday,
Binyon, whose *Painting in the Far East* (1908) was the first book on its
subject in any European language, was a pioneer in the movement that
introduced oriental arts to the West, and a connoisseur in particular of
eighteenth-century Japanese wood-block prints or ukiyo-e. The rhapsodic
style of Binyon's prose writings in the field have made them obsolete as
art criticism; but they constantly suggest the sort of effect he strove for in
his own creative practice. Take his description of Kiyonaga's supremely
elegant bijin-ga (pictures of women):

> It is an impersonal art, this: no violence of expression or of restless line dis-
> turbs the poise of these harmoniously moving or statue-like goddesses, or
> the adjusted folds of their garments.

Such a spirit might find an English literary equivalent in what Binyon
described, in an undergraduate essay unearthed by Hatcher, as 'the pale
beauty, bathed in moonlight air, of Matthew Arnold's muse of marble'.
And no disciple of Arnold can have buckled further than Binyon under
the appeal in the 1853 'Preface': 'Let us, at least, have so much respect for
our art as to prefer it to ourselves'. The lack of individual colouring in his
writing has been fairly attributed to a deficiency of imagination; but it has
also to do with an enduring taste for his master's moonlight. Not that he
always had his influences under sure control. For Ezra Pound, Binyon's

poetry was doomed from the start, not drained by Arnold, but 'poisoned in the cradle by the abominable dogbiscuit of Milton's rhetoric'. Yet the poems in the early *Books of London Visions* (1896 and 1899) incline towards the fashionable urban experiments of W. E. Henley, Arthur Symons and John Davidson, and proceed from particular visual experiences, though they are for the most part anaemically executed. Reviewers made the analogy with Whistler's paintings: for one, Binyon was an 'impression- istic word-painter' composing 'harmonies in grey and other sad tones'; to another, he resembled, squinting at tramps from the shadows, 'a phi- lanthropist with a camera'.

But in 1899, as if to disqualify his verse from consideration in the mod- ernist century, he told the critic James Douglas that he was abandoning urban themes because the 'wrestle ... with brute material' – and he is the least wrestling of poets – left his verse 'languid'. *Odes* (1900) forsook the people of London for the kings and queens and stock heroes of Western mythologies. 'The Death of Tristram' was singled out on publication by W. B. Yeats as 'a great poem'; thirty-six years later, Yeats took it whole as one of the longest single pieces in his *Oxford Book of Modern Verse*. Yeats praised Binyon in another context for writing 'as men had always written'; and his tackling Tristram certainly swelled the mainstream. That myth had been treated at length in the previous half-century by Arnold, Tennyson (in *The Last Tournament*) and Swinburne (to name only the most celebrated). Binyon's instinct was to join them in a project bigger than the individual, on a subject which 'partakes of the universal'; to position himself, putting it mystically, on

> The road that is before us and behind
> By which we travel from ourselves, in sleep
> Or waking, toward a self more vast and deep.

For the more vital and robust and relevant and ugly poetry of Binyon's times, as he may already have intuited, this was the road not taken. In 1904, Binyon, apparently still 'sinless' in his thirty-fifth year, married Cicely Powell, the daughter of a banker, who was not immediately converted to his Franciscan ideal of living with the minimum of possessions; but all Hatcher's evidence suggests that the marriage was a wonderfully happy one. If the union had an effect on Binyon's poetry, it was only to banish still further the claims of the first person. When twin girls were born at the end of the year, he wrote to his wife: 'I feel the babies are going to deepen life for us & that will make my our poetry better' – the 'my' struck out, though Cicely, among her several accomplishments, wrote only Sunday poetry. The *Morning Post* declared in 1909 that 'as a poet of marriage Mr Binyon has few equals'; which masks the fact that as a poet of marriage Binyon had few competitors.

As a poet of war, he made the least of his disadvantages. 'For the Fallen' is one of a number of honourable exercises by Binyon in that discredited genre, the poem from the Home Front. (In fact, it was finished when the war was barely a fortnight old, and the scale of the falling unknowable.) But it was only his age that kept him from fighting; and he spent what leave he could take as a volunteer ambulanceman and porter at a French military hospital on the Marne. A fine and surprising poem written there, 'Fetching the Wounded', yields nothing to Wilfred Owen in directness of observation; and in the place of the stronger poet's indignation is a passive tenderness which is just as affecting and true. Yet the slaughter of France did not destroy his instinct for civilization, nor inhibit his catching after 'beauty'. He heard in *The Waste Land*'s (1922) 'jangled music and deflated rhythms' a 'sense of desolation and sterility and confusion', which he did not share, though he had seen the cause closer than Eliot or Pound; and he was even drawn into a mild-mannered campaign against them. 'In contrast to the poetry of Mr T. S. Eliot', as the *Sewanee Review* put it, 'Mr Binyon affects a reconstruction of beauty against the forces of disintegration'. Hence, when Binyon applied himself to the major work of his maturity, the long poems of the 1920s, he chose the extended ode, not so much a traditional form as a dead one. He had his supporters: 'I ... feel while I am reading [it], that I am in the very presence of the spirit of the age', wrote one in 1925 – not of *The Waste Land* but of *The Sirens*, Binyon's monotonously pitched ode to the airy heights explored by contemporary mountaineers and aviators, as if the war had never been. Yet those who took Binyon's side in the sporadic debate – Gordon Bottomley, Henry Newbolt, Lascelles Abercrombie – are themselves gone into the dark with him, even a poet as fine as Robert Bridges; the terms in which they praised him – 'noble' etc – are now seen to have been mortally damaged by the war. 'The great thing about Binyon', said Bridges, as if it were also the trouble – and the same might be said of himself – 'is that he has such a beautiful mind.'

But if the new, transatlantic generation eclipsed Binyon and his peers, they had always a sneaking regard in particular for the stubborn purity of his technique; and latterly he earned their explicit approval. Retiring from his museum duties in 1933, he embarked on his complete translation of the *Divine Comedy* in terza rima. Strikingly successful and uncharacteristically rugged in itself, this seems also to have had a helpfully astringent effect on Binyon's original verse: Pound thought Dante had cured him at last of his Miltonic 'bustuous rumpus'. Whatever the cause, the poems of Binyon's last five years confirm him, in John Masefield's ambiguous estimate, as 'one of the very few whose poetry got better as he got older'. There was even the balm of a late friendship with his erstwhile antagonist, Eliot. In 1940, as poetry editor at Faber, Eliot proposed to publish Binyon's *Selected Poems*; when Macmillan refused to grant copyright, he offered instead that Faber should publish a collection of new poems. Binyon was delighted, though (as he told his wife) 'a little embarrassed by such warmth toward a belated Victorian like me'; and the kindling of respect was mutual. Eliot sent Binyon the *Four Quartets* as they appeared, and Binyon admired them, noting acutely how 'when symbol and image come, they are enhanced by the bareness which foils them'. And Binyon re-modelled his austere, aromatic new wartime sequence 'The Ruins', published later as 'The Burning of the Leaves', with the structure of the Quartets in mind; and with quietly powerful effect.

If Binyon's temperament must be judged in the end to have been inimical to the production of great poems, he gives us in several places the sense of what very good poetry sounds like when it is too beautifully refined to be better. He was still working at the time of his death on a poem called 'Winter Sunrise'; it must therefore be considered a fragment, but it is perfect as it was left: the last of a thousand pages of verse, and miraculously the finest. With its own delicate reflections on the tricks of remembrance, it might stand, though written in 1943, as the closing signature of all Edwardian poetry:

> It is early morning within this room: without,
> Dark and damp: without and within, stillness
> Waiting for day: not a sound but a listening air.
> Yellow jasmine, delicate on stiff branches
> Stands in a Tuscan pot to delight the eye
> In spare December's patient nakedness.
> Suddenly, softly, as if at a breath breathed
> On the pale wall, a magical apparition,

The shadow of the jasmine, branch and blossom!
It was not there, it is there, in a perfect image;
And all is changed. It is like a memory lost
Returning without a reason into the mind;
And it seems to me that the beauty of the shadow
Is more beautiful than the flower; a strange beauty,
Pencilled and silently deepening to distinctness.
As a memory stealing out of the mind's slumber,
A memory floating up from a dark water,
Can be more beautiful than the thing remembered.

G. K. Chesterton

Too Old to Woo

Poems for All Purposes: The Selected Poems of G. K. Chesterton
Edited by Stephen Medcalf, Pimlico

When pressed as to why a talent as exceptional as Chesterton's would not apply itself to the higher forms of literature, his wife remarked 'He is bent on being a jolly journalist, to paint the town red … All he wants is buckets and buckets of red paint'. Many of the poems in Stephen Medcalf's handsome new selection display the same emphatic colouring; intense, martial, convivial, Roman Catholic: like the hordes of 'Lepanto', they 'rush in red and purple from the red clouds of the morn'. The poetry is also, as Medcalf's choice of title suggests, related to the journalism in another way: Chesterton was pleased to be able to turn his versifying hand to whatever the moment required (except, that is, for what his own generation – he was five years Yeats's junior – began to expect from poetry proper). Medcalf has whittled away most of the more plainly occasional material from the *Collected Poems* of 1933, and restored some of the early nonsense verse that 'enchanted' W. H. Auden. The centrepiece of the chronological arrangement is inevitably 'The Ballad of the White Horse', an eighty-page allegorical narrative of King Alfred, where the poet's ruddy vein of Saxon warfaring is at its most exposed: 'the hands of the happy howling men / Fling wide the gates of war'. This sort of thing (1911) had not long to live; a modern reader is likely to be drawn instead to the comic material, of which the pick is the series of parodies of English poets as sharp and funny as any of their kind on the theme of 'Old King Cole'.

But of the straighter-faced work, the stalwart trio of anthology pieces – 'The Rolling English Road', 'The Donkey', the madly belligerent

'Lepanto' – deserve to be joined in more general knowledge by a handful of other poems brought to light here: 'The Sword of Surprise', with its startling opening appeal, 'Sunder me from my bones, O sword of God'; the magical projections of 'A Second Childhood':

> Men grow too old to woo, my love,
> Men grow too old to wed:
> But I shall not grow too old to see
> Hung crazily overhead
> Incredible rafters when I wake
> And find I am not dead.

– and, from an earlier period, an historical meditation on the people of England, 'The Secret People', 'who have not spoken yet' and whose ale-regarding silence is a welcome break from the volume's prevailing clamour. Regrettably, the titles of individual poems are not listed, either in the contents or in an index, which discouragingly suggests that no one at this end of the century will want to look any of them up.

John Buchan

A Pretty Turn of Speed

The Leithen Stories
Introduction by Christopher Harvie, Canongate

Though he served his three countries – Scotland, Great Britain and Canada – conspicuously in law, politics and publishing, as well as in many branches of literature, John Buchan (1875–1940) is chiefly remembered now for his creation of Richard Hannay, his bulletproof Scots/South African adventurer. Hannay's domain was the spy thriller, what Buchan called the 'shocker'; *The Thirty-Nine Steps* was his rampantly successful debut in fiction, a novel whose classic status has been reinforced by several film treatments, including Hitchcock's entertaining takeover of 1935, and Don Sharp's colourful version of 1978, whose climax has Hannay wrenching absurdly at the hands of Big Ben: an agent of the Establishment, we are obliged to recognize, trying to hold back time. (Robert Powell, miscast here, resumed the role of Hannay in a short-lived television series of that title.) Hannay's popularity, meanwhile, generated a number of follow-up 'shockers', the best of them collected in *The Four Adventures of Richard Hannay* (1930). But Buchan had another serial hero: Sir Edward Leithen, who preceded Hannay on to the page, who dies at the close of Buchan's last novel, and who has the reputation of having a good bit of his author written into him. Now, under the enlightened editorship of Christopher Harvie, he has his own omnibus of four novels, *The Leithen Stories*. (Neither Leithen's first appearance, in the short story 'Space' of 1912, or his rather enervated political narrative, *The Gap in the Curtain*, 1932, which also involves 'Dick' Hannay, is called up here.) And where Hannay's adventures are effectively of a piece – *Greenmantle* (1926), for instance, reading like an epic or expensive sequel to *The Thirty-Nine Steps* – each of the books narrated by or featuring Sir Edward explores a different genre; and their tenor is likewise a little more refined and philosophical.

Leithen, as introduced in the short novel *The Power House* – serialized in 1913, and so pre-dating *The Thirty-Nine Steps* – is a new type of thriller hero: one who exploits what Graham Greene called the 'dramatic value of adventure in familiar surroundings happening to unadventurous men'. He is an MP and a high-ranking barrister; yet his buccaneering friends still josh him that 'Life goes roaring by and you only hear the echo of it in your stuffy rooms'. He describes his own routine complicitly as 'flat, chambers, club, flat', where the repeated word has a double meaning; himself as 'sedentary', 'prosaic', 'sober', 'dull' and 'dry'. He leaves London only once in the course of the novel, and that for a few days' motoring in the West Country with his 'sombre and silent' chauffeur. Yet peril seeks him out, and in passages which seem to anticipate the violations of the Blitz, he endures hairbreadth escapes in St James's, at Chancery Lane tube station, in a 'private' room in a Bloomsbury restaurant – and on his own doorstep. Like Erskine Childers's only novel, *The Riddle of the Sands* (1903) – from which Buchan derived, as he acknowledged, the temper and atmosphere of *The Thirty-Nine Steps* – *The Power House* capitalizes on the mixture of complacency and latent frenzy that grips the English in the face of a coming war with Germany. Here, though, the enemy is not a competing nationalism, but a global conspiracy masterminded by an English anarchist, the smooth and ruthless Andrew Lumley, whose brain (like that of Tuke, his 'Super Butler' – as villainous an epithet as Buchan ever conceived) was 'cut loose from the decencies that make life possible'. In one of their creepy chats, Lumley articulates, as a boast, the principal lesson of all Buchan's more missionary fiction: 'you think that a wall as solid as the earth separates civilization from barbarism. I tell you the division is a thread, a sheet of glass'. The novel is the first skirmish in a career-long punch-up between the top dogs of the Athenaeum and club-less, shifty intelligences who hood their eyes like hawks; and it establishes the delightful ascendancy in Buchan's narratives of the very improbable.

'The amazing and almost incredible thing about this story of mine', says Leithen, 'is the way clues kept rolling in unsolicited'. For all its deter-mined anachronism in the aftermath of the war and among the stirrings of what was to become the General Strike, *John Macnab* (1925) is the freshest and least perturbed of the tales collected here. A 'stale' Leithen, now in his mid-forties and 'former' Attorney General, heads north with two of his fittest Tory contemporaries, a leading banker (once a rugby international) and a member of the Cabinet, to shake off their mid-life ennui by announcing that on a certain date they will poach a salmon or a stag from named estates near the house of their ebullient young club-mate, Sir Archie Roylance, the Romeo of the piece, who happens to be their party's candidate for the vacant seat of Wester Ross. They sign their challenge with the joint alias 'John Macnab'. The book is unyielding in its celebration of an elite at play. All four gentlemen have gone through Eton, Oxford and the Athenaeum, and three own their parcel of Scotland; beyond that magic circle there is not much in the British Isles (including Harrow and Cambridge) to be regarded, until we reach the very lowest classes, if they show warmth, courage, local cunning and loyalty, like the twelve-year-old fish-seller, Benjie, in *John Macnab*. The poachers run the legs off a bunch of hired and hapless navvies (some of whom, it emerges, served 'under' them in the war); even the 'sedentary' Leithen ('long ago at Eton I had won the school mile ...') shows a 'pretty turn of speed'. Catching the national mood, they declare themselves, over drinks, to be 'on strike against our privileges'. But *John Macnab* is conceived as a holiday, and its mission is that of a feudal fairground. Given the poach-ers' status, there is no danger that the local landowners will do anything but offer them their daughters once their identities are uncovered. After the game is over, the local papers dutifully announce that it was the work of 'a nameless monomaniac – a gentleman, it was hinted, who had not recovered from the effects of the war'. But this may be more indicative of the book's intention as a whole than the jolly narrative might instantly convey. The chapter headings – 'The Assault on Glenraden', 'Haripol – The Armistice' – echo those of the popular history of the war – as it happened that Buchan wrote for the publisher Nelson, much of it from his sickbed. And as well as several gorgeous late-summer landscapes, the portrait of the Highlands takes in depopulation, the breakdown of the great estates and their purchase by alien speculators, and the despoliation of the wil-derness by tourists of all classes. London, from which they fled, is 'dead'. Their harmless playtime past, the 'boys' must return to the certain failure of their cause, and, increasingly, to the consolations of religion. Several of Buchan's novels have been described as his personal favourite; *The Dancing Floor*, a religious romance, is one of them.

Certainly the author seems half in love with both his younger protago-
nists: Kore Arabin, the blameless only child of an artistic monster (based
on Byron, some of whose unpublished letters sickened Buchan) who had
turned his castle on the Greek island of Plaxos into a nest for every kind
of vice; and the 'beautiful' Vernon F. Milburne (Eton, Magdalen, winner
of the Varsity mile and the coolest officer on the Western Front), whom a
recurring dream has prepared to meet his destiny at Easter 192-. Leithen,
the narrator, functions as an avuncular catalyst. Outrageous coincidence
and a Shakespearean tempest bring Milburne's yacht to anchor off Plaxos,
just when the starving islanders, reverting to their pagan religion, are
about to incinerate the defiant Kore in the polluted castle. On Easter
Sunday, as Leithen scrambles about the rocks trying to effect his own
rescue, Kore and Vernon emerge from the flames in the guise of shiny
white Greek gods. In an explicitly Christian ending, the terrified peas-
ants hurtle back to their neglected church, where they plead with their
gratified priest that 'Christ is risen!'

Leithen's individual salvation is the matter of *Sick Heart River*, writ-
ten when Buchan was mortally ill and published posthumously in 1941.
Given months to live, the tubercular Sir Edward ties up his legal and par-
liamentary duties and takes off for Canada (where Buchan, now Baron
Tweedsmuir, had been Governor General since 1935) in wheezing pursuit
of a Canuck businessman who has suffered a mysterious breakdown and
disappeared into the freezing wilds of the north. There are few of the famil-
iar narrative fireworks here; their place is taken, first by an almost obses-
sive topographical detailing ('You've heard maybe of the South Nahanni
that comes in the north bank of the Liard about a hundred miles north of
Fort Simpson?'), second, by the fluctuations of Leithen's spirit in extremis.
The last act of the great man's earthly life is his grey faced appearance
among a settlement of diseased and demoralized Indians, on whom he
acts, as if from the pages of *The Golden Bough*, as a revivifying priest-king;
his quietus is the vision of a bull moose crashing out of a river, at which
epiphany 'He knew that he would die; but he also knew that he would
live.' The special seriousness of attention granted to *Sick Heart River* has
had much to do with our knowledge of its author's own simultaneous
facing-up to mortality. But how far can the identification be carried?

No one can have written 130 books, as Buchan did, without pretty often
sitting at his desk, which Leithen sees as his defining posture. There are
other superficial similarities: Leithen was born in Peeblesshire, the home

of Buchan's father, a minister, four years after Buchan was born in Perth; of an evening, Leithen appears 'as usual, deep in the works of Walter Scott' – of whom Buchan's biography (1932) remains the best – and there is no doubt of the moving personal investment in *Sick Heart River*. But in the big things of life, as they saw them, Buchan and Leithen diverge. Buchan went to a fine day school in Glasgow, Hutcheson's Grammar, and only went to Oxford (and Brasenose at that) as his second university. Leithen fought and nearly died in the First World War; Buchan was prevented from enlisting by a duodenal ulcer, though he later became a war correspondent for the *Times* and eventually, as Director of Information, an associate member of the War Cabinet. Most strikingly, however, Buchan was happily married, from the age of thirty-two, to Susan Grosvenor, with whom he had four children; Leithen, like many of his 'pals', remained a bachelor. On the third page of the first novel, Leithen mentions the wife of a dodgy clubmate as the 'only person ('person'?) to have captured my stony heart'; by *The Dancing Floor*, this has been purified to the claim that 'I had never been in love in my life'. The girls in this omnibus are of the regular Buchan type: 'slender', vivacious, respectably unconventional, 'like an adorable boy' or 'like a wild boy'. Janet Raden (in *John Macnab*) would have made 'a dashed good soldier'; Kore Arabin, springing from her burning tomb like 'a mailed virgin', is naturally admired by a hero who had 'always preferred Artemis to Aphrodite'.

Yet Leithen's chaste regard for the latter is no different from his warmth towards her future husband, Vernon Milburne, whose name suggests a common ancestor for Buchan's leading ladies: Diana Vernon, the gloriously overwritten warrior-heroine of Scott's *Rob Roy*. On the other hand, Leithen's celibacy is quite consistent with Buchan's awareness of their resemblance; it wouldn't do for a character based on his wife's husband to fall in love all over the world, or to marry, say, a spirited young redhead. A similar gallantry may explain Susan's peripheral presence in his posthumous memoir, *Memory Hold-the-Door*. Besides, Leithen, 'dry old stick' as he says he is, may seem to protest too much: any half-awake post-colonial reader would have him for a homosexual. John Buchan's Tory heroes were becoming obsolete even as he wrote them. And yet, it is partly – as well as by the brilliantly suspenseful scenes and crisply realized settings in which they appear – through their pungent 'incorrectness' that they continue to transmit the unnamed quality of 'life' that Sir Edward Leithen groped for on his deathbed.

Edwin Muir

'Late In the Evening'

Edwin Muir – Selected Poems
Faber and Faber

My childhood all a myth
Enacted in a distant isle …
    ('The Myth')

Edwin Muir was born in 1887, the youngest of six children, on a farm rented by his father in the island of Deerness, Orkney. Two years later, the family moved to the neighbouring island of Wyre, which was to supply the contours for Muir's 'myth' of a childhood Eden. When he was only seven, though, the family began to shift again, as their fortunes stuttered, from better farms to worse. At last, in 1901, the Muirs gave up the land and set out for Glasgow: an event he would equate, in his rather determined scheme of things, with the Fall. A parallel conceit of Muir's was that he had been born before the Industrial Revolution: 'In 1751 I set out from Orkney for Glasgow. When I arrived I found that it was not 1751, but 1901.' His place in this new age was to do clerical jobs, first in a beer-bottling plant, then in a factory down the Clyde for reducing animal bones to charcoal. The shock of the exchange was aggravated by – and, in Edwin's mind, to blame for – the loss of most of his family: 'My father and mother and two of my [three] brothers died in Glasgow within two years of one another.' These calamities, and Muir's nervous dread of the slum life he observed in the city, are recorded in his memoir *The Story and the Fable* (1940), whose six chapters were supplemented to make the celebrated *An Autobiography* (1954).

Conditions in the poorer parts of Glasgow (which were much of it) at the end of the Victorian era were the worst, it seems, ever to blight a British city. They had come as a shock to the elderly Friedrich Engels, himself a former citizen of industrial Manchester, who visited in 1888: 'I did not believe, until I visited the wynds of Glasgow, that so large an amount of filth, crime, misery and disease existed in one spot in any civilized country.' To Muir, too, the city's evils had an absolute quality. As late as 1956, when his Glaswegian trauma was forty years in the past, he published a sonnet, 'Milton', in which Glasgow and Hell are freshly synonymous; in which the utmost trial devised for the blameless Milton is to submit his ears to the riot of Argyle Street at closing time, 'the steely clamour known too well / on Saturday nights in every street in Hell'. A personal 'myth' is one thing, and Muir's helped him vitally. But he would never have pretended – after most men of his generation had gone into the trenches – that the forms of his own Fall were especially steep or severe. For one thing, he had already been sharply disillusioned by the second half of his Orkney boyhood: this is Garth, near Kirkwall, the fourth of his father's farms, as it is described in *An Autobiography*.

> We moved into it when I was eight. From the start everything went wrong. The land was poor and had constantly to be drained; the dwelling-house was damp; in the rooms where we slept worms writhed up between the stone flags in wet weather. My mother was always ill; my brothers and sisters, one after another, left to take up jobs in Kirkwall or Glasgow or Edinburgh; the family slowly broke up; horses and cows died; my father grew more and more discouraged, strained his heart, and was unable to carry on his work. We all hated the dreary place, which gave a spiteful return for the hard work flung into it. We were five years at Garth.

From here, the particular Glasgow to which his family moved was the 'respectable' southern suburb of Crosshill near Queen's Park, described in Muir's *Scottish Journey* (1935) as inhabited by 'the better-paid clerks, shopkeepers, foremen, buyers, commercial travellers'; the houses had 'sofas, armchairs, pianos, pictures and knick-knacks of all kinds': no intellectual paradise, but not an unkind place in which to grow up; deserving, perhaps, the gentle mockery of a poem like 'Suburban Dream'. The 'damned' themselves are another story: the city's slum dwellers and no-hopers, 'kicking a football in a tenth-rate hell', are given rough treatment in Muir's prose. Muir went to his first job by tram, through Eglinton Cross, where some insanitary streets ran under the traffic. In the auto-biographical novel *Poor Tom* (1932), the first of his writings to deal with his Glasgow experience, a commuter peers down on these fleetingly, and remotely, as if at an underworld:

> Astonishing the number of dirty squalling children that were down here … and the way they yelled and screamed was enough to scare you; wasn't a human sound at all. Yet you never heard them when you were passing on the tramcar.

In the *Autobiography*, the Dantesque notes of distaste and disdain for 'the arrogant women, the mean men, the terrible children' are assuredly Muir's. And the horrible work with bones and maggots and so on, which sticks to the mind from his appalled account of it, is actually done by others: 'I worked from nine to five in the pleasant, boring office.' The reader of his memoir is shown further that Muir was in these uninspiring or vicariously revolting jobs, for years and years, because he would not or could not rouse himself to get anything better or to get out of Glasgow altogether. The two brothers in *Poor Tom* are quick to blame their sepa-rate problems on the 'corrupting influence of Glasgow'; but we can tell that one had been a drunkard, the other a chronic prig, before they ever left 'home'. Muir says of his own state, in his last year in Orkney: 'I was now fourteen, and, except when I was reading, very unhappy.' He allows us to see that his youthful paralysis had internal causes.

Muir was neither coy nor unduly specific about the many physical illnesses that punctuated his career. He had major problems at different times with his lungs, heart and stomach, and there is a steady drizzle of incidental ailment – 'I had bronchitis at the time'; one might call his an unlucky constitution, except that it failed him when he tried, in 1915, to enlist in the army. But of greater relevance for readers of his poems is the current of nervous illness from which he rarely found relief. His memoir records a persistent dread of testing but ordinary experience. At seven, it was going to school: 'It was about the time when my first world was crumbling and I was frightened and ill that I was sent to school … I dis-liked school from the start.' But the childish sensations of 'terror', 'fear', 'guilt', persist into adulthood: spared the war, he is none the less afflicted with the symptoms of shell-shock:

A jagged stone or a thistle seemed to be bursting with malice, as if they had been put in the world to cut and gash; the dashing of breakers and rocks terrified me, for I was both the wave and the rock; it was as though I were both too close to things and immeasurably distant from them.

These neurotic symptoms would not have been less painful or debilitating because they were 'privately' generated, because they could not be attributed to battlefield noise or even, in truth, to the 'steely clamour' of the modern city. And Muir's development, social and literary, was unusually hesitant. He did not make a serious start as a poet, for instance, until he was well into his thirties. As a younger man in search of guiding principles, he had tried and discarded, in turn, evangelical religion, socialism, and the philosophy of Nietzsche. In 1918, however, he met Willa Anderson, a Shetlander by birth, then teaching at a college in South London; they married the following year, and set up home in Bloomsbury. It seems that his wife's enthusiasm helped Muir to redeem his own potential. He had already begun to write essays and reviews for the journals, and now took a post as assistant to A. R. Orage, editor of the influential journal *New Age*. Soon after, at Orage's suggestion, he underwent a course of psychoanalysis. This involved the recording of his dreams, a discipline which was to cross over, with mixed results, into his writing. He describes how his analyst warned him that his unconscious 'was far too near the surface for comfort and safety, and that I should hurry to put something soundly substantial between me and it'. The 'something' they hit upon was poems.

In 1911, Edwin and Willa Muir decamped for a prolonged sojourn in German-speaking Europe. It was in Dresden that Muir – 'too old', as he claimed (though he managed later), 'to submit to contemporary influences' – began in the manner of an apprentice to compose the verses that were published in 1925 as *First Poems*. The same year, he and Willa began their important collaborative translations of contemporary German literature, including the standard English versions of Franz Kafka, and Muir was soon able to claim a higher profile as a critic and reviewer. His dismissal, in *Scott and Scotland* (1936), of the Scots language as a literary medium provoked a ferocious counter-attack from 'Hugh MacDiarmid' (Christopher Grieve) which Muir seems not to have minded. After the Second World War, he held British Council posts in Prague and then at Rome, where he became (he would say 'at last') a practising Christian. The Norton lectures on 'The Estate of Poetry', which he gave at Harvard in 1955–6, gave him the means to buy the cottage near Cambridge where he spent his remaining years.

Since his death in 1959, Muir's reputation has been sympathetically tended. On the biographical side, to the special attributes of his own account have been added the diligent biographical support of *Edwin Muir: Man and Poet* (1966) by the late P. H. Butter, a gentleman-scholar from the Scottish Borders, who also edited the *Complete Poems* (1991); and Willa Muir's loyal testimony in *Belonging* (1968). The quiet personal virtues honoured in these have moulded some of our responses to the poems. In the last months of his own life, T. S. Eliot supplied a preface to a posthumous selection of Muir's poems (1965) which praised the work for its 'integrity' – meaning, in Muir's case, the construction in the face of distressful circumstance of a particular artistic regime – a judgement which has long held sway. And while fears of an atomic catastrophe have yielded to fears of an ecological one, poems like 'The Horses', with its wholesome apocalypse, continue to be trotted out in schools. But the signs are that Muir's special dispensation is coming to an end. Normally generous readers have begun to protest that much of the poetry is 'unexciting' (Patrick Crotty) or of 'low wattage' (Seamus Heaney). In particular, no one would now suggest that our estimate of the poems improves the more of them we read. Muir benefits, more than most, from being read in selection. For though he purged a lot of earlier work – the whole of *Chorus of the Newly Dead* (1926), for instance – when he came to prepare his *Collected Poems*, still much of what remains has the indistinct quality of juvenilia. It is no exaggeration to say, if he was thirty-eight when he published his first book, that he did not come of age as a poet until he was over fifty. But if only because the problems of the earlier work are also present, in modified form, in the later, it is instructive to see what they are.

If we approach Muir's poems as a mass, the first obstacle to greet us is the kind of title he gives them, which does nothing to appeal to a visiting interest. Nine consecutive poems in *Journeys and Places* (1937), for example, have the titles 'The Unfamiliar Place', 'The Place of Light and Darkness', 'The Solitary Place', 'The Private Place', 'The Unattained Place', 'The Threefold Place', 'The Original Place', 'The Sufficient Place' and 'The Dreamt-Of Place'; the writer's idea is of course to differentiate between these abstract 'places', but the effect on the reader is rather to lump them uninvitingly together. And Muir is not finished: he called his next collection *The Narrow Place*. When the late Donald Davie complained that

Muir 'does not say a thing once for all, then move on fast to another thing', this is the start of what he meant. There are similar features elsewhere. Formally, Muir is conservative, with a repetitive streak. Numbers of rather colourless linked poems may be presented as a poem-sequence, such as *Variations on a Time Theme*, or as parts of a longer poem, such as 'The Journey Back': in either case the dimensions and divisions seem arbitrary. (Nor does the merging between poems stop at this: who can easily tell 'The Journey' from 'The Journey Back', 'The Return' from 'The Return'?) Within single poems, the repetition of certain words manages to be unsettling, without seeming experimental: how the word 'Time', for instance, clangs against itself, without changing, in 'Variations on a Time Theme', a poem whose mechanical end-stopping is its most apparent meaning; or the way three preceding references to 'Paradise' defuse the revelation of the fourth in the sonnet 'Milton'. On one level, it is clear that Muir knows what he is doing. His oft-repeated dictum that 'the life of every man is an endlessly repeated performance of the life of man' chimes with an apparent belief that the diction of every poem should be consistent with the diction of the poem preceding it. As late as 1949, the title poem of Muir's collection *The Labyrinth* – playing and replaying, through an endless opening sentence and beyond, its verbal stock of 'roads' and 'tracks', 'maze' and 'echoes', 'shepherds' and 'flocks' – offers a perplexing model of the poet's difficulty in getting into and out of his narrow creative place: how his imagination will snag, stop, then press on again in some version of the same direction. But still one is unsure about this preoccupation with repetition: whether it is truer to say, in general, that the poet makes art with it, or that he suffers from it, as from a tic or another ailment.

To put it another way: if Muir did not stutter in person, he habitually stutters in his poems, up to the last and best of them – in 'The Horses', for instance (though here the cadence is borrowed from Eliot):

> ... But now if they should speak,
> If on a sudden they should speak again,
> If on the stroke of noon a voice should speak ...

And it is not too fanciful to draw a further physiological parallel. An intriguing passage in the novel *Poor Tom* describes the internal effects of a brain tumour, which Muir might have gleaned from his afflicted brother

Johnnie. It seems at the same time to offer an analogy to the balked or superfluous articulation of Muir's less successful poems.

> And even when he opened his mouth to say something, the words seemed already said before he heard, as in a dream, his tongue laboriously and quite unnecessarily repeating them. Everything he did seemed to be an unnecessary repetition, retarding him, obstinately delaying his thoughts before they could move on to something else; or rather everything seemed already done, and all that was left for him was to watch this repetition, this malicious aping of each one of his actions after it had already taken place.

Muir's poetry may have had strange origins. It is certain, too, that the process of its articulation was, for a long time, extremely laborious or labyrinthine.

The *Autobiography* makes an uncompromising distinction between the 'story' of individual lives and the recurrent 'fable' of humankind with which we occasionally connect: 'There are times in every man's life when he seems to become for a little while a part of the fable, and to be recapitulating some legendary drama.' Muir's poetry, distinct from the individual or prose part of him, is chiefly concerned with these moments of recapitulation. And so it begins, severely as it seems, by refining all the particulars of experience into the timeless, placeless and impersonal formulae of a dream.

The first chapter of the memoir relates an episode from Muir's childhood, in which he has to run away from a rough boy called Freddie Sinclair. 'I got rid of that terror', he tells us, 'almost thirty years later in a poem ['Ballad of Hector in Hades'] describing Achilles chasing Hector round Troy.' Muir's code – his therapy, you might say – required him more generally to absorb the particular properties of Orkney, Glasgow, Dresden, Prague into the psychic pits, the indeterminate towers and rubble of generalized mythology; to lose Sinclair and Hitler, personal and historical demons alike, in the stuff of legend. (It is not, either, as though the myths to which he turns are revitalized in the process. One poem, 'The Town Betrayed', blurs the heroes of Classical, Teutonic and Arthurian myth in one faceless, inimical line – 'Inland now / Achilles, Siegfried, Lancelot / Have sworn to bring us low' – while the mental landscape of the poem is rendered in the same tolling, fatigued rhythmic package, 'the sea, the hills, the town', its elements not so much realized as ticked off.)

What disconcerts the reader further is that the very words of which the bulk of these poems consist seem to have undergone an allied process of purging or refinement. Verbally, with their many returns of rock or wall, good and evil, earth, world, death and enemy, and so on, they are something of a desert. Muir will rarely surprise us with a magical touch of music or colour, a colloquial turn of phrase or a sharply observed detail; it is as if such luxuries had been put aside to establish an austerity of outline, the 'featureless plain' of allegory. (Readers may feel here the long reach of his Presbyterian upbringing. His parents objected to 'profane' literature; hence his formative over-reliance on *Pilgrim's Progress*, 'a book which thoroughly terrified me'.) He seems almost to take words for granted, to use them again and again for the senses they already have. The outcome of these choices or characteristics is a body of work which is determinedly, and with few exceptions, not 'of the world'. Muir's poems are in this sense anti-social; they are not designed to delight or move the reader. This is a rather large concession for us to make; but it sets us on the road towards the special virtues of the best of them.

Until about the outbreak of the Second World War, Muir's awkward, victimized poems are places in which the creative process is not really revealed – is not, perhaps in most cases, truly working. But the poetry which comes after, while it is still true to the sturdy laws that Muir has made for it, is generally looser round the edges, more relaxed and capable in its traffic with externals; and if it is still not really 'meant' for us, it appeals to us more. What we must call Muir's late period produces almost all his best work. Of the sixty poems in this selection, for instance, all but eight were written after his fiftieth birthday. One can think of others who wrote their best when they were oldest – Robert Bridges, for one. But only Yeats, among significant British or Irish poets of their century, enjoyed a creative surge in later age to compare with Muir's; and though the whole level of Yeats's achievement was higher, Muir's trajectory was more simply one of improvement. A new effect of concentration is achieved by the preference for shorter forms, especially the sonnet, which suits Muir's emblematic instincts while curbing his tendency to run on.

There are, notably, excursions into different types of poem. Muir belies his gentle reputation in a number of cussed satirical pieces. The theme of Scottishness, in particular, seems to get him going: 'Scotland 1941' strikes at the cult of Burns and Scott, those 'sham bards of a sham nation', and

'Scotland's Winter' ices over the bones of her warriors. Muir discovers his ease, too, in a lighter, less harried, personal mode, in which he writes a number of poems for his wife ('The Commemoration', 'In Love for Long'), some for himself ('A Birthday'), and the surprising and affecting elegy 'For Ann Scott Moncrieff' – where we catch Muir giving 'Princes Street' of all places a transcendent value. (Still these personal pieces are few and reticent enough not to tell us whether Muir was a father: he was, of a son.) And there are new materials, even machines: motor cars, aeroplanes and battleships appear in their own image, where once they might have been wrought up into dragons or a stranger.

Yet it would be misleading to say that Muir is at his best where he is least like his younger self. Part of his growing authority derives from the respect he continues to show to the narrow poetic personality with which he started, and to which we begin to yield as we might to a Presbyterian minister. And indeed, there is a religious flavour to some of the upward patterns in the late poems, and not only in the overtly Christian pieces, such as 'Transfiguration', which unveils Christ 'discrucified', or, indeed, in the strikingly bitter 'The Incarnate One'. The heavenward surge is more modestly located in a little poem called 'The Bird', where it comes with a skip over a rhyme-word in a spiralling final line:

> The wide-winged soul itself can ask no more
> Than such a pure, resilient and endless floor
> For its strong-pinioned plunging and soaring and upward
>   and upward springing.

And part of the puzzle of Edwin Muir is that it is easier to explain the failure of certain inferior poems than it is to explain the success of the best: why poems like 'The Bird', 'The Face', or 'The Question', or 'Double Absence', have more beauty and durability in store than a first glance at them seems to promise.

The rare qualities of these quietly powerful poems can be brought out by comparison, again, with prose antecedents. It has been fashionable lately to disparage the poems in favour of the sum parts of the prose works. Thus, though the novel *Poor Tom* is structurally a rag-bag, such a view might excerpt the memorable passage in which, on a nocturnal walk, 'Mansie' encounters the statues in George Square, the heart of Glasgow:

Tall shapes rose round him in the fog ... High up, the electric lamps flung
down cones of bluish light on the stony heads and shoulders of the smoke-
grimed statues ... Must seem a queer world to them if they were to waken
up now, frighten them out of their wits, think they were in the next world ...
Like johnnies frozen stiff and cold; the last fellows left on earth might look
like this ...

And the novel closes with a visionary thrill that expands the suggestive-
ness of these stone figures once more: '... and the dead stood about in the
mist like the statues in George Square.' In the poem 'The Rider Victory',
on the other hand, which we may locate (though the poet doesn't) in the
centre of Prague, sculpture seems to lose its suggestiveness, its latent,
dimension of moving and being, and stay emphatically stone:

Suspended, horse and rider stare
Leaping on air and legendary.
In front the waiting kingdom lies,
The bridge and all the roads are free;
But halted in implacable air
Rider and horse with stony eyes
Uprear their motionless statuary.

Many of the poems are given static resolutions like this one: 'heraldic'
is a term they like to use. It may be a disconcerting direction for the
modern reader. But to say that the poems are more emblem than flesh
and blood, more statue than rider, is only to reiterate their purpose as
Muir perceived it. In the *Autobiography*, there is an admired passage in
which Muir recalls the forms of life he knew as a small child combing
the undergrowth. (It does in prose what Seamus Heaney – another who
grew up on a farm – does in the verse of *Death of a Naturalist* for the
tadpoles of his own childhood.)

... most of the time I lived with whatever I found on the surface of the earth;
the different kinds of grass, the daisies, buttercups, dandelions, bog cotton
(we did not have many flowers), the stones and bits of glass and china, and
the scurrying insects ... These insects were all characters to me, interesting
but squalid, with thoughts that could never be penetrated, inconceivable
aims, perverse activities. I knew their names, which so exactly fitted them

as characters: the Jenny Hunderlegs, the gavelock, the forkytail, the slater – the underworld of my little underworld ... Some were not so horrible, such as the spider, impersonal compared with the others, whose progress was a terrifying dart or a grave, judge-like, swaying walk. Unlike the others, he was at home in the sun, and so did not need to scuttle; I thought of him as bearded and magistral ...

It is strange to find in the work of a celebrated poet such a relish for words – the Dickensian allure of the insect names, the personification brought off by the fancy term 'magistral' – and such successful tricks of scale; and to find them not amongst the poems. (Or see by comparison how faint and abstract is the use of 'magistral' in the poem 'The Emblem'.) But the verse, too, has its lowlife, though this may be seen through gauze or a misted lens or rheumy eye. 'Late Wasp' is a late poem – its subject, too, is lateness. A sonnet of loose, liquid, form, it is short enough to quote in full:

> You that through all the dying summer
> Came every morning to our breakfast table,
> A lonely bachelor mummer,
> And fed on the marmalade
> So deeply, all your strength was scarcely able
> To prise you from the sweet pit you had made, –
> You and the earth have now grown older,
> And your blue thoroughfares have felt a change;
> They have grown colder;
> And it is strange
> How the familiar avenues of the air
> Crumble now, crumble; the good air will not hold,
> All cracked and perished with the cold;
> And down you dive through nothing and through despair.

Here the poet's normal procedure does not quite stick his subject in amber: what is caught is not a posture but a dying movement, whose finish is out beyond the poem. Every word of the last line, which you cannot always say with Muir, seems perfect in its place. And so the rare singleness of his writing passes into another medium: 'Late Wasp' could not be improved, rewritten in verse or prose, repeated, repointed or recapitulated.

The last word on Edwin Muir belongs to 'The Horses', the poem which has been read more widely and praised more highly than anything else he wrote. It was picked out by T. S. Eliot as 'that great, that terrifying poem of the atomic age': and it has been accounted the most frequently anthologized Scottish poem of the whole twentieth century. It revisits, in Muir's way, an earlier poem (though freer in line and diction), 'Horses' from *First Poems*. It imagines a brief, catastrophic war that has brought an end to 'that old bad world', and the arrival a year after of a group of strange horses ready to be 'owned and used' by the surviving farmers of a new Orkney. The poem is not free of certain familiar weaknesses: the guileless plagiarism (here of Eliot himself); the heraldic tendency ('Now they were strange to us / as fabulous steeds set on an ancient shield'); and the unguarded wishful thinking by which the end of modernity sets up the speaker with his loamy acres and willing team of workers. Perhaps it appeals most to the adolescent or early student mind, itself half-eager to annihilate the facts of life. But it also stands decisively for the break-through of Muir's poems, 'late in the evening' and in spite of all, to a field of unforced imaginative fluency and an unexpected common cause:

Stubborn and shy, as if they had been sent
By an old command to find our whereabouts
And that long-lost archaic companionship.

'In the Dorian Mood'

The Myth of the Decadent Poet

Decadents, Symbolists, Anti-Decadents: Poetry of the 1890s
Edited by R. K. R. Thornton and Ian Small, Woodstock Books

It was Arthur Symons who brought the dubious example of the French Symbolistes with him from Paris, and who was the presiding spirit at the meetings of the Rhymers' Club at the Cheshire Cheese in Fleet Street; it was Symons who edited the *Savoy* magazine, which ran for eight months in 1896, folding when W. H. Smith's objected to Aubrey Beardsley's 'disgusting' engravings and withdrew it from their shelves; Symons who defined 'The Decadent Movement in Literature', and drew in the Savoy the archetypal '90s portrait, of Ernest Dowson a 'demoralized Keats', racked by tuberculosis, 'in search of new sensations' (through absinthe, hashish, prostitutes) to transfigure with his lyric gift; and it was the skilful craftsman Symons who, with Dowson, wrote the few good English poems in the impressionistic, minor mode he perversely championed.

For Yeats, the myth grew with retrospect. In his *Autobiographies* (1920), he wrote blithely (in the immediate aftermath of the First World War) of a 'Tragic Generation' of singers; though of the Rhymers, only Lionel Johnson, slain by whisky ('much falling, he'), and Dowson in 1900, the same year as Oscar Wilde, died young. Later, in his introduction to the *Oxford Book of Modern Verse* (1892, 1935), Yeats observed gratefully that 'in 1900, everybody got down off his stilts; henceforth, nobody drank absinthe …': grateful, because when he himself emerged blinking from the frenzy and the folly of the '90s, he at once discovered the harder, graver manner that served him for four decades of great poems. *Decadents, Symbolists, Anti-Decadents: Poetry of the 1890s* is a distinct series within

Woodstock Books's valuable ongoing project of facsimile reprints. It consists in all of twenty-seven volumes, reprinting thirty-eight books by twenty-two poets; and a survey of those being published or written around the time of Wilde's trial, which began a hundred years and two weeks ago, gives a rich sense of a confused poetic culture: authors who espoused Decadence, others who deplored it, some who ignored it, one or two who might never have heard of it. From several points of view, none of them literary, the most interesting volume in the series is that which binds together *Silverpoints* (1893) and *Spiritual Poems* (1896) by John Gray; Gray, who strenuously denied that he was the original of Wilde's decadent anti-hero, but who signed at least one letter to Wilde 'Dorian'. Elkin Matthews and John Lane's original edition of *Silverpoints* – its very title suggestive of book design rather than verbal substance – is introduced by Thornton and Small as 'an icon of the 1890s'.

It has all the hallmarks of the exquisite book, being slim and select, only forty pages long and published in an edition of two hundred and fifty copies. Its format is distinctive and elegant, only about eleven centimetres wide and twice as tall. It was bound in vellum or green cloth with a chaste design in gold by Charles Ricketts of leaf or flame shapes against a wave pattern, and it was printed at his instructions in imitation of the old Aldine books in an italic with Roman capitals at the beginning of the lines. The margins were lavish and the paper was handmade Van Gelder. This is the book which prompted Ada Leverson's suggestion to Wilde that he should publish something which was 'all margin'; but what is left in Woodstock's smart but uniform edition are the words in the crabbed and minuscule italic which would be maddening if it carried poems you wanted to read. And these words seem hardly to want to matter. Thirteen of the twenty-nine pieces are translations from Symons's Symbolistes; and the remainder deliver frissons that are equally second-hand, made bathetic by euphemism or careless rapture:

> I was a masseur; and my fingers bled
> With wonder as I touched their awful limbs.

Yet three years later, this card-carrying Decadent, having embraced the Catholic religion which for several of these poets, with their taste for Frenchness, perfume, music-hall and sexual torture, was a not unnatural step is producing *Spiritual Poems*; and by 1907, 'Dorian' Gray is the parish priest of Morningside. It was not only in *Silverpoints* that the words seemed of secondary importance. This is how Wilde greeted the publication of Vincent O'Sullivan's *Houses of Sin*: 'I received today Vincent O'Sullivan's poems: they are beautifully bound and printed: I like the format of the book intensely ....' But when you come to turn O'Sullivan's pages, you move without relief through one stone dead lullaby after another:

> Sleep, sleep, baby sleep!
> Baby sleep in thy trundle-bed!
> Sleep, sleep, baby sleep!
> The wee one laughs in dreamyland.

The editors make no claims for such writing; and O'Sullivan's place in the series is surely earned by his friendship with Wilde (about whom he later wrote a book), rather than any sense that his poems deserve to survive more than, say, John Todhunter's, or T. W. Rolleston's, or those of others whose names have gone fairly into oblivion. Their resurrection a century on in such a desirable (if not actually exquisite) form, like that of the other quainter titles in the series, Theodore Wratislaw's *Caprices*, for instance, or Victor Plarr's elegant *In the Dorian Mood* books which in their own day sold as few as a hundred copies seems half whimsical, half miraculous. O'Sullivan may be terrible, but he is not Decadent; and it is interesting to see how many of the Rhymers challenge the attitudes that are generally held to define them. Said O'Sullivan of Symons: 'Though he was perhaps the only decadent in London ... (he) has managed to pass into history as the leader of a definite movement called Decadent.' Richard le Gallienne, for all his surname, countered Symons's francophile Silhouettes with his hearty *English Poems* (1893), pronouncing that 'decadence is merely limited thinking, often insane thinking'; and the Catholic Lionel Johnson's sense of his own moral failure was the very opposite of his credo.

And, of course, there was life beyond the Cheshire Cheese, 'younger poets' in whom E. K. Chambers found no trace of decadence: 'Mr Robert Bridges, Mr William Watson, Mr Alfred Austin, Mrs Woods. They are sane and healthy and "English" enough: they have not made cayenne pepper of their souls.' None of Chambers's nominees makes it into the Woodstock series, but the muscular Henley, Kipling and Newbolt do; and so does *A Shropshire Lad* (1896), to remind us that great poetry was even then being made in the open air.

Robert Graves

Unrest Cure

Complete Poems, Volume One
Edited by Beryl Graves and Dunstan Ward, Carcanet

Robert Graves felt drawn away from the straight and narrow at an early age. In *Goodbye to All That* (1929) he recalls climbing as a schoolboy on a precipice in Snowdonia: '… a raven circled round the party in great sweeps. This was curiously unsettling, because one climbs only up and down, or left and right, and the raven was suggesting all the diverse possibilities of movement.' His career in poetry now seems to be characterized by just such a restless individuality, his determination to choose his own path 'Flying Crooked', as one poem has it. Living in Majorca for most of his life, detached from what he called the 'godawfulness' of our civilization, he scorned fashionable contemporaries and past masters alike; and he developed a system of mythological convictions 'written up in *The White Goddess*' which no one else could easily share, and which gave him as a by-product a love life both rich and strange. But the pattern of Graves's early life 'at public school, as an officer in the First World War, as a student at Oxford, in his friendships with Siegfried Sassoon, Robert Nichols, John Masefield' was standard for an English poet of his generation: and it was not until he was into his thirties that his personal and literary eccentricities, his instinct for rebellion, began to muster in a single direction.

Hence, in the first volume of Carcanet's handsome, important new *Complete Poems* ('two more are to come'), the craft and exuberance of the writing do not always disguise a thinness or uncertainty of purpose. 'A volume of Collected Poems,' Graves wrote, 'should form a sequence of the intenser moments of the poet's spiritual autobiography'. He could not have felt the war more 'intensely': he was so seriously wounded in action on the Somme that he was announced dead in the *Times*. Yet he was to expunge his war poems from his collected works on the grounds of 'inauthenticity': 'One of the realistic war poems for which I was best known in those days ... was written at my regimental depot in Wales some weeks before I had a chance of verifying my facts.'

Poetry, for Graves, happened outside history, arising out of personal conflict; and we can conclude from the shape he gave his own corpus that, whether or not it blew him to the brink of death, war, as a mass experience, was on that level important to him. So one value of the first Carcanet volume is to allow us to see in all its details Graves's resistance to what he called the 'fashion' for war poetry. There are flashes here as harshly documentary as anything in Wilfred Owen; but more often Graves opposes a dream of innocence, as the tension in the title of the volume *Fairies and Fusiliers* suggests. In the aftermath of Graves's war, the poems served a therapeutic aim: those of *Country Sentiment* (1920) were 'products of the desire to escape from a painful war neurosis into an Arcadia of amatory fancy'. And yet the war can be seen to inform Graves's love poetry in unsuspected ways. The symptoms of shell shock are identical with 'The Symptoms of Love' described in the poem of that title, or those of 'Lost Love', written in 1919 when Graves's nerves were most raw:

> His eyes are quickened so with grief
> He can watch a grass or leaf
> Every instant grow; he can
> Clearly through a flint wall see
> ... Across two centuries he can hear
> And catch your words before you speak.

This closely resembles the condition of agonized supersensitivity which, in a letter of 1942, Graves says he has to enter when a poem is on him: 'Writing a poem for me is putting myself in a very odd state indeed in which I am excessively sensitive to interruption; I can hear, or I think I can hear, people doing disturbing things behind shut doors three houses off ...' So if the war was not the making of Graves as a poet in the tragically direct way it was of an Owen or an Ivor Gurney, he would have recognized artistic compensations in the damage it did him. This substantial volume covers the same span as Graves's own first collected volume, the much thinner *Poems 1914–26*. For that Graves jettisoned more than half the material he had published to date, the first exercise of the 'ruthlessness of suppression' instilled in him by his lover, the maligned American poetess Laura Riding. By the time he came to assemble his 1975 *Collected Poems*, Graves had boiled down the fruits of these first twelve years to a mere forty pages. Yet while it can't be pretended that much of the best of Graves is to be found here, nor that there are not off-putting stretches of ballady-whimsy, there is the pleasure of variety that his later fastidiousness, in pursuit of the 'true' poem, did away with. Aside from the war poems, there are curiosities like 'The Clipped Stater', a taut narrative blending the story of Alexander the Great with the post-war predicament of T. E. Lawrence; the chatty 'Northward from Oxford: An Architectural Progress', which you would not believe was by Graves did it not end up in his own house; and most intriguingly, 'At the Games', the poem with which Graves won the bronze medal for poetry at the 1924 Olympic Games in Paris. There are also enough hints of the Graves that is to come, like the enchanting quatrain whose theme anticipates the whole devoted lyric enterprise:

> Love without hope, as when the young bird-catcher
> Swept off his tall hat to the Squire's own daughter,
> So let the imprisoned larks escape and fly
> Singing about her head, as she rode by.

Graham Greene

The Chap Who Told Tales in his Sleep

A World of my Own: A Dream Diary
Viking

The trouble with dreams, from a literary point of view, is encapsulated in one of Graham Greene's:

> Studying the moon's surface through binoculars, I suddenly discovered a human face on a great crag. I was immensely excited by this discovery and all that it suggested, but I couldn't get anyone else to see it.

Not only have we not seen the face, but neither, in a sense, has Greene, and he is powerless to control 'all that it suggested' unless he converts it into fiction. A whole diary full of such short-lived private excitements is hardly a reader's dream, but there are several reasons why Greene's little book, which he prepared in the last year of his life, is more indulgent to the public than it sounds. The first is that he has risked the contradiction involved in editing his subconscious and slimmed his diary – compiled between 1965 and 1989 – down from 800 pages to nearer 100, getting rid of we shall never know what inconsequential nonsense. Another is the generous shortness of most of the entries. A third is that these dreams are largely inhabited by famous people – he groups them under categories: writers, actors, statesmen and royalty – so that they build into a pantomime of celebrities caught off guard: Alec Douglas-Home in sticky pyjamas, Edward Heath expansive in the pub. This might rouse suspicions that Greene has simply edited out his mother, his children, his lawyer, his publisher, waiters and cab drivers – until we remember (and he tells us) that famous people were the people he knew.

Hence, the section on 'Statesmen and Politicians' is prefaced by a list of those he met (and 'liked') in 'the Common World' – 'Ho Chi Minh, Daniel Ortega, Allende, Fidel Castro, President Mitterrand, and Gorbachev' – a list every bit as powerful as the cast of the dreams that follow. He encounters three Popes in his sleep, but then he knew two of them upright; and, as for exotic travel, his dreams can't hope to outdo his actual experience, as he implies in this complex boast: 'I have travelled as much, I believe, in the World of My Own as I have in the Common World.' His life, his dreams and his fiction are equally exciting, so that a phrase 'I was taken by car across a frontier to Havana' could belong to any of the three.

These privileged experiences make his dreams paradoxically accessible: his portraits of the great, whether they offer strange psychological insight (Andropov's withered right hand), vengeful irony (W. H. Auden as a guerrilla fighter) or mere defacement (T. S. Eliot with a moustache) have the unusual effect of a sort of impartial satire. These are evidently the dreams of a man who knows himself to be famous, but one doesn't get the impression that he has shaped them for posterity. He seems confident that his psyche is too healthy for analysis, asserting, or commanding, in his Introduction that 'no biographer will want to make use' of this material. The two most revealing kinds of dream are absent: erotic ones, ostensibly to protect his 'partners', and nightmares, because he claims not to have had any. Even bodily disorders – the '12 crevettes' and 'one langoustine' that come out with his urine, or the 'large scampi wrapped in a transparent caul' that a masseur (a masseur, mind) extracts from his buttocks – appear to have their roots in nothing more traumatic than too good a lunch at the Colombe d'Or in St Paul de Vence.

It is also amusing to watch such a well-fed subconscious tough out the classic nightmare situations. Confronted with the Actor's Nightmare – 'I was given no dialogue and the script gave no explanation of my actions' – he simply shrugs off the problem: 'I decided to extemporize.' Similarly, ill-equipped to direct a film of an Ibsen play, and challenged on that score by Ralph Richardson, he goes exhilaratingly on the offensive: 'I shan't appeal to anyone,' I told him, 'I shall cut your face open with a riding whip' – enough to wake Ralph Richardson in a cold sweat. Even in old age, 'a little frightened' (he concedes) of a yapping dog, his response is to scold it until the emotion is transferred: the dog ends up whimpering

'Are you going to punish me?' and making 'a little pool of spittle in his fear'. Much more typical is the scene where he impatiently jabs a poisoned cigarette up Goebbels' nose. This is the dream life of a man who claims to have found fear – in Haiti and Vietnam – a source of 'adventure and pleasure'; as a sleeper, he is an absolute hero. And anyone else who wants to publish a 'dream diary' should be made to play Russian Roulette.

Henry Green

Dash and Melancholy

Romancing: The Life and Work of Henry Green
Jeremy Treglown, Faber and Faber

'I was born a mouthbreather with a silver spoon in 1905.' So begins the memoir *Pack My Bag* (1940) of the novelist 'Henry Green'. That pseudonym is a lasting mark of Henry Yorke's uncomfortable dealings with his background, specifically, with what Jeremy Treglown calls, in a long-awaited and sharply executed critical biography, his 'crushingly grand relations'. Henry's mother, Maud Wyndham, was the daughter of the second Baron Leconfield, owner of Petworth, the finest house in Sussex: a woman whose diction was so superior, as Maurice Bowra observed, that she managed to leave the gs out of words that didn't contain them, 'such as Cheltin'ham and Chippin'ham'. His father, Vincent Yorke, who inherited Forthampton Court near Tewkesbury, was an industrialist and country sportsman, a rugged performer with whom Henry, nervous and uncompetitive as a boy, grew to be at odds. While part of him kept the family name, went to Eton and Oxford (where Nevill Coghill fell in love with him), joined the family business (principally, the manufacture of beer-bottling machines) to please his father, and married well, his individuality began to disclose itself in writing: first (at school) as Henry Michaels, then as Henry Browne.

With the publication of his first novel, *Blindness* (1926), while he was still an undergraduate, he emerged as Henry Green. (Harold Acton quipped at the time, 'There are Greens of so many shades writing novels that one wishes he had chosen another colour.') Yet, even in his early prose, one can see an instinctive cancellation of the author's ego, a strikingly negative view (in Keats's sense) of what fiction might be. The fantasy of blindness is not confined to the novel of that title. In an early short story, 'Adventure in a Room', a blind boy sits on a lawn, listening to birdsong: 'He lost all sense of personality, he was just a pair of ears and a brain, absorbent as a sponge.' Henry Green, with his proclaimed mistrust of knowing narrators, aspired to just such a dumb relationship with his characters, as his novels advanced towards the condition of pure and rivetingly inadequate dialogue. In life, too, Henry (as Treglown even-handedly prefers to call him) seems to have preferred to absorb than to project. His dislike of publicity or exposure was symbolized in Cecil Beaton's portrait (after Magritte) of the back of his head (not reproduced here, among a rather mean selection of photographs). His son Sebastian Yorke once noticed how difficult it was 'to find people to give a really true account of what he was like'; and while Sebastian himself withdrew his co-operation from this biography, Treglown calls plenty of other witnesses to a peculiar passivity or indeterminacy of character. Anthony Powell, an associate from Eton onwards, remarked that 'although we knew each other so well, of all the people I've ever known I never really got to the bottom of him'. Rosamond Lehmann seems to have modelled the character Rickie in her novel *The Echoing Grove* on Henry: 'fading out at will, slipping his identity … Any piece of humanity could invade him like a cloud and like a cloud pass through and out of him. Any woman could move him. "Anything in skirts".'

  Treglown takes his Green-ish title, *Romancing*, from the listing under 'Recreations' in the Who's Who entry for 'Henry Green': 'romancing over the bottle, to a good band'. And while there was certainly a physical element to his pursuit of so many women – Isaiah Berlin found his presence 'rich, aloof, lascivious' – it seems that it was only in such unstable relationships that he could find a self agreeable to him. One of his girlfriends, Mary Keene, wrote harshly of him in retrospect:

> He didn't really exist … There was a hole there. He only really existed in other people. He was living off the fat of other people and once the fat was gone, he would go.

'Romancing over the bottle …' Henry's philandering tailed off in his forties; he talked 'dotingly' of his last serious fixation, Lucian Freud's first wife, Kitty, ever after. But the bottle remained. Henry had drunk gin through the day all his working life, and in the 1950s it broke him. The closing words of *Doting* (1952) – 'The next day they all went on just the same' – were Green's last as a novelist. He was forty-seven. Interviewed in 1960, he confirmed that he would never write again; he found the effort involved 'too exhausting'. He had already been eased out of his position in the family firm when – his erratic demeanour increasingly causing concern – his water-glass at a morning meeting was discovered, when he left the room, to contain raw spirits. At home, his loyal wife 'Dig' took the same euphemistic approach to his drinking as she had to his 'romancing'; various breakdowns and hospitalizations were passed off as 'the most frightful cold' or suspected diabetes. Raymond Carr, a friend and stalwart admirer from this period, put it simply: 'He drank because he couldn't write and he couldn't write because he drank.' The last ten years of Henry's life, until his death of pneumonia in 1973, were practically empty.

In his memorial address at Forthampton church, V. S. Pritchett referred to the 'strange mixture of dash and melancholy' that people encountered in the man. Readers of *Romancing* will feel that the one gradually annihilated the other; writing in the 1960s, Henry's old mocking adversary Evelyn Waugh recalled, as if subdued by pity, the 'lean dark, singular man named Henry Yorke' he had met at Oxford, who went on to 'dazzle us' with his writings. And what survives of Henry Yorke is, of course, the fiction of Henry Green: nine novels, which mark him out, however remote and defensive his private character, as one of the most forceful personalities in English fiction of the modernist century.

Not the least valuable sections of Treglown's book are his generous and acute discussions of each of the major works; these he rehearsed in his capacity as editor of the Harvill Press edition, which has now succeeded in getting all the novels simultaneously in print – a satisfaction denied their author in his lifetime. In particular, Treglown argues convincingly that the muddling of detail for which Green has sometimes been reproached – is Ilse, in *Caught* (1943), Norwegian, Swedish, or both? – is integral to the writer's project, rather than 'exhausted' incompetence. But with a proper biographical detachment he leaves it to another – Green's heartiest advocate, the American novelist Terry Southern – to convert this into a larger claim:

> The reader does not simply forget that there is an author behind the words, but because of some annoyance over a seeming 'discrepancy' in the story must, in fact, remind himself that there is one ... The irritation then gives

way to a feeling of pleasure and superiority in that he, the reader, sees more
in the situation than the author does – so that all of this now belongs to
him ... Thus, in the spell of his own imagination the characters come alive
in an almost incredible way, quite beyond anything achieved by conventional
methods of writing.

*

Doting
Harvill

Doting (1952) was Henry Green's ninth novel, and his last; though he was
not yet fifty, and had more than twenty years to live, he subsequently
found the work of writing too difficult and unrewarding. Like its pre-
decessor, *Nothing* (1950), it is a bitter-sweet sketch of emotional inad-
equacy, conducted almost entirely through dialogue, brilliantly caught
and piercingly flavoured with folly, selfishness and helplessness. Arthur
and Diana Middleton are a middle-aged, upper-middle-class couple in
a London exhausted by the war. Though each of them, and the reticent
narrator, talk of their 'love' for each other, the limitations of their life
together and their bewilderment at growing older push them into silly
'doting' elsewhere. Their charmless teenage son Peter provides a natural
outlet for their feelings; but when Arthur begins to indulge his weakness
for Annabel, who could be but isn't his daughter, the tender inarticulacy
of the marriage is compounded by 'fibs'. The scene in which he half-
heartedly begins to seduce Annabel has two brilliant surprises on top of
one another: she suddenly tearing off her skirt to prevent a coffee stain,
and the next moment Diana appearing at the door with news of Peter's
injury in a car crash. But the injury is nothing serious; neither Arthur
nor, later, Diana commits the adultery to which they are partly drawn;
and the novel is expertly petered out. Its whole dramatis personae of six
people spend the last evening of Peter's school holiday in a nightclub,
where the main act, a wrestling bout, fails to materialize. Jeremy Treglown's
introduction talks of middle age and disillusion, and compares Henry
Yorke's own domestic situation to that of the Middletons. We might go
further, and suggest that certain unconscious repetitions and flashes of

unpleasantness – Annabel has 'fat' legs, her friend 'fat' features – are signs of a writer confused or needled by the encroachment of his own 'dotage'. Treglown points out the irony of the novel's final words, 'The next day they all went on very much the same', in relation to its author, on whose literary life they bring down the curtain.

Gavin Ewart

Wise Satires

Selected Poems 1933–1993
Hutchinson

> When I am old and long turned grey
> And enjoy the aura of being eighty,
> I may see the dawn of that critical day
> When my lightest verse will seem quite weighty
> To pilgrim admirers my wife will say:
> Ewart is resting.

When he wrote this poem in the late 1960s, Gavin Ewart imagined himself as he might be today. Sadly he died last winter, a few months short of that eightieth birthday. In the years between, however, there was such a phenomenal outpouring of verse enough for two separate *Collected Poems*, with plenty to spare that he really did achieve the eminence he pretended to desire: the most, at any rate, that could reasonably be due to an art so free of seriousness. It was around the age that most poets look to their laurels that Ewart hit his stride. And when, last month, his widow hosted a party to honour the late poet, it was packed with 'pilgrim admirers', drawn, it must be said, as much to recall an unusually lovable personality as to hail the most productive, gifted and entertaining light versifier of our times.

When a reviewer measured the output and reckoned he must produce two or three poems per week, Ewart pointed out in all modesty that he wrote much more than that. For every published poem, there were several bits and pieces thrown off as social graces or on the most trivial pretext. The *Times Literary Supplement* was in regular receipt of squibs about Scottish sporting heroes (Ewart, the most English-mannered of men, enjoyed his Scottish blood: 'Wha dreams that I am nae a Scot / Yon is a blastit Hottentot'). The duds and the daily nonsense were all part of the Ewart project, which is why this new *Selected Poems* is a rather chastened memorial bringing to mind the spectacle of the author frowningly culling hundreds of the 'Little Ones' conceived in jest.

But the book is a generous sampler, and its variousness of metre and verse form, of content, of scale (he made a speciality of the one-line poem, yet he could be as garrulous as McGonagall), of dialect and even of language will still seem remarkable. New readers may be most struck by the bawdy poems: some merely giggly, others like the rewritings of the limerick about the young man of St John's, using definitions provided by the *Oxford English Dictionary* and Johnson's dictionary lastingly funny. But there are political poems, too, which, while seldom relinquishing lightness of tone or the characteristic air of innocence that was both real and strategic, are heartfelt censurings of Thatcherism and other cruelty. There are wise satires on poets ('We all want total praise / For every word we write / Not for a singular phrase'), and sweet love poems, especially a sonnet to his daughter. There are poems we couldn't imagine were written by Ewart, such as the photo-poem, 'Afrokill', about a zebra's carcass. There are sharp poems like the desolate 'Back', about the effect on an ageing couple of children's voices rising from another garden; or 'The Moment', about the first sight in battle of the advancing enemy:

> This is it, you think, these are the ones
> we've heard so much about.
> Like old people when, for the first time,
> they confront the unambiguous symptoms.

It may be the timing of the publication that pushes a mild melancholy to the fore. The longest poem here, 'The Sadness of Cricket', reflects on a number of sportsmen's lives gone wrong after the idle glories of their youth. Ewart may have been particularly responsive to this kind of sadness because his own verse was a sort of extended summer sport, most of it written in extra time, a refusal to bow to the earnest, though the length-ening shadows and the growing chill were always a part of its subject. As the title of another poem ambivalently has it, 'Every Doggerel Has Its Day'. And one of the most touching poems in the new context of the Selected is Ewart's prayer for 'A 14-Year-Old Convalescent Cat in the Winter':

> I want him to have another living summer,
> … an Old Age Pensioner, retired, resented
> by no one, and happinesses in a beelike swarm
> to settle on him.

Amen.

Philip Larkin

Selfishly yours, Philip

Selected Letters of Philip Larkin, 1940–1985
Edited by Anthony Thwaite, Faber and Faber

Philip Larkin's executors and publishers have made an odd decision in putting the Letters before the Life. Anthony Thwaite promises in his introduction to the former that Andrew Motion's biography – due out next year – 'will fill in some of the apparent gaps'. Which is one way of putting it. Meanwhile, we read the Letters as inefficient biography, and they do serve up some mysterious fragmentary evidence: the sudden switch of addressee from 'Colin and Patsy Strang' to Patsy alone ('Dearest Honeybear …'); and the unexplained break in Larkin's regular correspondence with his oldest friend, J. B. Sutton, which then goes unmended for thirty years. Through what the poet himself called the 'Larkin Drama' – his illness and death – the letters are naturally muted; and so are the footnotes. Thwaite, presumably anxious not to steal the biographer's thunder, has left such gaps honourably vacant.

His introduction acknowledges gaps of another kind. This 'selection' amounts to more than 700 letters, which – given the nature of the life, its single mood and almost constant non-event – feels far too many. But then Larkin wrote a lot of letters, and the editor has tried to balance the requirements of the lay reader with those of (say) Larkin's *next* biographer. (One is reminded of the conflict of interests in Thwaite's edition of the *Collected Poems* which sacrificed the integrity of the finished volumes for a scholarly inclusiveness.)

And yet three significant groups of letters are noted as missing: those to Bruce Montgomery, Larkin's closest correspondent for many years (lodged in the Bodleian by Montgomery's widow); those withheld by

George Hartley, the unyielding publisher of *The Less Deceived*, with whom Larkin's disaffection ('I don't say Hartley is a phoney, exactly – well, I do') is never as thorough as you'd expect; and those to his mother. We're told that Larkin wrote 'regularly' to her through the last three decades of her life (he refers himself to 'daily' letters), but Thwaite chooses to exclude this correspondence on the grounds that it 'would have swelled the book to unmanageable proportions'. Most of it must be very dull, but something could surely have been salvaged to represent the subject's family life.

Half a dozen favoured correspondents are represented by fifty letters or more. The first of these is the invisible Sutton, whom Larkin used through his university years and beyond as a sounding board for ideas about himself ('It's hard to say whether I improve or not with keeping and living'). The most inventive letters are those to Kingsley Amis, conducted in a private mutation of Greyfriars style, with its own conventions like their method of signing off – a phrase from any sphere of life with the last word replaced by 'bum' ('Smoking can damage your bum, *Philip*', etc). The high spirits of this exchange endure over four decades, though schoolgirls gradually yield place to strikers and immigrants ('keep up the cracks about niggers and wogs'). The correspondence with another politically like mind, Robert Conquest, is built on bawdy verses and a shared pursuit of pornography; sending Conquest the poem entitled 'Annus Mirabilis' was asking for the parody it got. Barbara Pym, by contrast, generates parsonical fan letters of a unique gentleness and generosity: after a typical outburst to Amis about what the Permissive Society hadn't delivered, 'LIKE WATCHING SCHOOL GIRLS SUCK EACH OTHER OFF WHILE YOU WHIP THEM', the note of 'My Dear Barbara' falls with a sort of comic grace.

With each of these Larkin enjoyed, for some time, satisfactory postal relations; and the products have the literary interest of things that he wanted to write. But there is another style of letter to women, intermittently represented here, which seems to have been squeezed from him as a guilty substitute for the sort of relationship he preferred to do without. A sour, unfinished poem of August 1953 analyses this phenomenon:

> letters of a kind I know
> Feel most of my spare time is going on:
>
> I mean, letters to women – no,
> Not of the sort

The papers tell us get read out in court,
Leading directly to or from the bed.
Love-letters only in a sense: they owe
Too much elsewhere to come under that head.

Too much to kindness, for a start ...

But the effect of this kindness is to disgust the kind:

Another evening wasted! I begin
Writing the envelope, and a bitter smoke
Of self-contempt, of boredom too, ascends.
What use is an endearment and a joke?

At which the poem is abandoned. Thwaite prints two letters to women
in the same month as these lines. The more trivial and laborious is to
Winifred Arnott, the girl behind 'Maiden Name' and other poems, to
whose virginity Larkin laid unsuccessful siege ('Wish I had some of the
money back I spent on her, and *the time*', he moans later). Winifred dog-
gedly kept up the correspondence after she married, and would eventu-
ally get replies with less-than-urgent sentiments like 'I'm sorry you had
such a dreary winter, and I hope you aren't having another'. The other
August letter is to Patsy Strang (with whom Larkin was still having a
sort of affair); this mocks Winifred as 'Miss Mouse'. Reviewing Evelyn
Waugh's letters critically at a later date, Larkin finds himself wondering
'how my own wd rank for charity – not very highly, I should imagine';
and in cases like Winifred's, his chief 'kindness' seems to have been to
disguise the boredom or unkindness he really felt.

The 'Miss Mouse'/'Winifred dear' effect is a common one in the book,
especially in Larkin's Belfast period (1950–5): on one page, we read about
'horrible craps like Arthur', on the next it's 'My Dear Arthur'. The poet
was to dramatize such a slide nearly twenty years later in 'Vers de Société',
where the poet's gut response to a dreary invitation – '*Dear Warlock-
Williams, I'm afraid*' – is transformed by lonely fears into hapless accept-
ance ('*Dear Warlock-Williams: Why, of course*'). The poem and its real-life
counterparts – the more furtive or disengaged of Larkin's social letters –
show an essential selfishness doing its penance.

One of Anthony Thwaite's dilemmas is that the last major correspond-
ent of Larkin's life seems to have been Anthony Thwaite. Larkin's praise

of his future editor's poems and personality is here in full: in one place, he chastises him for leaving himself out of his book on Contemporary Poetry. One can hardly blame Thwaite for printing this; it is, after all, a letter from Larkin about poetry. But the message to Thwaite from Larkin's secretary, even if it is about the poet's final illness, ought not to be here.

The most questionable aspect of Thwaite's editing at the local level is the way he omits parts of letters without indicating how much material has gone, or of what sort, or why. Some cuts are evidently to avoid libel ('In my experience it's easier to [...] than to get a publisher to accept anything he doesn't like'); others look as if they have been made to protect Larkin himself. The footnoting, kept deliberately 'light', is sometimes too reticent: when Larkin, reading Virginia Woolf's *A Writer's Diary*, exclaims, 'What a sentence about Isherwood!', it would be easy and helpful to supply that sentence, especially as it appears to be a very rare instance of Larkin approving another writer.

Indeed, in all these pages, there is hardly anything to supplement the astonishingly meagre list of approved reading that Larkin used to offer interviewers. His student passion for D. H. Lawrence burns surprisingly brightly – 'the greatest writer of this century, and in many things the greatest writer of all time' – but is renounced at the age of twenty-four, by which time he was already unreceptive to new writing ('My mind has stopped at 1945', as he wrote later, 'like some cheap wartime clock'). Among poets of his own generation, only Betjeman, Amis, Gavin Ewart and *Patience Strong* merit praise, along with a few poems each by J. C. Hall and Jonathan Price. Everyone else – from Sidney Keyes in the 1940s, through Lowell, Gunn and Hughes in the 50s and 60s, to Heaney in the 70s ('"the best poet since Seamus Heaney" which is like saying the best Chancellor since Jim Callaghan') – is entertainingly dispatched. Larkin confronts the idea of new writing with wicked structures of horrified multiple abuse:

> Today I bought *The Breaking of Bumbo* by Andrew Sinclair at a Boots' chuck-out – Good God, every 'new young' writer I read seems worse than the last. John Braine – there couldn't be anyone worse than him. Oh yes there could: John Osborne, And now Andrew Sinclair: soft-headed hysterical guardee. Like an upper-class John Wain.

The editorship of the *Oxford Book of Twentieth-Century English Verse* involved Larkin in some especially fruitless reading: the likes of W. W. Gibson ('*never wrote a good poem in his life* ... People like this make Rupert Brooke seem colossal'); or Laurie Lee ('Xt, he's absolutely no good whatsoever'); and Alun Lewis ('not really so good as some would have you think ...') or MacDiarmid ('Is there any bit ... that's noticeably less morally repugnant and aesthetically null than the rest?'). The chief value of most other writers for Larkin is the understanding that they aren't 'any good' – no elaboration needed – as the basis for other jokes: of T. F. Griffin, 'Of course I don't mean that he is any real *good*, just that he seemed well up to publishing standard'; or of a conversation with George MacBeth, 'He replied to my question "Do you think William Golding is any good" with "I prefer to bypass that aspect of his work". Rather nice, don't you think?' (His self-criticism is only a modification of this rule of thumb; as he told the *Paris Review*. 'My "secret flaw" is just not being very good, like everyone else.')

What is most unusual about this monumental correspondence is how – since Larkin so soon recognized his need for stable employment and domestic solitude – its concerns and attitudes remain so much the same. Just as he laughs with Amis about those life-changing letters he never received – 'Something starting "I am directed to inform you that under the will of the late Mr Getty ..." or "Dear Philip. You'll he interested to know that old Humpley is at last giving up the library at Windsor, and HM ..." or "Dear Mr Larkin, I expect you'll think it jolly cheeky for a schoolgirl to –"' – so his own seldom have any news to break or passion to declare or end to achieve. What they restate, richly and poorly, are: the impossibility of letting another person into his life; his depression at writing so much less than he wished; his innate meanness, which characteristically places the cost of his pleasures before them ('I spent 7/- yesterday on [two art books]'), involves him in long disputes with publishers over halves of one percent, and makes nastily plain sense of that ambiguous adjective at the end of 'The Building' – 'With *wasteful*, weak, propitiatory flowers'; and, above all, his consuming fear of ageing and death. The refrain 'What have I done to be [gives his age]?/It isn't fair' recurs with variations from twenty-six to sixty. And even the death of his former lover, Patsy Strang, from an overdose of Cointreau and Benedictine elicits only a hard joke ('Fascinating mixture, what?...') before leading him anew to the subject of his *own* mortality. Still, self was his life (of which more later): and in it he made not only – incidentally – hundreds of sharp and sad and funny letters to others, but also (and this was the paradoxical point of it) dozens of the most generally enjoyed English poems of the century.

Christopher Logue

Poet of Protest

Review / Profile

Not for Christopher Logue the subsidized readings, the punitive residencies in psychiatric wards, the bland reviews and zero sales that are the miserable lot of most of England's practicing poets. Indeed, such has been the variety and glamour of the various phases of his seventy subversive years – the army and military prison; Fifties' Paris and swinging London; *Private Eye*; performing at the Isle of Wight Festival; appearing in the films of Ken Russell and in his own plays at the Royal Court – that it would once have been true to say that his life was larger than his poetry. Then, in 1969, he published the first part of his *War Music*, an ongoing free-verse recreation (rather than a translation) of selected parts of the *Iliad*: an astonishing display of unsuspected imaginative brio, structural daring and bold anachronism which has since earned him the reputation to go with the rest of it. George Steiner, for instance, who uses such terms sparingly, has hailed it as a work of 'genius'. One instalment of the sequence, Kings – a treatment of the first two books of Homer's Trojan epic – is to be staged next month at the Tricycle Theatre, Kilburn, in a production for two voices: Alan Howard's and that of Logue himself.

Howard's voice is famously magnificent, 'like a cliff' to quote Logue on the sound of Agamemnon's. But meeting Logue at his house in Camberwell, where he lives with his wife, the critic Rosemary Hill, you find his own voice is an instrument to be reckoned with: charged, emphatic, but with a pantomime curl, gathering every so often into goblin shrieks of delight or outrage or mockery – a scathing Thersites, perhaps, to Howard's Agamemnon. (I must be careful here, as Logue edited the

Pseuds Corner column in *Private Eye* for 30 years.) In short, he barks; but he is neither mad, nor vicious, and if he talks abundantly it is because he has much to talk about and everything he says is his own.

Logue was too individual for his mother, who told him: 'We always wanted a girl, but we must accept what God sends us.' He was born in 1929, the only child of liberal-minded Catholics, and brought up, after his father's retirement, in Southsea, near Portsmouth. What he most wanted to be at school was a nuisance: 'I was difficult to discipline ... I had very little respect for what was going on, unless it had some private appeal to me.' He stole from shops; he 'created disturbances'. In 1944, because he didn't know what to do with himself, he volunteered for the army, lost the sight of one eye in a training accident and fetched up in Palestine in 1946 amid the chaos of demobilization. 'You had a million and a half soldiers, whose units were suddenly disbanded and sent home, and yet you had these contracts, which had to be honoured, to supply them with equipment. So there's all this gear mounting up which was to be thrown away ... I helped myself to all sorts of stuff, including these six Army Pay Books – which were a sort of ID card for the common soldier – and I announced that I was going to sell them to the Jews; it might as well have been the Arabs, it wasn't an ideological thing. Anyway, when the business came to light, I could have gone to trial and that would have exposed the shambles of it all, but there was a masochistic impulse in me – I *made* the military put me in prison.'

The sixteen months he spent in gaol, holed up with Wilde and Chesterton, Pound and Baudelaire, gave him a glimpse of a vocation: 'I became aware that if you said you were a poet, you could get away with murder – and you could be a sort of justified nutcase and no one would expect you to get a job.' But when he emerged from prison, he found his unemployment strictly prosaic. 'I had no way into the literary establishment and no contacts to help me into university – I wasn't in the swim. And you can't imagine what London was like – grey, depressed, everything rationed, utterly demoralized. It was as if the war had been lost. Then I found my way to Paris, and I couldn't believe the difference in outlook – and these people had had the Germans on their bloody necks.'

Logue's career began to take off with his arrival in Paris in 1951. He met the Scottish writer Alexander Trocchi, founder of *Merlin* magazine, for which he began to write. The Olympia Press published his first books of poems, the derivative but promising *Wand and Quadrant*, and, subsequently, his pornographic novel *Lust*, written under the pseudo-nym Count Palmiro Vicarion. *Lust* was commissioned by the legendary publisher and hypochondriac Maurice Girodias: 'He would come into the office muttering about his liver, or what a doctor from Brussels had made of his urine – he wanted 10 pages a day and each 10 pages had to have two sex scenes. So he'd read them through and if they were okay he'd peel off £10 or £20 from the roll in his pocket.' But these were also the years in which Logue's political conscience came of age. In 1953, *Merlin* published in English translation 'the memoirs of an Hungarian doctor who had worked for the Nazis to save his own life and the lives of a few others. And, of course, this had an overwhelming effect on us. We knew that there had been something wrong, but what we knew was Dachau and Belsen, spectacular, vindictive hatred against political enemies – but this was something even worse than that – the operation of an ideology that demanded the destruction of whole groups of people'.

This discovery and the influence of Brecht, whom he met in 1956, convinced Logue of the need for poetry to assume political responsibility, at the very moment when English poetry in general had consented to give it up. 'There was this species of literature developing which completely ignored the terrible things that were happening around it – and that seemed extraordinary to me. Nothing has changed. Our current poetry is hopeless. It's fostered and sponsored and given money and treated as a humiliating promotion. Of course there are a lot of people around who've learned to write very well, but what comes out at the other end is only feelings. It's all so subjective, there's no argument, or intellectual power – there's nothing in the poetry that actually cuts.' (He admired, by contrast, Harold Pinter – 'at least he's got some guts'.) 'Take an exam-ple. At this moment our politicians have got to work out how the future of this country is going to develop in reaction to Europe. This is a very important decision. But you wouldn't know that the issue even existed from the poems people are writing today. And the public behaves accord-ingly and ignores them completely. I'll often find poems that I like and clip them for my 'Poems Liked' book. And they're good poems. But they don't make you think, I've got to do something like that. Look, if some poet were to be arrested and hauled into prison for something he'd writ-ten, I'd damned well do something about it. But it isn't going to happen.'

The poetry of protest Logue wrote in the Sixties found exactly the audience he sees other poets abandoning. The poster-poem *I shall vote*

Labour ('because / deep in my heart / I am a Conservative') sold 30,000 copies; at the Isle of Wight, he read to a field full of 180,000 people ('I suppose most of them were just eating their sandwiches – I didn't have banks of 100-watt speakers to help me out'). He has never been bothered by the difference between writing for the page and reading aloud. 'When my mother gave up on me entering the priesthood, what with this strange voice of mine and her interest in the theatre, she thought I might make an actor. And there is a bit of the actor in me. So she sent me for elocution lessons to someone called Miss Crowe, whose procedure was to make me learn by heart wonderful poems – *The Lady of Shalott, Gunga Din.* So from Day One I had the idea that verse was to be performed and I've always written verse with the idea in my mind of someone speaking it.'

Hence, in Logue's versions of Homer even the metaphysical bits are made to feel like oral events: 'His soul / crawled off his tongue and vanished into sunlight.' And this sense of performance is augmented by a dislocated narrative technique that is strikingly cinematic. The action is mostly present tense, with instructions to the reader that mimic screenplays: 'Reverse the shot. Go close'; 'Cut to the rocks … west side'; so that the chief concern for those adapting *War Music* for the stage must be the extent to which it is already conceived as a drama for the reader. The first instalment to be staged in 1971 was *Patrocleia*, in a production at the Royal College of Art which amazed the author: 'This young man had written to me, and I'd just said yeah, go ahead and do it, without great expectations, and I rather forgot about it; anyway, I went to the first night, and there was an orchestra! – and there were girls without any clothes on and they'd taken the rood out of the theatre and the place was full!' Subsequent productions may have been less memorable; 'the olde worlde Greek thing came creeping in, with people carrying vases around the stage and so on'. But anyone who has 'felt the force' of *War Music* – to borrow Logue's description of the effect the best poetry has on him – 'coming off the page', will relish the prospect of that same charge roaring out of Alan Howard's mouth.

Harold Pinter

The Chaotic Energies of Youth

The Dwarfs
Faber and Faber

Harold Pinter wrote a novel called *The Dwarfs* in his mid-twenties, before he had the better idea of writing plays. In 1960, he stripped it down and converted it into a radio drama, and three years later adapted it further for the stage. Now, to fill the regrettable absence of important new dramatic work from Pinter, the original work has been published as his 'first and only' novel. 'The text is fundamentally that written over the period 1952–56', he says in a curt note, but admits to axing five chapters and reorganizing some of the rest in preparing it for the press. This dabbling sacrifices one potential interest of the book: we can't make definite comparisons between the text of the novel and the play that came out of it (not even to speculate on trivial matters such as why Euston becomes, on second thoughts, Paddington. Perhaps Paddington has become Euston.) But while the revisions don't go far enough to upset the careful balance of owning and disowning in Pinter's stance towards the work, they do indicate that he wants it to be read as a novel rather than as a curiosity, as a novice work of art rather than the débris of a false start.

As novels go however, it is not much like one, or not much of a good one. The bulk of it consists of the interplay between three mentally energetic (not to say bonkers) young Jewish men in indistinguishable East-End rooms and pubs. The narrative is so sparse that it takes us many pages to know the characters: Mark Gilbert, an occasional actor and incorrigible seducer; Pete Cox, a chilly, inward intellectual who works in the city; and Len Weinstein, a gabbling fantasist, musician and loser whose latest odd job is as a railway porter. There is also Virginia, Pete's passive girlfriend, the catalyst of the minimal plot. (Her role was excised from the play, which as a result is almost entirely abstract.) Pete's mental breakdown sunders their relationship. She then has an affair with Mark; and what she tells him about Pete brings the two men into their first and last honest confrontation. In a long, stylized exchange (fourteen pages, which the play sensibly trims to about thirty seconds) Mark and Pete wind up their friendship and so conclude the 'action'. Len, meanwhile, has absconded to Paris (if we are meant to believe him) and returned with Camembert poisoning (we are hardly meant to believe him). In a poetic resolution, Len's voice slips into authorial mode to lament the dwarfs: a running symbol of the chaotic energies of youth, which at the close have departed the yard with their shit, rats and garbage and left a lobotomized spick-and-spanness:

> Now all is bare. All is clean. All is scrubbed. There is a lawn. There is a shrub. There is a flower.

Pinter himself noted (in 1961) how his unpublished novel 'incorporated too many styles, so that it became rather hotch-potch'. Passages of embryonic Pinter are interspersed with exercises after Joyce. Alongside exaggerated plainness, there are eye-catching epiphanic inversions ('By the tray of flowers the nurses talked'); and whole chapters are given over to experiments in the presentation of disordered consciousness. Pete stares into a canal:

> Glass how can you to the grit? Eyeball sum up in wax. To say so. To say no. To pull and parley I chat I am swabbed to now. God and his leak. Cocaine Christ. Now bolt.

This is especially frustrating from Pinter, whose best work embodies the lessons that words have to be chosen most carefully when any words will do. Elsewhere, verbal patterns are assembled for their own sake. In one scene, Pete meets an old schoolfellow, Derek, whose unwelcome face is said successively to be 'shining', 'spreading', 'breaking', 'folding', 'shutting', 'foaming', 'scalding', 'grinding', 'flaking', 'singing', 'chanting', 'sprouting' and 'ceasing'. But there is no reason why Derek – who has no other part in the novel – should have a face at all, let alone such a superfluously expressive one. The overall effect of *The Dwarfs*, however, is of a novel written by someone striving to write plays. The narrative with which the book begins is only a series of stage directions rendered into the past tense:

> Len unlocked the front door and pushed it open. A pile of letters lay on the mat. He picked them up and put them on the hall table. They walked down the stairs. Pete opened the living-room window and took a packet of tea from his pocket. He went into the kitchen and filled the kettle …

We don't read this; we watch it. When the dialogue takes over, as it impatiently does, it is punctuated with speech tags rather than quotation marks (as though speech was the substance); the odd 'Len said' is there to make up for the lack of a name in the margin; and it is up to the reader to interpret how and why the words are spoken. The dialogue predicts Pinter's characteristic rhythms, but as yet it is mostly without comic spark or the strange portent he will later wring from the dullest speech:

> – Give me the tea
> – Without milk?
> – Come on.
> – Without any milk?
> – There isn't any milk.

It's no wonder that Pinter was able to transplant most of the best things in the novel – i.e., Len's exuberant fantasies – almost verbatim into the play; so these are already familiar (or at least available) in a tighter form. But one or two other elements in the 'hotch-potch' give warning of unusual powers. In particular, there is a tremendous scene, lost from the play with the character Virginia, in which Pete berates her at incredible length for daring to offer opinions on *Hamlet* in front of his friends. Pinter's budding instinct finds a chilling end to the chapter: Virginia apologizes quietly, Pete manfully forgives her ('No … it's all right. It's all right'), and the monstrous rant is displaced by the silence of the last, unhappy tenderness between people who have finished with each other.

Alasdair Gray

Potently Venomous

The Ends of our Tethers
Canongate

In 'Miss Kincaid's Autumn', the best and most old-fashioned of the stories in Alasdair Gray's latest collection, a brother and sister in a Lowlands town express contrasting views of the Scottish 'fall'. 'For sheer dull depressing misery', the former reckons, 'a damp Scottish November cannot be surpassed'; he sees the decay there, 'a thin carpet of rotten old leaves with some recent ones the colour of dung'. His sister, a maturing spinster, persuaded that 'Autumn could be quite a satisfactory season', prefers to dwell on the glowing colours of remaining leaves, seen to best advantage in the mild Northern light: 'I'm sure they would damage our eyes if we saw them by the strong sunlight of Tahiti'. Neutral readers of *The Ends of our Tethers* may find some cranky local cheer got in a pretty gloomy setting.

Ten years ago, the notes on the cover of Gray's second volume of short stories, *Ten Tall Tales and True*, already October in mood, described their author as 'an elderly Glasgow pedestrian'; the new book, subtitled 'Thirteen Sorry Stories', presents him as 'a fat, spectacled balding increasingly old Glasgow pedestrian'. (He is sixty-nine.) Both books in fact contain fourteen pieces, and number is not the only area in which their titles are genially misleading: some items are less (if at all) like 'tales' or 'stories' than others. It would be unlike Gray's published persona to exaggerate the richness of this late harvest: that said, two or three pieces here are reminiscent of the page with which *Ten Tales* began, 'Getting Started: A prologue', in that they show an author surveying his options rather than executing a plan. A certain sympathetic silliness has been part of Gray's business from its beginning, in *Lanark* (1981): his trick has been to make this seem connected to the suffering, personal or Glaswegian, that we sense underlies the fiction. The strands are pulling apart by now, and the signature whimsy and 'pedestrian' withdrawal begin to hamper what he presents (in '15 February 2003' at least) as serious political commentary. In particular, the party put-downs of Scotland ('Ours is a comic opera wee country with several comic opera imitations of English establishments'; 'What chiefly characterizes my nation … is arselicking') sound increasingly worked up.

Given the teasing fanfare of Gray's artwork, the effect of the book as a whole is boldly insubstantial, and not just because there is so little text on each of its pages. Only four or five of the pieces seem designed to be memorable: generally, those that deal most plainly with the depredations of age. 'Pillow Talk' is very brief because it offers no narrative route out of its bitter bargain: 'You're an alcoholic bore but not violent and I'm too old to find anyone better'. By contrast, 'No Bluebeard' tracks a career of sexual loneliness through three failed marriages and into a fourth, in which dwindling expectations are at last rewarded: 'but we cuddled at night and steady cuddling has always nourished me more than the irregular pleasures of fucking'; the 'great contentment' of the close stems from the narrator's sense, as he 'fell asleep on the floor beside our bed', that his new wife's insanity makes his presence a necessity to her. In 'Job's Skin Game', the narrator's two sons have died in the attack on the World Trade Center: he loses control of his company, his drinking and his marriage. But the imaginative heart of the tale is the nomenclature he invents, in a late flowering of eczema, for the types of scabs on his body: cakes and crumbs, hats, bee-wing, parchment, moss, paper; lace, fish scale, snake-skin, shell, biscuit, straw and pads. With an Old Testament aptitude for indignity, he starts to collect his daily pickings, and cremates them on the hob, as if to say: even the death of the flesh, like old age or Scottishness or bereavement, is an affliction, worse in others than oneself, to be borne with creative curiosity.

There are some cunning observations on writers and writing. The most potently venomous line in the book is reserved for the lecturer on modern Scots literature in 'Miss Kincaid's Autumn': 'an enthusiast who tried hard to hide a conviction that the best things about his subject had been his meetings with the authors who wrote it'. The second-longest story, 'Aiblins', is based, we are told, on Gray's experiences as a creative writing instructor at Glasgow University, 1977–9: it figures the writer's lot as passing on market know-how to no redeeming purpose: 'if you persisted with your writing, and got some of it into magazines … eventually, at the age of forty, you could end up sitting behind a desk like me talking to somebody like you'. The phases of the action follow the contact of this cynical narrator with Luke Aiblins, a dashing young student (when first encountered) convinced of his greatness as a poet. Luke does not get the praise or help he thinks he deserves; and when we meet him for the third and last time, twelve years on, haggard and homeless, he believes that the government is jamming his brain electronically to break up his inspiration. Our narrator is briefly bothered by the thought, 'It might emerge that I have driven a great poet insane by suppressing his earliest works. For the same reason I fear to destroy them'. The information given in the characteristic after-notes, that the poems quoted in the text as Aiblin's are those of Gray's own apprenticeship, gives an added twist to the dilemma the story seems sardonically to propose: how the selfish individual can determine where excellence or worth might lie; and what, if he finds it, he can get out of it.

Tony Harrison

Dead Men's Mouths

The Shadow of Hiroshima and other Film Poems
Faber and Faber

From the vandalized gravestones in Leeds of *V.* (1986), through the many cemeteries visited in the four-part *Loving Memory* (1987), with its quatrains modelled on Gray's 'Elegy', to the 'Bradford Tomb' in *The Blasphemer's Banquet* (1989), places of burial and markers of the dead have been at the centre of Tony Harrison's 'film/poems' for television. Now Hiroshima offers him its awful variant (and a relative for the charred, upright corpse in his Gulf War poem, *A Cold Coming*): the 'shadow' of a man, printed on the stone steps of a bank by the blast that vaporized him, and now cased in the Peace Memorial Museum. It is this unidentifiable 'Shadow San', released by the poet for 'a day's parole', who acts as his guide to the city as it prepares to mark the fiftieth anniversary of its destruction, though Harrison, who for the first time has directed a film as well as providing the commentary, uses footage shot on the forty-ninth.

As you would expect from Harrison, the dead condition of Shadow San is sharply conceived: he is speaking out now because, literally and ironically fading away from the stone, he might not 'make' the full centenary; when the poet's shadow lengthens in the late afternoon, his own stays 'just the same' until it retires, as darkness falls, on the eve of the anniversary, 'to face once more the flash and fire'. The film's other chief symbols, the Dome and the doves, are more ambiguous, partaking of the contradiction between the ubiquitously proclaimed 'Peace' and terrible memory. Writing in last week's *New Yorker*, Murray Sayle wonders whether any significant message is given out by the A-Bomb Dome, the one carefully preserved skeletal survival of the old city centre. Here it appears from dozens of different viewpoints, and as the obsessive subject of a local artist, as if it were a hellish mutation of Hokusai's Mount Fuji. The main business of the film, though, is the preparation by pigeon-fanciers of their birds – the so-called 'Peace Doves' – for release in the Peace Memorial Park, a ceremony repeated each year at 8.23 on the morning of August 6. Harrison makes them harbingers of peril: they panic throughout, and, after their release, get lost or caught by hawks, fight amongst themselves, or (in one crisp detail) burn, claws up.

The metres of Harrison's commentaries are always taken from a telling model; in this, the grimly spoken tetrameter couplets are revealed halfway through to have their source in a Japanese version of 'Twinkle, twinkle, little star', sung by the pretty successors of perished schoolchildren. Harrison has approved the publication of his film/poems in an edition introduced by his long-time collaborator, Peter Symes of the BBC; but the commentary on *The Shadow of Hiroshima* is not calculated as, say, that of *V.* was to work independently on the page. A passage like

> Dead men's mouths make only M,
> the M in Dome, the M in Bomb,
> tuned to the hum that's coming from
> the A-Bomb Dome that I hear hum
> all round this baseball stadium

may not seem much in the reading, but Richard Blackford's musical effects, Harrison's grinding delivery, and shots of a ringing bowl of empty seats give it an electric force. Indeed, Harrison takes as many pains with his visual materials as he does with the writing, and verse and image are inventively contrasted, taking turns to apply the greater pressure. When the verbal pictures hot up (of 'those / whose skin slid off their flesh like clothes. / Like clothes, three sizes oversize / their flayed skin loosens from their thighs. / Burns and blisters, bloated blebs'), the camera dwells reflectively on the surface of the river Motoyasu; later, these lines are echoed visually by two lovers slipping off their dressing-gowns without remark from the narrative.

The aim of Harrison's toils for television, as declared on the back of the Faber volume, is no less than 'to confront the major horrors of the twentieth century'. Hiroshima is one of the most complex of these, as the city's own confusion testifies whether in the evasive inscription on the cenotaph ('Rest in peace, for the error will not be repeated'), or in the presence there of a pinball arcade called Parlor Atom. Harrison's effort is not without its moments of strain, a late flash of context – 'Japan in her aggressive guise / taking Pearl Harbor by surprise' seems either unnecessary or inadequate – but the whole casts its dark imprint firmly on the mind.

Ian Hamilton

Other Men's Glowers

Against Oblivion: Some Lives of the Twentieth-century Poets
Viking

'A nice idea, if somewhat gimmicky', was Ian Hamilton's own estimate of his last published project. *Against Oblivion* is a collection of forty-five obituary length essays, appraising the lives and work of the twentieth century's most famous dead poets in English (with a representative sample of the writing of each), after the model of Doctor Johnson's *Lives* (1779–81). There is no tokenism: no Irish (though Patrick Kavanagh's current reputation is surely healthier than that, say, of James Wright); no Australian or whatever (though these nationalities were not disqualified); seven are women; none is black (though we're reminded that William Carlos Williams, whose mother was Puerto-Rican, was called a 'dago immigrant' by Ezra Pound). A loose half of the poets are American, the others British. Hardy, Yeats, Eliot and Auden are exempted, as being secure from the title's 'oblivion'; the rest are figured as competing, more or less aggressively, to join them, against odds (using Johnson as a yardstick) of about three to one. It is something, of course, to have carried the first hurdle.

Yet *Against Oblivion* might equally be compared to another Augustan classic, Pope's *Dunciad*. While Johnson's choice of subjects – from John Milton to Thomas Tickell – was largely imposed on him by the booksellers, Hamilton's is his own; but his own exacting judgment has not been applied in the selection process, which makes for a longer book and a much livelier one. Boswell was dismayed by Johnson's submissive attitude to his commission: would he write a Preface and a Life for any dunce's works? 'Yes, Sir', was the reply, 'and say he was a dunce.' – Hamilton was not one

of those editors – at the *Review*, the *New Review* or on the *TLS* – whom
one could have accused of championing individual poets; his count of
the number of his contemporaries he thought 'any good' varied between
'about two' and 'maybe three'. Of the eighty poems he reprints here, it is
safe to assume his whole-hearted admiration for no more than a couple:
Robert Lowell's 'Home After Three Months Away' and Philip Larkin's
'Mr Bleaney'. Sometimes the samples seem chosen with ambivalent intent
(is that windy extract from 'Preludes to Memnon Two' really the best of
Conrad Aiken?). A handful of poets – Charlotte Mew, Dylan Thomas,
Norman Cameron – escape with their reputations slimly enhanced. More
often, Hamilton uses the forms of praise humorously, or over-precisely,
in order to lay open larger failings. Roy Fuller, for example, exhibits 'a
curiously formal manner of despair which, in its stiff, bleak, rather stilted
way, can be quite powerful'. And, of Robinson Jeffers, if 'it has to be con-
ceded that his tireless eye for oceanic detail and expanse is one of his
most lasting strengths', then the concession itself seems to go on forever,
and the critical commonplace of 'lasting' is refreshed with mimetic and
sarcastic overtones.

Outright abuse is not Hamilton's style, though he comes close in
appraising the work, early and late, of 'Hugh MacDiarmid' and in the last
two sentences of his unillusioned dispatch of John Betjeman:

> In 1976 came his autobiography – in verse and on TV – a work both tedious
> and twee called *Summoned By Bells*. Betjeman died in 1984. He prefers in
> general to delegate execution to others; and in this he is well served by his
> subjects, especially by some of his Americans, who in their lust for 'rank-
> ings' seem routinely to have rubbished one another.

(See Stevens on Frost: 'His work is full – or said to be full – of human-
ity'; Allen Tate on Randall Jarrell: 'a self-adulating little twerp'; Jarrell on
Tate, Theodore Roethke on everybody, etc.) One sentence, in the essay
on Norman Cameron – 'It was Cameron who described Stephen Spender
as "the Rupert Brooke of the Depression" – a jest that (Geoffrey) Grigson
treasured, and repeated as often as he could' – can thus convey some-
thing unfavourable about as many as four authors. It is remarkable that,
through so much eager deployment of his own scalpel and the vitriol of
others, Hamilton hardly ever seems mean-spirited or off-puttingly nega-
tive; rather, his insistence that no poet should be honoured as of right

is felt as a gift to the reader. (He dares to call Pound's *Cantos* 'a "major work", which the whole world found incomprehensible but somehow got bullied into taking seriously.' Hurrah!) It is also, he convinces us, a just reaction to the effects of excessive self-promotion. If a position emerges from the biographical portions of *Against Oblivion*, it is a stand against megalomania.

Hamilton pounces on the most literal instances of poets cultivating a name: stating baldly that 'John Berryman's real name was John Smith'; making mincemeat of the pose that was 'e. e. cummings'; and gleefully appending, to R. S. Thomas's denunciation of his mother's failure to teach him Welsh, the parenthesis '(R. S. stands for Ronald Stewart)'. The uncomfortable truth of the matter, however – as embodied in Pound, in Frost, in the drunken ravings of Hart Crane ('I am Baudelaire! I am Whitman! I am Christopher Marlowe! I am Christ'), and particularly in Robert Lowell – is that the urge to make poetry often goes with an unstable conviction of the superiority of the gifted self (or genius) to others. In the case of Lowell, whose *Life Studies* (1959) had been Hamilton's exemplary book, the genius bit was so destructive to those around him that it led Hamilton, in a disenchanted biography (1982), to join Elizabeth Bishop in wondering whether even these poems were worth it. In other cases, the swollen ego may forget the poetry that inflated it. If Theodore Roethke, in whom 'inspiration was supplanted by ambition', is therefore 'a typical mid-century case study', it follows that it is not with the poems, but with the business of poetry, the clamour for status and the competitive shenanigans, that Hamilton's survey seems centrally engaged.

In an interview with his friend Dan Jacobson given shortly before his death, of cancer, in December 2001, Hamilton declared that 'every book I've written has some strong autobiographical element in it'. If this book is no exception, it is the stealthiest of autobiographies. There is, for a start, no hint of valediction, beyond the rugged joke of the title. And beside its cast of gushers, drunks and maniacs, his own poetic 'career' seems almost absurdly reticent. His *oeuvre* – 'gratifyingly compact', according to his publishers – consisted of the same collection of poems reissued at intervals with additions; *Sixty Poems*, in the last revision, and short ones at that. If this reflects Hamilton's demandingly narrow idea of what, in our time, a poem should be – (to paraphrase) the as-if-spoken record of an intense personal experience with general interest or application – it also suggests he was too interested in others to be a poet of realized reputation: others, that is, who confirmed to him something about him-self. One of his poems, 'The Poet', catches him, as if cribbing, 'listening for other lives / Like his'; and so it was that biography of his own kind absorbed him. One of his late poems, 'Biography', is certainly about both self and another subject:

> Who turned the page?
> When I went out
> Last night, his
> Life was left wide-open,
> Half-way through, in lamplight on my desk:
> The Middle Years.
> Now look at him.
> Who turned the page?

Against Oblivion lets us see both enterprises – the creative and the bio-graphical – as putting to use such a fear, of being not neglected, or dried-up, but dead.

Seamus Heaney

Nostalgia for World Culture

The Redress of Poetry
Faber and Faber

Seamus Heaney's third volume of prose consists of ten of the fifteen lectures he gave over five years as Professor of Poetry at Oxford University. Yet because everything he has had to say in public about the poetry of others stems from his own deep convictions about the art he shares with them, it reads as a coherent single work of something more vital than we usually mean by criticism. (For the same reason, he has avoided reviewing, except as an occasion for celebration: one who has felt Osip Mandelstam's 'nostalgia for world culture' will not be inclined to local disparagement.) The keynote of the lectures is a remark borrowed from George Seferis's notebooks about poetry being 'strong enough to help' – a considerable statement of faith disguised as a small claim. But as often in these pages, the generous precedence Heaney gives to the saying of another is soon overtaken by the subtlety, charm and humane force of his own formulations.

By the 'redress' of his title, he means one definition in particular: 'Reparation of, satisfaction or compensation for, a wrong sustained, or the loss resulting from this.' His subjects, broadly speaking, are thwarted individuals made good by poetry, those who have mastered, in Elizabeth Bishop's ironic phrase, 'the art of losing'. Hence Hugh MacDiarmid's 'A Drunk Man Looks at the Thistles' figured as wresting artistic victory from the defeat of his political ideals, achieving 'something equal to and corrective of the prevailing condition'. 'Poor' John Clare, whose loss amounted to nothing less than himself ('I am – yet what I am none cares or knows') is celebrated for his exemplary rejection of any official version of how poetry should behave; the measured enthrallment of Heaney's essay continues the reclamation of Clare, a task which has been accomplished – with respect to the editorial work of Geoffrey Summerfield and others – less by academic critics than by the impassioned advocacy of poets like Heaney and Tom Paulin.

Elizabeth Bishop returns Heaney's close artistic sympathy by supplying him, in 'One Art', with a perfect enactment of another, obsolete meaning of 'redress' – 'to set upright again':

> It's evident
> the art of losing isn't hard to master
> though it may look like (Write it!) like disaster.

Says Heaney, 'The pun in that final nick-of-time imperative – "Write it!" – is in deadly earnest … the poem is asked to set the balance right'. Heaney is in his element with poets as watchful (for all the apparent gulf in sophistication between them) as Clare and Bishop, whose 'attention to detail' – Clare's 'one-thing-after-anotherness', Bishop's engagement with the movement of a sandpiper's toes – 'can come through into visionary understanding'. His own sense for the weight of the unconsidered magnifies their successes, and wittily, too: 'I am reminded of a remark made once by an Irish diplomat with regard to the wording of a certain document. "This," he said, "is a minor point of major importance."' Heaney concludes of Bishop, in perhaps the plainest statement of the principle behind these writings, that 'she does continually manage to advance poetry beyond the point where it has been helping us to enjoy life to that even more profoundly verifying point where it helps us to endure it'. Which you would not easily say, whatever his virtues, about Philip Larkin. The lecture in which Heaney's convictions lead him closest to disapproval deals with Larkin's late poem 'Aubade', that supremely bleak admission of the terror of being dead. Heaney proceeds to his position through a gracious appreciation of the poem's 'heartbreaking truths and beauties'; he notes the reappearance in harrowed form of words like 'unresting' and 'afresh' from earlier poems by Larkin, less, perhaps, to stress the new hopelessness of 'Aubade' than to allow that the poet has after all been more affirmative elsewhere. But finally, following (this time) Czesław Miłosz, he objects to the poem's central proposition that 'Death is no different whined at than withstood'.

One of the recurring ideas in this sequence of lectures is that poetry exists on the frontier between the world we know and 'the domain of the imagined'; whatever the balance of its movements, its work is to go to and fro. In such a dark night as Larkin's, W. B. Yeats looked up and 'Suddenly ... saw in the cold and rook-delighting heaven'; Heaney notes, in contrast, how 'when Larkin lifts his eyes from nature, what appears is a great absence'. 'Aubade' is accused, not for its loss of religious faith, but for its lack of faith in poetry's redress. Heaney is a believer. The force of his book is as much spiritual as critical; there is a priestly glow beneath its intellectual sparkle. No one who has absorbed its reverence for consolation, its steadfast attachment to possibility, will succumb quite so readily again to the seductions of Larkin's No.

Douglas Dunn

Grave and Muffled Beats

Dante's Drum-kit
Faber and Faber

Douglas Dunn likens his craft to gardening; but there are times when his verse seems too thickly planted with phrases, not all of them closely connected to the syntactical stem of a poem. One particular variety, the free-standing possessive with an abstract, classical flavour ('Infinity's emigrant', 'Eternity's acoustics', 'Pity's Statistic', 'Discovery's digits'), crops up in otherwise very different poems in this new collection; and the first section of 'Dressed to Kill', a sequence about Scottish soldiering, consists of sixteen rhymed kennings for bagpipe music ('Xenophobia's solo', 'Chauvinist's wallow' etc). There is virtuosity in this, but 'Dressed to Kill' as a whole exemplifies Dunn's venial overindulgence: written originally for television, it lacks the finish its place in the volume requires. Its inclusion, and that of say a dozen other pieces, may make the book more various (or perhaps just more – 145 pages), but tends to obscure what is happening in the fine poems at the heart of it: Dunn's exploration of what the forms and conventions of ghost poetry can and can't offer him.

'Dante's drum-kit' is one of Dunn's several phrases for terza rima, the verse form of Dante's *Divine Comedy*, and ever since the measure in which we can expect the dead to speak. In this century, T. S. Eliot (in 'Little Gidding') and Seamus Heaney (in much of the 'Station Island' sequence) have developed versions in English as a medium for encountering the ghosts of other writers; now Dunn uses it in 'Disenchantments', the longest and most ambitious poem here, described on the jacket as 'a meditation on the afterlife', though it's more fun than that.

But Dunn – most celebrated as the author of *Elegies* for his first wife, and a thoroughgoing secularist – won't pretend that the dead come back. His 'ghosts' don't talk: 'Only in life's interior extra sense / Are they glimpsed, tending a geranium.' They appear here instead to serve the poet impersonally with intuitions about history and continuity. In the key poem, 'Body Echoes', the shapes of ordinary Scotsmen and women evoke those of their predecessors through the ages, until Dunn is made to register a 'monstrous permanence' of drizzle and deprivation, each local incarnation one faceless line among others that multiply as his phrases do elsewhere: 'I've seen her headscarfed, / Soaked, by the door of a spectral byre, or / Hearing her weight against a frosted pump / Or beating passive cattle with a stick.'

The archetypal Janet and Jock that emerge are called 'national halves', and they feature in a number of remarkable poems, in the third of the book's five sections: on one side, in 'Queen February', the wintry spirit of Northern girlhood unleashed in vengeful weather; on the other, in the solemn and impressive 'Bare Ruined Choirs', a blind beggar-minstrel, whose tapping stick Dunn takes up as a prosodic baton. They are united in 'Poor People's Cafes' as a moving emblem of unending humiliation, their daily round rendered in a poll-tax-pinched and straitened stanza:

> He talks to a cup;
> She stirs their tea
> Then holds it up,
> A wedded pity
> In how they share –
> Her sip, his sip:
> It looks like a prayer,
> Companionship
> In a belief
> In the unknown,
> Elderly grief.

In 'Preserve and Renovate', another particularly well-made poem, the language of perpetual torment (that of the head-eating Ugolino, in a portion of the *Inferno* that Heaney has translated) adheres briefly to the author, while the ghost that is released – through looking at another old man painting his garden fence – is that of his industrious father:

I could gnaw
At that facsimile for ever more;
But I know who I lack
Not him, but that dead, distant door
Who looked like him, who draws me back and back.

But this grieving note is untypical. If Dunn's vision of a 'monstrous permanence' has none of the consolations of religion about it, if it disdains the supernatural, still its recognition affords him moments of what you might call spiritual pleasure. In 'Body Echoes', tremendous claims are made for a Vermeeresque glimpse of 'a girl shaking her hands / at a sink' (though this is certainly an instance of a poet telling what he might be showing): 'It has a very deep sweetness, / This moment, colossal sugar, brilliant / Ambrosial light'. And Dunn's own prospective afterlife is imagined less as something out of the *Inferno*, or the sixth book of Virgil's *Aeneid*, than as a dream from the latter's *Georgics*, his celebration of agricolas or husbandry (a word which appears several times here). Given his unlikely choice, this most Augustan of Scots poets would settle forever in a smallholding whose virtues would be those of his own verse, a type he has defined as 'native classic':

make mine pagan, please, Republican,
Domestic, set in very private grounds,

A spacious grave where all five senses quicken.

Julian Barnes

Revenge of a Tortoise

Love, etc
Cape

Julian Barnes's *Talking It Over* (1991) introduced us to two old friends and adversaries: Stuart, a chubby, unimaginative banker, and Oliver, the feckless but witty bohemian. The novel plots their related fortunes as the third main protagonist, a picture-restorer named Gillian, somehow chooses to marry Stuart, and then, on return from their honeymoon, dumps and divorces him in favour of his irresistibly persuasive best man. In an unusual manoeuvre – did Barnes always have a sequel in mind? – *Love, etc* revisits this triangle, to see how it has developed in the real time since. This book too is made up of the characters' alternating (and sometimes inconsistent) versions of events, addressed in appeal to a judgmental 'reader'; and although, as before, what happens is largely trivial, the psychological drama is constantly refreshed by Barnes's invention and intelligence.

Naturally, neither of Gillian's husbands (each now in his early forties) is quite what he was. The novel (or the second phase of it) is launched by Stuart's return to London from a long sojourn in America, where he has run a successful organic grocery business and worked his way satisfactorily through a second marriage and divorce. Toned by exercise and smartened up by money, he now knows not only his limitations but also his particular if prosaic advantages: 'My key words are transparency, efficiency, virtue, convenience and flexibility.' We see in Oliver, meanwhile, for all the frantic energy of his expression, how his purely verbal riches have failed to sustain him into maturity. He has not 'got on': the black-and-white spat-like shoes that were his statement are scuffed and worn. His crea-tive 'projects' – screenplays, whether written or imaginary – have come to nothing, and it emerges that he has had what his wife incuriously calls 'his – what? episode? illness? depression?' His reflex of condescension towards ('boring') Stuart no longer damages or diminishes its target. He jibes here that 'the novel of Stuart's life is, frankly, unpublishable'; but while Oliver dominated *Talking It Over* with his high-powered bullshit, Stuart just as surely rules *Love, etc* by application to the task. Gillian and Oliver (and their two suspicious daughters) allow themselves to become dependent on Stuart's financial support, a situation which vexes Oliver towards a repetition of his 'episode'; and it is with Stuart that Gillian is destined to have her only sex of the book.

That said, Oliver has a usefulness for Barnes the novelist that Stuart cannot offer, as an outlet for his own mental exuberance, a licence to go over the top, to inhabit and write like 'a sprite who'd been at the mar-garitas'. Even as they register his breakdown, Oliver's 'riffs', flourishes and flytings are memorable literary entertainment. The highlights of his performance here include the fable of *The Revenge of the Tortoise* as it might be retold in various literary genres (for Oliver, the hare wins every time); his take on the parlour game of *Would You Rather* ('As in, would you rather be buried up to your neck in wet mud for a week or compare all the recorded versions of the New World symphony? Would you rather stroll down Oxford Street bollock-naked with a pineapple on your head or marry a member of the Royal Family?'); a revelation of the principal English Romantic poets, Wordsworth (1770–1850), Coleridge (1772–1834), Shelley (1792–1822) and Keats (1795–1821), as Russian dolls ('The man with the longest name lived the longest, the one with the shortest lived the shortest, and so on in between. Better still, the first born died the last, the last-born died the first!'); and this unimpressed observation (part of a dig at Stuart's environmental concerns):

> Nomads aren't nomads because they like being nomads, but because they have no choice. And now that our modern age has given them the choice, see what they nobly prefer: the off-road vehicle, the automatic rifle, telly and a bottle of hooch. Just like us!

Yet Oliver's style, his poetry, is defeated. It takes one modest piece of liter-ary criticism from Stuart to puncture the whole operation: 'Now I think all these fancy comparisons were a way of not looking at the original object, of not looking at the world …' With this perception, Stuart consigns an inimical world view to the past. 'Oliver used to have a theory he called Love, etc: in other words, the world divides into people for whom love is everything and the rest of life is a mere "etc", and people who don't value love enough and find the most exciting part of life is the "etc". What is this wisdom now to Stuart? 'Boastful bollocks.' He supplants it with his own theory, that some, like him, love only once, and acts on that conviction. Gillian is a more reserved witness than the contending males, as if resistant to the notion of herself as battleground or spoils. If unreliability is a factor in the novel, that is especially because we can't quite gauge her motive for talking to us. Intriguingly, she gives two different accounts of the novel's climactic event, her seduction or rape in the kitchen while Oliver shivers upstairs. Are they true and false, false and true, or (if we are to believe Stuart's rhapsodic account instead) both false? In their supposed coupling, the characters diverge the most, are shown to be marooned after all in their own desires or pretences. As Oliver has it: 'truth mostly does not out. It mostly ins.' And the novel ends in deepening uncertainty, a fog of relativity from which, it is nice to think, a further sequel might one day appear.

James Kelman

After Closing Time

The Good Times
Secker and Warburg

'In this factory in the north of England acid was essential.' So begins 'Acid', one of the pieces in James Kelman's first collection of short stories, *Not Not While The Giro* (1983). By the end of its third sentence, a 'young man' has fallen into a vat of this acid; by the end of its eighth sentence, an 'old fellow', who is coincidentally the young man's father, has used a pole to push the obtruding dead head and shoulders beneath the surface. The whole is fewer than 150 words long, not much more than this precis of it; it is story boiled down to the bones. 'Acid' exemplifies an approach to fiction that Kelman has since rejected. The prizewinning *How Late It Was, How Late* (1994) is a long novel in which little is allowed to happen; and his recent shorter fiction seems likewise organized to avoid what we recognize (in every word of 'Acid', for instance) as event. His fourth collection, *The Good Times*, consists of twenty interior monologues, presenting twenty different men and boys from Kelman's native Glasgow. Some of these monologues are shaped by a particular non-event: in the opening story, 'Joe Laughed', the child narrator is anticipating a kick-about on waste ground, when he wanders off instead to explore a derelict building for his story's uncertain duration. Other tales begin and end, as if arbitrarily, at points of an average evening in, or at stages of any old session in the pub.

The embattled Kelman's mission to date has been to construct a serious literature for the experience of working-class Glaswegians. His politics now seem to require further that his stories should deliver the least remarkable hours of these unregarded lives. We know that men in Glasgow as elsewhere play football, get drunk, fight, win and lose the Lottery, fall in love and tumble into acid; but what we see of them in *The Good Times* is their walking to get the milk, sitting up in bed, sipping their pint, waiting for the Drumchapel bus. Kelman additionally relieves his narrators of the constraints of polite storytelling; they are not made to get to the point, or find a point to get to. This pursuit of inconsequence has its risks. While Kelman's exceptional ear for the accents of individual lives makes all his Glaswegians seem separately authentic, some of their narratives are so deprived that their being is scarcely registered. It is a mark of the power and conviction of his writing that so many of their stories still have an emotional impact. The longest piece, 'Comic Cuts', seems related to the rest of the project while not quite belonging within it. Originally conceived as a radio drama, there is a lot of Beckett about it. Four rock musicians, after a night (we guess) in the pub, are whiling away the early hours in a flat, waiting for soup, which throughout will be ready in ten minutes. There are intriguing hints of menace and revelation, which come to nothing; fifty pages are otherwise filled in with virtuosic but aimless 'blether': 'one can say many things, very many things, very very many things'. When at last it stops, no reason has emerged (other than to fit the piece for this collection) why one of its characters (the one who does most of the talking) has been awarded the first person. The overabundance of 'Comic Cuts' is a function of its being set after the pub has shut.

Every story Kelman sets in a pub seems to be successful: perhaps because our consciousness of closing time reassures us, against his own practice, with its shadow of authorial control. 'Every fucking time', for one, brilliantly evokes the atmosphere of an unnamed bar, while offering its own anguished critique of repetitive 'blether'. The exasperated narrator is talking (or mostly listening) to two brothers:

> What were they rabbiting on about now? The price of drink in general. What else. Their all-time favourite topic. Some pub in the Calton that used to supply the cheapest glass of Eldee in the entire city. I had heard it all before. A fucking thousand times. A million. Only it used to be a pub down the Garscube Road, or was it Garriochmill Road. Who knows; who gives a fuck. It was this kind of patter drove ye nuts.

At another point, this narrator jokes bitterly, 'sometimes yew felt like dropping deid, just to escape the company'. Yet, while he does in the course of his tale suffer heart pains, his story exists to display his routine, not to vary or break or end it. The fragments of *The Good Times* do not resolve themselves. The end of 'Joe laughed', for instance, leaves the boy hanging: 'I wasnay sure what I was gony do, no from now on, I maybe no even do nothing, it would just depend.' A number of subsequent pieces leave a similar mixed aftertaste of impotence and opportunity, though the promise wears thinner as men grow older. In the last lines of the volume, the narrator of the title story signs off his bleak little account of illness, nightmares and a wife withdrawn to a separate room, 'But these are the good times.' One interpretation of Kelman's not wholly ironic title is 'not dead yet'.

Women are withdrawn, marginal, or mysterious in many of these monologues. The most memorable of them is the invalid wife in the troubling 'Strength', who cannot be helped from chafing over, in her sinister habitual terms, an incident of thirty years ago, involving her husband, a motorbike, and his teenage girlfriend of the time: 'I know ye loved that wee lassie … Even if ye had got killed the gether, the two of ye, it still would nay bother me. I just admire ye both, I do.' When her husband counters, in the closing moments of the story, with irritation at her posture – 'I wish ye wouldnay put yer feet on that damned pouffe, I said, ye'll suffer for it' – his words also carry the general wish for suffering to be postponed: a lashing-out of tenderness which is the spirit of this radical, uneven but often moving collection.

Peter Reading

Thanoptic Designs

C
Peter Reading, Secker and Warburg

5x5x5x5x5
Peter Reading and David Butler, Ceolfrith Press

Intimations of *C* – Peter Reading's brilliant but ruthless new book of 'poems' about cancer – are to be found in the pamphlet *5x5x5x5x5*, produced last year in collaboration with the Sunderland artist David Butler. In five sections, each of five poems, each of five stanzas, each of five lines, each of five syllables, we meet five dismal drunkards in the 'Railway Hotel', each of whom suffers some more or less terminal misadventure before the end. Jock, for instance, is a noisy Poly second-year, a rugby braggart with 'too much confidence, / no respectful fright / or awareness, yet, / of mortality'. He is heavily tackled in a spontaneous rugby fantasy of our author's (scribbled on a beermat) and chokes to death on his gumshield. A few pages later, though, Reading has compassionate second thoughts, and brings in a surgeon to help repair the MS damage: 'Tipp-ex and scalpel / joined forces to clear / a throat obstruction.' Jock's life is restored on one utterly disabling condition: 'EX-SCOTTISH PATIENT / EXHUMED AS *ENGLISH*'. Meanwhile, a daft logician has been amusingly destroyed by a 'sub-species' of skinhead in the pub bog.

We look on these kinds of death and pain as the legitimate fictions of the light-verse black comedian; grotesque retribution on those who are only invented to deserve it, redeemable in joke resurrections. In 5^4, poet and surgeon alike have the power of life and death; in *C*, by a bold intensification of its author's morbidity, poet and surgeon have no power at all. The difference in atmosphere is pointed by the presence in each book of a stock Reading figure; when the weak-hearted palaeontologist comforts himself in 5⁴, 'What's 40 years / here or there on the / chronostratigraph?' he sounds drunk, but when the cancerous palaeontologist comforts himself in *C*, with the same phrase, he sounds insane.

C is an even more demanding numerological structure. It pretends to be the work of a versifying cancer victim, charting his last 100 days in 100 units each of 100 words; and around this central figure Reading builds fossil layers of 'poor frail dear frightened little vulnerable creatures' dying in isolation (the excellent acrostic 'IN THE SAME VERTICAL COLUMN' follows five storeys of hospital suffering down to the stoker in the basement). The strange excitement of the book lies in the inappropriateness of the admirable design, and especially of the medium of verse, to such a very unliterary subject. Verse, indeed, is *C*'s first casualty: 'Verse is for healthy / arty-farties. The dying / and surgeons use prose' chimes an early haiku; and prose subsequently outweighs verse three to one. Where they survive, verse forms are gruesomely misapplied, so that we relish all the more their impotence to explain, console, or cure. There is a sixteen-liner on bedsores (from two angles); a limerick plus 'cutely-adapted Adonic' for fatal haemorrhage; 'catalectic' (truncated) tetrameters to lament cut-off breasts; a Japanese sonnet on a 'stiff' in the chip shop; the thirteen-line sonnet, invented 'for unlucky people' in general; and a limerick with 'pretty Choriamb' to hymn the after-effects of a botched colostomy. In a different admission of verse's inadequacy, other pieces are hidden away in prose settings; as the stunned craftsman instructs himself, 'Run them together, set as justified prose,/ the inadequately blank pentameters'. Harder puns than these link the breakdown of verse and body. Can metre and punctuation contain the leakage of collapsed bowels? No – 'pentameters, like colons, inadequate'. Likewise, after the operation, '*ars*' is '*brevis*'.

Still, we ought to detach Reading's *ars* from the arse of his persona. Its most apparently reductive flourishes are carefully placed and prepared for. The last words on verse, for example, are spoken by the tramp Tucker who, in various guises, and in contrived partnership with the 'pale horse' from Revelation, attends gloatingly on death throughout. Watching another one borne away in an ambulance, he pulls at a whisky bottle (White Horse) and guffaws a perfect pentameter: Ha há / ha há / ha há / ha há / ha há.

– and perfect that unambiguously is. Besides, verse is not uniquely picked on by the impartial cancer. 'Not just me, but all of us …'; not just the poet, but the palaeontologist too. These instructions for home care show food and clothing to be just as 'incongruous':

> Phrase questions to receive very simple answers, e.g.: 'There is jelly and ice cream or egg custard – would you like jelly and ice cream?' Pyjamas should be absorbent.

So Reading, with a barrage of 'Shit, blood, puke', etc., takes us as close to the facts of disease as any work of literature – including the medical dictionary which supplies some of his text – is likely to want to do. He has no interest in the distancing demeanour which more reverent poets might adopt to deal with dying subjects; the dying 'hate' us (Reading's word) and want our life, not our verse. His solution – sick in its way, no doubt – is to join them, posing as 'the Master of the 100 100-Word Units' who '*chronicles his death in the third Person*' in a game which is deadlier by far than the average earnestness. His daring even induces a certain dread for his health – a peculiar achievement for imaginative writing. Section Eighty-seven, a letter to his publishers (advising them chirpily that it forms part of his last book, and that he is dead as they read it) is awesomely unsuperstitious: '*P. S. Seriously though, my wife will deal with proof correction*.' More than Reading's, though, our own health concerns us, and the book tweaks and probes at the general anxiety. One of its truest episodes is that of a victim, not of cancer, but of fear of it, who kills herself with twenty pills in Section Forty-four. There is the merest shadow of an ironic triumph in the fact that our nameless hero, who contemplates a bowery Virgilian suicide throughout, and collects the same twenty pills, is too weak by the close – too nearly dead – to do the job. And if the book's coda displaces poetical emphasis, nevertheless it borrows something of poetry's affirmative habit as it moves unexpectedly to its muted ten-thousandth word: 'My wife patiently washes my faece-besmirched pyjamas, for *prosaic* love.'

Christopher Reid

Modest Metaphors and Tiddly Riddles

In the Echoey Tunnel
Faber and Faber

Tidy, subtle, faintly surreal poems of a domestic character have established Christopher Reid as a master and advocate of the diminutive; 'little' is his favourite adjective, as in 'our little red Renault'. Like Alan Brownjohn of the preceding generation, he sometimes borrows the manner and materials of children's literature, and the first few pages of this new book are full of innocent perfect spheres: the 'tiddly ball' of a teacher's game, balloons, chubby seals, bubbles blown across a playground. The bubbles are stamped on by a fat boy; and against the implied opposition of braggarts and bullies, Reid has developed an almost provocatively tiddly poetic.

Since *Pea Soup* (1982), with its unstated promise of a main course, Reid has published only *Katerina Brac*, daringly but also diffidently presented as a set of translations from an unworldly poetess. But with *In the Echoey Tunnel* he has begun to extend himself. There are two long poems and five sequences, though one of the latter, the series of tiny 'Pips', renews the idea of the poem as the thing before the real thing – the 'perfect / prelude to whatever next' of an earlier volume. Here 'Forebodings' locates 'Intimations of thunder / in my little toe'; and 'Knowledge' sardonically promotes the seed:

It's the cleverest trick
Eve taught Adam
you bite the pip
and taste the whole tree.

The two long poems are whole trees all right, though Reid has chosen subjects which suit his taste for fragmentary structure. In the remarkable 'Memres sic of Alfred Stoker', a 100-year-old mental patient looks back on his unusual religious upbringing in the East End. It's not clear whether this material is in any way 'found', or all impressively invented; it purports, anyway, to have been written by Stoker (if not 'Stocker') with a 'pesil' or 'pensel' and its main point is its illiteracy. The creatively wayward language that Reid foists on Stoker – the blurb calls it 'accomplished argot', as if either of them were getting it right – offers the local pleasure of riddles ('cubed' is cupboard, 'moggne' mahogany) and gives the simplest recollection the glow of pathos ('Pa Holed my Hand'). It also increases the novelty of the narrative: when Stoker's preacher father is pelted by unimpressed Glaswegians, the 'cabige' they throw is somehow more humiliating than the standard vegetable. The 'Memres' end disconcertingly with the boy's admission to the 'ofinick', ninety years ago.

The other long poem, 'Survival: A Patchwork', leads Reid into a different kind of new territory, the explicitly personal. It deals with his wife's recovery from cancer, and imitates the design of the patchwork quilts she makes. The form embodies Reid's aversion to 'big', rhetorical writing; there is no punctuation, minimal syntactic connection between the short lines, and loose, bathetic strands like the line 'your steady achievement' are all part of the fabric. By the close, the asymmetric presentation, with its recognition of 'two pulses/inevitable variance', becomes a formal metaphor for the rough harmonies of a marriage: what Reid calls, in a relatively fluent passage,

> the frequently-trumpeted
> republic of two
> with its improvised constitution
> and merry folk-culture.

Technically and otherwise, displaying its flaws, it is a brave poem. Reid's respect for other arts and artists is sometimes expressed in terms detrimental to his own craft. In 'Survival', his jottings are compared to the paper templates the quilt-maker throws away. But his modesty now seems less of an attractive gimmick, more a genuine discipline from which works of increasing value will emerge.

Martin Amis

Return Ticket to Auschwitz

Time's Arrow
Cape

Martin Amis's language has always been able to summon surprises from the most familiar subject matter; in his extraordinary new novel, he uses structure to the same effect. For *Time's Arrow* flies preposterously 'bassackward', telling the story of a single life from its first nauseous flicker on an American deathbed to the mortal blow of its German conception. The body belongs to someone known in his dotage as Tod Friendly, whose various aliases fall away over the years to reveal him as Odilo Unverdorben (the name means 'Undepraved', and the novel undepraves him), a doctor in a Nazi death camp.

The narrator, though, is not the doctor, but a baffled, impotent witness, a 'passenger or parasite' trapped inside his head, whom we are encouraged to identify as a dislocated or aborted soul. This easy-going and sentimental companion has no idea where the doctor's past is taking him, and is at odds with him throughout, except when they join in the buoyant 'I' who recounts his repair of the dead at Auschwitz. Robert Jay Lifton's book *The Nazi Doctors*, which Amis cites as his prime inspiration, discusses the phenomenon of 'doubling' in the psychology of its subjects; it also records the sense of Auschwitz as 'a different planet', whose unnatural rules (especially the relation between doctor and patient) 'totally reversed those of ordinary society'. That is the point of Amis's strenuously perverse exercise: one way to conceive the non-sense of the Holocaust is to tell it backwards. But the first, more innocent half of the novel is its own justification of the backward procedure. Meeting a structural challenge stiffer even than the amnesia of *Other People*, Amis has imagined regressive forms with a thoroughness which makes light of the mere impossibility of telling a story this way. Of course he cheats. He allows his narrator a partial understanding of normal sequence, craftily varied for the benefit of momentum or a good joke.

Speech, for example, is first encountered as a 'pitiable chirruping'; but while we puzzle at a misogynist mutter of 'Shtib ... Shtib', we are also asked to hear the self-loathing implicit in the sound of the German 'Ich' ('like the sound a child makes when it confronts its own ...'). Dialogue is presented, with due consideration, as fully decoded speeches, but set in their proper reverse order; so that after sampling one or two for their arbitrary comedy (or strange pathos), we tend to enter all spoken exchanges at the bottom. The pursuit of an alternative life-logic is energetically sustained. All sustenance is called up by the toilet handle, and ingested anally; daily needs are got from the trash that is distributed in the 'morning' (i.e, the hour before bright bedtime) along with the shit for the dogs. Eating we do in vomitoria (restaurants) or at home, where, once we've filled our plates, we put the food back together to take to the shops, which give us the money to take to work, etc. Love affairs begin with bitter silences in car parks or with shouting matches: 'You can go up to a woman on a street corner and start yelling at her and 10 minutes later she's back at your place doing God knows what'. All is powered along by a matey, confiding prose shamelessly alert to our language's stock of reversals: from broad puns like 'he knows this town backwards' and 'I'm head over heels' to tiny felicities like the 'decaff' the doctor drools in the morning (to remove the caffeine and get to sleep, though we're left to work this out for ourselves).

In a world where creation is 'no trouble at all', the medical profession does its laborious damage. Victims back dopily into the casualty ward; doctors rip off bandages, swab on the blood, insert the grit and glass, and send the bodies out on stretchers to be dumped in town by ambulances. Twenty years of sitting in on such atrocities in American hospitals and even this mustard-keen narrator confesses himself 'tired of being human'; now the doctor heads for Europe, with a new sharpness of an old fear, to cure that fatigue. The twenty-page chapter on events at Auschwitz must have been the hardest for Amis to write; but, though it stops short of the magical fluency we might expect as things outrageously start 'making sense', it is the easiest (in a sense) to read. The lull of the first few pages, after the narrator-cum-doctor, in his eerie new first-person conjunction, has screeched on his motorbike into the grimmest of abandoned land-scapes, is dreadfully enthralling: 'the ruins begin to smoke and glow, the sprinkler-rooms compact out of the rubble, and the sweet smell of creation begins to rise.' Under the charismatic Mengele (here 'Uncle Pepi'), the exhausted, devoted, ingenious doctors set about their 'preternatural purpose': to make an entire race of people out of the ground and the sky.

Amis the writer has preferred to keep his distance from straightforward feeling; and he has discovered a way of treating the Holocaust that protects him from making explicit a compassion we can take for granted. Ironic inversion is essentially a comic device, but its trickery here yields results that are rigorously grave. The worst of stories are conveyed in a spirit of whistle-while-you-work: 'I saw the old Jew float to the surface of the deep latrine, how he splashed and struggled into life, and was hoisted out by the jubilant guards ... Then they put his beard back on.' Above the do-gooding ruck of his assistants and their orthodox medicine, Mengele becomes a worker of casual miracles, whose beauty is a new damnation of his incredible offence:

> He can knock together a human being out of the unlikeliest odds and ends ... It was not uncommon to see him slipping out of his darkroom carrying a head partly wrapped in old newspaper ... the next thing you knew there'd be, oh, I don't know, a fifteen-year-old Pole sliding off the table and rubbing his eyes before sauntering back to work.

Amis's comic skills – at work in the banal enthusiasm of the whole, in the good-humoured shrug of 'Oh, I don't know', in the stunning dailiness of 'sauntering' – contribute as much to the power of this passage as the horror they oppose. As the dazzled Jews migrate from the camps into ghettos, one last 'happy' anecdote explains a bad dream that has been thickening like a plot towards fruition. Decanting one batch of thirty, led by a howling baby, from a mass grave into their 'rude hamlet', Unverdorben stands aside as they huddle instinctively into an empty shed and back their way, one by one, through a missing panel in the wall. 'This panel,' recalls the narrator fondly, 'I myself replaced with a softly spoken "Guten Tag"' – and he lingers awhile, listening avuncularly to the child's muffled wails and its family's soothing, communal 'Schhh ...'

After the Holocaust (as the narrator asks, partly of Amis, 'How do you follow that?'), *Time's Arrow* declines, though it never falters, towards

the enveloping zero of Unverdorben's own birth. This is the sort of dia-
grammatic cancellation that Amis has favoured in the past; but the rever-
berations of this mighty little book are not so easily hushed up. For the
unnatural daring of its technique, at first (apparently) only ingenious,
has had after all to oppose the Unspeakable.

Paul Muldoon

Abandoned Origins

Meeting the British
Faber and Faber

It is a surprising fact that the most exciting feature of perhaps the most eagerly awaited book of 1987 should be its rhyme – given the word's usual connotations of traditionalism, decorativeness, jingle, levity, consolation. But *Meeting the British*, Paul Muldoon's fifth and most ambitious collection, is a long way from Pope, and a very long way from Wendy Cope. Where Pope has a couplet, Muldoon has this: 'or lemon / (all those afternoons in the Ashmolean)' – which is two rhyme-words supplanting the idea of a line with whatever it takes to divide them – drawing attention even more emphatically than usual to the end-words. Another difference lies in the nature of his rhymes, the best of which have never been aware of how unexpected consonantal and assonantal pairings will amuse or disconcert the reader, and it is a measure of his success with these that his (less frequent) use of ordinary full rhyme seems relatively underpowered. Add to these an ability to trap a theme in the lexical space (often not very much) between two words, with effects that make up Eliot's celebrated 'trumpets' / 'crumpets' look naïve, and you have a technique of rhyming which is in every way essential to a difficult and delightful body of poetry.

Muldoon's previous book *Quoof* made explanatory use of words' proximity to one another; in 'The Right Arm', for example: 'I would give my right arm to have known then / how English was itself wedged between / *ecclesia* and *église*' – typical in the way it invokes and fends off the cross weight of 'English' with words that *aren't* English. *Meeting the British* has several poems whose last rhyme-word is matched with the first, so that the whole has the appearance of being 'wedged' between them. Indeed, a single Muldoon rhyme can be all the substance of a short poem (remember, from *Quoof*, Nairac / anorak). 'The Mist-Net' is the slightest here:

> Though he checked the mist-net
> every day for a month
>
> he caught only two tiny birds;
> one Pernod-sip,
>
> one tremulous crème-de-menthe;
> their tiny sobs
>
> were his mother's dying words:
> *You mustn't. You mustn't.*

Context and echo transform this 'mist-net' from a bird-trap into some mythical object more worthy of the word: a drizzly hymen, or a film where family tears condense; a delicate and unreal property, like another poem's 'bucket of steam', whose mysterious significance is pressed from a single accident of consonance. The illusion sticks that the rhyme-words are joined by something more essential than the letters they have in common; so the poem works.

A build-up of pairings like this creates an atmosphere where words are actually likely to destabilize and slip into the words close to them. At low pressure, the trick can seem corny; when a character in '7, Middagh Street' cites Yeats's line about 'two girls in silk kimonos', the gazelle is bound to turn out a 'gazebo' (though this may mean to point out unconscious Muldoonery on Yeats's part.) Elsewhere it releases an almost unbelievable lexical abundance. The most spectacular rhyming stunt occurs in 'Sushi', where the 'scrim-shandering' of a carrot is interrupted by this isolated outburst (by whom?) of variations on the consonantal theme *r g n*:

> Is it not the height of arrogance
> to propose that God's no more arcane
> than the smack of oregano,

orgone,
in the inner organs
of beasts and fowls, the mines of Arigna,
the poems of Louis Aragon?

This fragment (which might convey a complaint against Muldoon's indis-
criminate plundering method) is only joined to the rest of the poem by
its rhymes with (again) the first and last lines of the poem – 'arguing' and
'Scotus Eriugena' – and with 'erogenous' in the middle. When we find
further variants ('organza', 'Oregon') dispersed through *other* poems, an
enigma presents itself; and though there is no need to solve anything
(Muldoon is less of a puzzler than he can seem), it does make sense if the
origin of this rhyme-sequence (which like the theme behind the *Enigma
Variations* doesn't itself appear) is the word 'origin'.

So a daft rhyme-glut can lead us straight to the heart of the book, for
abandoned origins are what much of it is about. They provide the back-
ground to '7, Middagh Street' (the long poem we have come to expect
at the back of a Muldoon collection), an ambitious sequence of mono-
logues re-creating the experiences, fantasies and ironical meditations on
art of a group of famous floaters and migrants, who meet in a New York
house for dinner on Thanksgiving Day in 1940. It has seven parts, one
each in the 'voices' (scarcely different) of W. H. Auden, Gypsy Rose Lee,
Benjamin Britten, Chester Kallman, Salvador Dalí, Carson McCullers
and (a strong finish) Louis MacNiece, each at one or more removes from
original sonnet form. In the monologue given to Auden (rhyme: 'I would
gladly return to *Eden*'), America is figured as a 'great void' to be filled by
voluntary and involuntary exiles:

> we are all now dispossessed:
>
> prince, poet, construction worker,
> salesman, soda fountain jerker –
>
> all equally isolated.
> Each loads flour, sugar and salted
>
> beef into a covered wagon
> and strikes out for his Oregon …

The poem is more intriguing for the fact that Muldoon himself has recently swapped (as it were) his Irish origins for his Oregon, and gone to live in America for some time. Its airy meandering structure (the monologues are shackled together like trailers by little twists of familiar quotation) is part of its free-wheeling declaration of cross-cultural freedom. Those who prefer the supercharged local narrative of 'The More a Man Has …' (*Quoof*), and who doubt the marketability of the huge cultural cargo that Muldoon seems prepared to take on (a move that involves much abuse of ancestral Yeats and his stationary tower) will at least note how rigorously not only this departure but the procedures of the book as a whole are in keeping with a poetry that has deliberately uprooted itself ('Ireland has moved', notes one poem. 'They haven't').

This is especially true of the treatment of proper names – the most fluid part of the lexicon because they are attached to mortal cargoes. Nothing places us more reliably; yet in the second poem ('The Coney'), when a cartoon rabbit summons the narrator as 'Paddy Muldoon', we are already unsure whether this is a nickname for Paul, or whether the son is mistaken for his dying father Patrick. In '7, Middagh Street' identities are disrupted largely for fun. The emigrant hero swears he 'will not go back as *Auden*' but in his absence he has already begun to cease to be that: 'The Minister, in his reply, takes Wystan / for the tennis-star H. W. Austin … [nicknamed 'Bunny' – compare Auden as 'albino rabbit' – compare 'The Coney' – compare 'Soutine's *Hare* …' etc]'; Chester Kallman is invoked as W. H. A's sonnet-lover, his 'Mr. W. H.'; Benjamin Britten ('Britain' to Carson McCullers) is in danger of slipping (literally) into André Breton; and so on.

These dissolving names link with the first principle of Surrealism, given in the first line of Salvador (O'Daly) Dalí's part of the poem as 'This lobster is not a lobster.' In a remarkable elegy, 'The Soap-Pig', Muldoon's own frequently surreal or 'Ovidian' method and the death of his friend Michael Heffernan fix an imaginative charge behind a review of familiar ontological problems (set in the terms of packing and flitting that characterize the book):

> For how he would delib-
> erate on whether two six-foot boards
> scaled with ship's
> varnish and two tea-chests
> (another move) on which all this rests

is a table; or this merely a token
of some ur-chair,
or – being broken –
a chair at all …

Ergo we are only precautionary ourselves, and *Meeting the British* finds
new and memorable metaphors for the process of our dissolving and dis-
appearing. In 'The Coney', the fatal illness of the poet's father is charted
through the simultaneous diminution of a scythe and a whetstone wrapped
in his old cap:

This past winter he had been too ill
to work. The scythe would dull
so much more quickly in my hands
than his, and was so often honed,
that while the blade
grew less and less a blade
the whetstone had entirely disappeared
and a long-eared
coney was now curled inside the cap …

From the same mould as this whetstone comes the 'Soap-Pig' itself, a gift to
Muldoon from Michael Heffernan and now, on its donor's death, reduced
by use from pig to bar to sliver to lather. Such emblems are at the core of
the book's pathetic preoccupation with clothing. 'There's more enterprise
in walking not quite / naked', observes Gypsy Rose Lee, sticking tassels
on Yeats, and Muldoon offers this slippery justification for reticence; we
are only the thing we wear, and that briefly.

Meeting the British isn't an easy book, sitting too happily in its pain-
ful mode of *in transit* for the reader's comfort. In addition, one group of
poems takes Muldoon's associative method too far. In 'Crossing the Line',
'The Earthquake', and 'The Toe-Tag', bits and fragments are disjoined
by hefty asterisks, as though the writer has presented us with the raw
materials of a possible poem and left us to get on with it; trusting, with
the perplexed observer of 'Paul Klee, *They're biting*', that 'At any moment
all this should connect'; but these pieces lack the rhymes to make that
eerily happen; they're just baffling. It's no help either to feel that our
bafflement may be part of the author's calculation. Still, this mars only

a few pages in the book. At least half-a-dozen other poems, including 'The Coney', 'Gold', 'Brock' and 'Christo's', are unforgettable individual successes; and the whole – leaky, shifting, overladen – is a fascinating exercise in departure.

John Burnside

A Connoisseur of Rain

The Mercy Boys
Cape

'If you were lucky, you got to live a normal life, with somebody you loved, and work to do, and children to bring up. If you weren't, you were on your own ... You had to fill the spaces in your story, any way you knew how.' Each of the four 'boys' in John Burnside's second novel – four men from Dundee in their early forties – has arrived by his own loveless route at the death-in-life which is to spend every waking hour in the pub called the Mercy. While a scheme of four men in a pub invites comparison with forerunners such as Graham Swift's *Last Orders* (1996), and while Burnside's Dundee drinkers must bring to mind the alcoholic Glaswegians of James Kelman, the overall effect of *The Mercy Boys* is one of powerful individuality. Burnside's method as a novelist is grounded in his outstanding success as a poet. The narrative incorporates scores of the street-corner or riverside epiphanies which are the staple of his tender, traumatic poems; and where these occur, their fictional setting recedes from view. One character asks of the afterlife:

> Would there be rain, or first snow, or that moment when you came home from the baths and sat down at the table, and your mum dished you up leek and potato soup, and asked you how hungry you were?

Whoever's 'mum' is being summoned up here, the poignant relish of things past, the knack of giving a sacred sheen to the mundane, are borrowed from Burnside's own intense and delicate psyche; and the fact that he is of an age with his characters gives their stories the sharp suggestion of suffering transposed. The 'boys' have failed to find or make society, of which the pub is a poisonous mockery. The narrative visits each of them by turns in his isolation, and searches for the moment – the sight, in one case, of a first girlfriend being fucked in the bathroom by her uncle – that has doomed him to this condition.

The novel begins and ends in the mind of Alan, the soul of the piece, a dreamer, a connoisseur of rain and cloudscapes ('he could see the sky, pale and blue-grey, with streaks of ivory in places, like the sky in a Chinese painting, half-present, half-erased'); he lives alone, in phlegmatic contemplation of his hangovers, until he is shaken to discover his desire for Jennifer, a twelve-year-old who haunts his tenement building. Of the supporting 'boys', the structure pairs Alan with the hardest drinker, Rob, who has grown sick in body and mind. Scorned (as he sees it) by his wife and maddened by the barking of a neighbour's dogs, Rob's explosion into violence one weekend is the centrepiece of the novel. On the Saturday, he attacks a tramp and goes with a sorry, stoned prostitute; on Sunday, he gets home to find his wife's cousin at the table where his dinner should be. The pages which follow, rendering the boiling-up of a manic rage, its power and unreason, are brilliantly done:

> Rob couldn't believe it. It was the middle of a Sunday afternoon, he was hungry, still dirty from having stayed up drinking and fucking half the night, and here he was, standing above the telly, hanging up a picture of some kittens. The other boys were probably down at the Mercy, on their third or fourth drink, wondering where he was. He couldn't believe it. He just couldn't believe it.

As the plaster crumbles under the nail he is trying to fix to the wall, a jealous thought burns through him, and he is suddenly a murderer. 'It's amazing how things happen', Rob observes as he flees Dundee; and with the rule of limbo lifted, the boys are suddenly exposed to a glut of event. One is implausibly butchered by a religious cult; the same day, another finds his wife, who has long been dead to the world, to be dead indeed; Rob kills again (another tramp). The mode switches from alcoholic realism to allegory. By the end, Alan, touched with madness, is wading ecstatically into the waters of a sea loch, a suicide which is also a mystical arrival: 'he knew exactly where he was going'. This seems fantastic and willed. The two parts of this novel suggest that Burnside is a better writer, an extraordinarily good one, when he shuts out angel voices and looks squarely on the drizzle of men's days.

Michael Hofmann

No Pop, Still Fizzy

Corona, Corona
Faber and Faber

The death of the German writer Gert Hofmann this summer may seem to have deprived contemporary English poetry of one of its most productive enmities. The second half of his son Michael's brilliant collection of poems *Acrimony* (1986), dedicated 'For my Father and Mother', consisted solely of poems of hate for the incommunicative monster with 'anal pleats' beneath his eyes – an honest, vulnerable, unmalicious hatred, laid out with skewering precision. But the complete success of this sequence exhausted its source, and the long interval between *Acrimony* and its successor suggests that Michael Hofmann has already had to retrain himself to raise new poems without the presiding ogre of the old.

Corona, Corona is dedicated 'For my kids', but we don't see much of them; Hofmann will have found that better feelings don't necessarily make better poems. 'From A to B and Back Again' is a maternity hospital poem made from a typically clinical correspondence – between the scars on his wife after childbirth and the tracks on the underground line by which he travels to visit her; and the loyal address to 'my brave love' falls awkwardly among its scalpelwork. The small core of autobiographical poems here are buttressed on either side by ten pieces on other lives (though the choice of subjects – Marvin Gaye, slain by his father, and the father-slayer Richard Dadd – are consistent with the old acrimony), and by a lighter series based on the poet's travels in Mexico – a holiday from, or at least a displacement of, his essential concerns. The book as a whole may therefore look slight by comparison with its awful predecessor. Yet if the family stimulus is no longer such an unusually fruitful one, Hofmann is far too good a poet for us to be disappointed for long in any book of his.

There is, after all, the texture of the writing itself. Hofmann's line has been called prosaic. But while the rhythms are certainly depressurized, every word feels artfully chosen and placed, and the vocabulary is phenomenally rich. The syntax crumbles frequently into lists of nouns, into one-line inventories of landscapes or interiors: 'The soil was cedar chips, sprinkler heads and ants' (of poolside Florida); 'long panoptical / galleries, spider-plants, whippets and double-gaslights' (Bethlem Hospital); 'Dry air, manila light, cardboard and silence' (aboard the 'brick ship' of Victorian science). Such lines give their poems a dense physical grounding, but they are also capable of diseased lexical harmonies akin to rhyme: 'all pocked, opaque, Venetian, venereal'; 'ancillary, bacillary blocks of anthrax'; 'pruned willow, prunes and the WI'.

There is nothing prosaic, either, about an imagination whose way of thinking in shapes often brings geometry to mind: not just in incidental diagrams, like those of Hart Crane (the homosexual poet who drowned himself) as 'a power vacuum ringed with lifeboats', or 'standing on Brooklyn Bridge / with the US Navy steaming between his legs', but in the materials and organization of whole poems. 'Wheels' is a delightful understated meditation on time, working through television's round of ball-games and car-chases:

> the wheels turn very slowly backward,
> to convince the viewer that, far from wasting time,
> he's recreating himself

– to end in another choice scrapheap of nouns, of broken tellies, dumped cars and people whose wheels have come off: 'wheelchair hulls, rhombuses, stalled quartz'. If Hofmann has been afraid of stalling, there is enough evidence in *Corona, Corona* of tentative forward motion. It is present in the almost pretty closing quatrain of 'Shivery Stomp' (which pursues Malcolm Lowry – another lost father-figure – through a links landscape), the last two words of which suggest the territory of lesser trauma that his poems are now free to play in:

> The field, so comprehensively settled with starlings,
> the farmer might have sown them there, starling
> seeds, something perhaps like the frozen dew
> I chip ahead of me in the light rough.

Irvine Welsh

In a Chemical World

Ecstasy
Cape

At the close of *Trainspotting*, Irvine Welsh's prodigious first novel, the junkie Mark Renton, having stolen his pals' drug loot, is compelled to flee to a new beginning: 'He could now never go back to Leith, to Edinburgh, even to Scotland, ever again … The thought both terrified and excited him …' *Trainspotting*'s phenomenal success placed its author in a similar dilemma. He had found a winning fictional formula in the torrential, ribald expression of his own East Coast subculture; but in so doing had already used up the choicest parts of his experience. His writing had to move on or perish in repetition. The second novel, *Marabou Stork Nightmares*, with its mixed-in African settings, literally unconscious narrator and typographical experiments, may have striven a bit too ambitiously to be different. *Ecstasy*, on the other hand – his fourth book, counting the stories of *The Acid House*, in three years – seems to have been tossed together in a hurry and in ill humour. The new book consists of three pieces, each the length of a novella, each figured half-ironically as some sort of 'romance'.

The first, titled 'Lorraine Goes to Livingston', is a puerile and pointless satire on what it fancies to be London life. It concerns Rebecca Navarro, a predictably fat, cloying, middle-class writer of more traditional romances, who is made to suffer a stroke; in hospital, she makes improbable best friends with a young nurse down from Welsh's territory. Together they uncover her husband's interest in pornography and prostitutes, and their revenge is to turn her work-in-progress into a saga of bestiality – the joke being that while this should appeal to her husband's tastes, it will be rejected by the publisher and topple him into penury. The pantomime subplot introduces the necrophiliac host of a television show which 'sorts' treats for kids, who makes large donations to the hospital trust in exchange for access to its dead bodies. When the ruined husband is knocked down and killed by a car, a further indignity therefore awaits him. The silliness of the conception is matched by the sloppiness of the execution. A second nurse, Yvonne, is seen 'greedily devouring the last two pages' of one of Mrs Navarro's novels; some hours later, interrupted while 'still engrossed' in it, she is seen 'earmarking a page'. This same nurse is chatted up at a club by a man, of whom it is pointedly said that 'He didn't know her name, all he knew of her was that she was Lorraine's friend', with the line 'Yvonne, innit?' This failure to follow the simplest of his own narrative instructions ties in with Welsh's declared loathing of work, something that he casually transmits to NHS nursing staff 'looking after decaying, incontinent people who had degenerated into sagging, wheezing, brittle, twisted parodies of themselves' – not the only point in the book where an ugly, antisocial fit convulses whatever consciousness the narrative happens to be passing through.

The horrors of the second tale, 'Fortune's Always Hiding', are spread through several countries but laid on with inexhaustible relish. It charts the revenge of a young woman, born with no arms, on the company which sold her mother an untested drug. First, in league with a similarly handicapped German terrorist, she kidnaps and dismembers the baby son of the Bavarian manufacturer; then, with a psychopathic West Ham fan – brought in to add his own weight of rapes, assaults etc – she chain-saws off the arms of the drug's British distributor. There are sporadic attempts, in these two stories, to reproduce Welsh's great gift for his own vernacular in other idioms: a Somerset drawl, a page of Brummie, the peculiar hybrid of a Cockney doing 'a Jock accent'. The result is to litter the stage with dummies. The reader of *Trainspotting* was drawn to identify with even the most depraved of its characters; but none of these tales' token beings engages the sympathies for as much as a moment. The plots masquerade as dramas of revenge, but the satisfaction is all Welsh's, working up hatred and devising gruesome punishments for characters he has hardly bothered to animate or differentiate. The Edinburgh vernacular itself is restored for the final tale, 'The Undefeated', as long as the narration is in the hands of Lloyd from Leith. He would have been at home in *Trainspotting*, and one scene of a drinking session in a bowls club has the boisterous comic momentum of the best of that book. But this being by contrivance a 'romance', Lloyd alternates with Heather, a bored housewife from Dunfermline, whose inner life, conveyed in standard English, is by comparison a short-winded, shrunken thing, a trickling complaint against her husband's neglect of foreplay. Their integration in a single tale, and their union at the end of it, is achieved only by demand of the structure – and by E.

If *Ecstasy* has anything positive to propose, it is about the redemptive effects of the eponymous drug. Lloyd and Heather come together when they are both 'E'd up' in a club, a scene duplicated exactly between protagonists in each of the otherwise disparate tales. Clubbing and drug-taking have a political dimension for Welsh:

> you had to celebrate the joy of life in the face of all those grey forces and dead spirits who controlled everything, who fucked with *your* head (my italics) and livelihood anyway, if you weren't one of them. You had to let them know … you were still alive.

We might object that these fine words are voiced by a character who has just pocketed a hefty bribe from a necrophiliac; but we are to understand that daily identity, one's role in the world 'of trivial, banal oppressions' is left behind at the doors of the club: 'We shared an insight and intimacy that nobody who hadn't done this in this environment could ever know about'; 'What you learn when people open up like this is that we are all' – romantic novelists, nurses, handicapped murderers, queer-bashers – 'basically the same.' And indeed, when their pills 'kick in', the chemical feelings and chemical speech of all Welsh's instant heroes and heroines are shown to be interchangeable. This sameness is a crippling assumption for any novelist, in particular one in search of diversification, to take on; yet Welsh seems increasingly prepared to embrace it. 'I just wanted tae blaw ma muck in (Nicole) Fenwick, then split from the whole depressing scene' (Roy Strang in *Marabou Stork Nightmares*); 'I just wanted to blow my fucking load and get on out of there' (Dave in 'Fortune's Always Hiding'); 'all ah wanted tae dee was tae blaw ma muck and git the fuck oot ay thair' (Nukes in 'The Undefeated'); 'that selfish bastard Lloyd did fuck all except blow his load and roll over' (Heather in 'The Undefeated'). Until Irvine Welsh can extricate himself from this community, and apply himself more generously to the task, his reader will feel at once put upon and excluded.

Douglas Galbraith

Taking Tincture with 'Claret Colquhoun'

The Rising Sun
Picador

The old name for the Isthmus of Panama, the narrow waist of what Douglas Galbraith calls 'the great hourglass of the Americas', is most famously preserved in John Keats's sonnet 'On First Looking Into Chapman's Homer', where 'stout Cortez' and his fellow conquistadors glimpse the Pacific Ocean from their awed vantage 'upon a peak in Darien'. In the black book of Scottish history, however, the name of Darien has more grievous and embarrassing associations, which Galbraith takes as the matter of his massive and thoroughly impressive first novel, *The Rising Sun*.

In 1697, the Company of Scotland Trading to Africa was founded and floated in imitation of the English trading companies of the day. Scots great and small flocked to subscribe. The following year, a convoy of five ships, carrying around 1,100 volunteers, set out from Leith to establish a Scottish colony ('Caledonia') in the virgin territory of Darien and, by forcing an overland route through the jungle from ocean to ocean, to clear a dizzying prospect of commercial fortunes for Scottish investors. Instead, the destruction of the enterprise – by in-fighting, disease, the machinations of the superpowers and the unbelievable malice of the elements – bankrupted the nation and so brought on the indignity of takeover by England in the Act of Union (1707). Galbraith's fictional recreation of the Darien catastrophe is presented through the chronicle, composed piecemeal like a diary, of Roderick Mackenzie, the young superintendent of cargoes on the expedition's flagship, the Rising Sun. A spirited, even flamboyant narrator ('the Herodotus of our comic tragedy', as he styles himself), Mackenzie is, by nature, at once cunning and naive, which makes his insight on the obscure rivalries at work in the settlement both rewardingly observant and intriguingly incomplete. Part of Mackenzie's journal is given over to an account of his own earlier history in Edinburgh, before he begged and conned his way into the company and aboard ship. His first position is as bookkeeper to the wine merchant 'Claret' Colquhoun, a red-faced volcano of self-righteousness, the best of a gallery of vividly realized male characters (the women are a sorry little group of dumb prostitutes and pinched wives). Like the rest of 1690s Edinburgh, Colquhoun speaks recent if not quite modern colloquial English ('Damn them all, damn that damned Dutchman!'). This may be strictly inaccurate, but it is also fresh and apt in its effect, not least because it protects Galbraith's city from the echoes of other historical Edinburghs – Scott's, Hogg's, Stevenson's. In other matters of material authenticity, though, Galbraith's reconstruction is as convincing as any of these.

Brought up in Scotland, Galbraith was a doctoral student in medieval history at Cambridge and it is his attraction to lost facts – menus, business practice, engineering, medicines, ways of thinking – that give his novel its depth of authority. An allusion, say, to the sequence of stages on the Bristol-to-London coach may be incidental, but the great stacks of documentary detail to which it contributes buttress the narrative and our belief in it. And none, or very little, of this appears as unprocessed research, for, besides being a responsible historian, Galbraith is a powerfully imaginative storyteller and a stylish writer. *The Rising Sun* is distinguished by its supple and characterful prose, full of lively figures: to quote just one of a thousand pleasing examples: 'I had a vision of myself with one foot on the Company and one on Colquhoun. They drifted apart like a boat from the quay with cold water threatening beneath.' And the rhythm of the collapse in Darien ('where the powers of corruption are so fantastically accelerated'), the satisfying crescendo of appalling incident, is masterfully controlled. *The Rising Sun* isn't quite perfect. The historian gets the better of the novelist when he extends the tale beyond its natural scope to encompass the affray about the Union. All but dead when he returns from Darien, Mackenzie has to kick his heels for nine years and sixty pages to witness it. And in their heyday, adventures in far-off lands would be fronted with maps: one here of 'Caledonia' would help us to enjoy detailing such as that of 'a fortified ditch across the narrow neck of the peninsula where it joins the mainland'.

But we finish the book with strong feelings of gratitude for the amount and variety of fictional entertainment it has provided. Its publication propels Douglas Galbraith to a place among the very best of our historical novelists.

'Auld Acquaintances'

More to a Language than Fine Literature

A Dictionary of Scottish Quotations
Edited by Angela Cran and James Robertson, Mainstream

It must be a healthy nationalism that can produce a volume as big-hearted as Angela Cran and James Robertson's *A Dictionary of Scottish Quotations*: for in all their other attachments, the compilers appear scrupulously correct. A number of writers are enlisted more for what they represent than what they said: so we have 'miller-poets' and 'miner-poets' as distinct from 'poets'; there is a measure of tokenism (Graham Woolaston: 'Scotland must be free, and lesbians and gays must be free within it'); and there is, as the introduction promises, a high proportion of women's voices, especially those speaking of women's rights. Hence the early nineteenth-century campaigner Fanny Wright, though all her work was done in America, has more space than either Robert Henryson or James Boswell. Yet though some of the more politic choices lack the necessary distinctness of thought or expression, they do not subtract from the big blocks of Burns, Scott and Stevenson; rather they enlarge the image of a national forum in which, as the editors might wish, there seems to be room for everyone to have their say.

Generous annotation sets intriguing but obscure quotations in some highly colourful contexts. Take the enigmatic 'I am he who will bell the cat', attributed to Archibald Douglas, 5th Earl of Angus, known as 'Bell the Cat', which Cran and Robertson illuminate: 'The story is that a faction of the nobility gathered to discuss how to counter the power of Robert Cochrane, Earl of Mar and favourite of James III. Lord Gray recounted the fable of the mice who wished to hang a bell round the neck of the cat to warn them of its approach: all were agreed on the plan, but none would volunteer to put it into effect. At this point, Douglas made his famous remark. Shortly afterwards, Cochrane and his associates arrived at Lauder, were seized and hanged over the bridge "there". The single monosyllabic phrase encapsulates the romantic savagery of late medieval Scotland: the same volatile culture that produced verse, in the Scots of William Dunbar, as sophisticated as any in Renaissance Europe.

Soon after Dunbar, the Reformation did for Lowland Scots as a literary language; just as the failed Jacobite enterprise did for the Gaelic culture of the Highlands. The most potent sentence in Scottish history, though it is not recorded here, is the one sent by Bonnie Prince Charlie to his forces at Ruthven, licking their wounds after Culloden, but mustering for more – 'Let everyone seek his own safety the best way he can' – enacting the dispersal of the cause and the splintering of the Highland community. Some of the tricks played by the book's alphabetical organization suggest that the Scots' historic fighting qualities have been sublimated in violent drinking, that fealty to the clan has evolved into allegiance to the football club, whose managers sometimes seem like beleaguered elective chieftains. Wallace Mercer's pathetic leave-taking of Heart of Midlothian – 'When we came to the end of the agenda and I handed them the letter saying I was going, there were tears in my eyes' – can only have been included for its echoes of other lost leaders, of more truly grievous departures. But from the quote-collector's angle the principal 'bewteis of the fute-ball', as the Maitland manuscript (1582) calls them, are comic: the Partick Thistle manager John Lambie's 'Brilliant. Tell him he's Pele' – 'on being informed that one of his strikers, Colin McGlashan, had suffered a head injury and could not remember who he was' – is typical of the bright cynicism of West-coast humour.

Indicative of the book's sociological bias, amid scores of football references there is only one rugby-related quote: nothing of Bill McLaren, though his 'Turnbull smashing on!' is surely common parlance, let alone 'They'll be celebrating in the streets of Kelso tonight'; while the baleful Murrayfield anthem 'Flower of Scotland' has been docked one of its two stanzas. From the world snooker champion Stephen Hendry we get the wonderfully boring 'As long as I still get the buzz from playing the big events, I'll carry on' – an anti-quotation, surely. Aside from arguments over the Union, the most significant of the dialogues going on in the *Dictionary* is that between two tongues, Scots dialect and standard English (with respect to Gaelic, whose small literature is inventively represented). As late as 1672, Scots, though seldom written, was still competitive in public life; the Lord Advocate George Mackenzie thought it the most suitable idiom for the law courts: 'Our pronunciation is like ourselves, fiery, abrupt, sprightly and bold.' Burns was to follow, but the fissure in his own works between Scots and English anticipates the limitations of the Scots revival in literature.

Edwin Muir observed in 1936, ignoring Hugh MacDiarmid, that 'Scots has survived to our time as a language for simple poetry and the simpler kind of short story ... all its other uses have lapsed, and it expresses therefore only a fragment of the Scottish mind ... Scotsmen feel in one language and think in another.' Muir is sadly borne out in the *Dictionary* by the reams of studied quaintness, of bonny, bonny lassies, that the compilers have had to include from the later nineteenth century: a national self-parody that culminates in the cult of Harry Lauder. But there is more to a language than fine literature, and the dialect does its work in other ways. For instance, its habit of adding a 'y' sound to nouns (as in sweetie) softens and diminishes the material world, making hard things silly and dear things more dear. Intrinsically sentimental, it helps the Scotsman indulge his primary impulse, his love of Scotland.

No country can have been celebrated so generally and intensely, so weepily and alcoholically, by its inhabitants as Scotland is in these pages; so Stevenson's quiet claim that 'the happiest lot on earth is to be born a Scotsman' is unassailable. She is, you have to admit, the greatest country in the world. She even makes a flower-worshipping fool out of an intellectual firebrand like Hugh MacDiarmid (writing in English, so he must have thought it as well as felt it):

> The rose of all the world is not for me.
> I want for my part
> Only the little white rose of Scotland
> That smells sharp and sweet – and breaks the heart.

'I Belong To Glasgow'

From Workshop to Cancer to Human

Growing Up in the West
Edited by Liam McIlvanney, Canongate

There is a locally provocative passage in Book Two of Alasdair Gray's novel *Lanark: A Life in Four Books* (1981), where the art student Duncan Thaw suggests that 'Imaginatively, Glasgow exists as a music-hall song and a few bad novels'. The allusions are to the alcoholic anthem 'I Belong to Glasgow' and to novels like the best-selling shocker *No Mean City* (1935) by McArthur and Long, in which the excitable Johnnie Stark led his razor gang out of the Gorbals and made that district lastingly synonymous with poverty, stupidity and violence. For Liam McIlvanney, who has edited *Growing Up in the West*, a retrieval of four neglected Bildungsroman set in the Glasgow region, *Lanark* is itself 'the greatest of all Glasgow novels' – his own volume happens to mirror its four-book structure, and he justifies one of his choices partly by its demonstrable influence on Gray's masterpiece – but he is still nettled by what appears to be its casual dismissal of a considerable tradition. (As usual Gray is being mischievous: *Lanark*'s 'Index of Plagiarisms' shows him to have read, absorbed, and in some cases directly reproduced the text of half-a-dozen of its predecessors in the field. In a later novel, *Something Leather*, Gray has a cultural executive from London observe: 'Some novels by Glasgow writas have had rave reviews in the *Times Lit. Sup.*, but I'm afraid they leave me cold. Half seem to be written in phonetic Scotch about people with names like Auld Shug'.) A first volume of McIlvanney's project – which admits the Ayrshire coalfields and lower Clydeside into its province – might have included George Douglas Brown's *The House with the Green Shutters*

(1901), George Blake's *Shipbuilders* (1935), Edward Gaitens's *Dance of the Apprentices* (1948) and Archie Hind's *The Dear Green Place* (1966); a third might sample the work of Gray's contemporaries, James Kelman, Alan Spence, Jeff Torrington, A. L. Kennedy and Andrew O'Hagan.

In fact, no other modern British city has had so much of a presence in its own literature. Glasgow novels are nearly always about Glasgow, in a way that you could not say Mary Barton was about Manchester. That is because Glasgow, which once built more ships than Germany and the United States put together, the 'Workshop of the World' then the 'Cancer of Empire', was the industrial city on an unprecedented scale, admitting comparison, if at all, with other urban freaks such as Calcutta, or with its own mythic progeny like *Lanark*'s 'Unthank'. It exceeded the darkest imaginings, anyway, of Friedrich Engels, himself raised in Manchester, before he saw it in 1888 at the age of sixty-eight: 'I did not believe, until I visited the wynds of Glasgow, that so large an amount of filth, crime, misery and disease existed in one spot in any civilized country'. To the fourteen-year-old Edwin Muir, arriving from Orkney to live there, it was, without metaphor or fear of exaggeration, 'Hell'. He had already raged at the blight of Glasgow in *Scottish Journey* (1935); he would tell of his family's dreadful misfortunes there in the early chapters published separately in 1940 as *The Story and the Fable of his Autobiography*; and the Hell of his pre-modern, allegorical verse is built on the Clyde. But it was in the third of his largely forgotten novels, *Poor Tom* (1932), that Muir first wrote about his adopted home. The narrative tells of Tom and 'Mansie', two brothers from Orkney who have come to Glasgow around 1910 after the death of their father. In the opening paragraph, Tom (an engineer, moody, tending to drink) glimpses his ex-girlfriend coming out of the park arm-in-arm with Mansie (a clerk and a prig). The brothers' subsequent estrangement deepens until the day Tom, the worse for whisky, falls from a tram and knocks himself out. Headaches follow; a brain tumour is diagnosed; Tom declines, and dies in the closing chapter. Readers of the *Autobiography* will recognize Tom's story as that of Muir's older brother Johnnie: Mansie is modelled on the eldest, Jimmie, with bits of the more sensitive Edwin (such as his weird dreams of horses) awkwardly imported. The fiction and the memoir are otherwise parallel in observation and detail: like the young Muir, Mansie passes by the sunken slums of Eglinton Street on his way to work; in each book, a 'head clerk' asks of such places, 'And what about the poor, bloody little children?'; and so on.

The novel is also, though short, unusually repetitive within itself sometimes in ways that point to other weaknesses. Five times in the space of 700 words Mansie is said to be 'quite incapable' of 'understanding' or 'grasping' what we are told is going on in his own mind. The narrative is interspersed with chapters of almost perversely generalized reflections, about 'a young man' who does this or suffers that. But while Muir's writing may seem to grind at us with the conviction of his own trauma, it has a sure and deep instinct – while resisting the horror stories that have elsewhere been used to enhance Glasgow's imaginative appeal – for the meaningful image: one noseless beggar at Eglinton Toll; Tom's naked iron bedstead. More centrally, the stages of Tom's sickness – the deceptive chubbiness of his face on his first release from hospital, his concentration on a ticking inside his head, the unruly kicking of his left leg as he walks – are realized with memorable precision. In his poem 'Milton', the worst torment Muir can devise for a blind poet is the din of Argyle Street at closing time, 'the steely clamour known too well / on Saturday nights in every street in Hell', a nightmare distortion of Burns's bucolic 'Cotter's Saturday Night'. It is a phrase from the latter poem – 'From scenes like these, old Scotia's grandeur springs / That makes her lov'd at home, rever'd abroad' – that supplies the parodic title for Gordon M. Williams's novel of 1968, *From Scenes Like These*, the other star item in this valuable collection. It treats the coming of age in the early 1950s of Dunky Logan, who has left school at fifteen to work on a dwindling farm on the outskirts of an imaginary industrial town (the model is Kilmarnock) in North Ayrshire. Dunky shows signs of independent thinking: a Protestant, he admires the style of the Celtic players; but experience presses it out of him. Caught between the aspirations of his family ('"We're middle-class," his mother said. "D'you want some more mince?"'), his fading dream of escape to Canada, and his workmates' habitual disparagement of aspiration ('Who's fuck'n skillt aboot here, eh?'), he settles into a confused desire 'to be like everyone else', which the novel, distinguished by its sympathetic presentation of the urge to violence, punishingly grants him. In one of the most authentic football games in fiction, Dunky charges an opponent with such animal malice that his own front teeth are knocked out and his nose broken. Soon afterwards he chucks playing, and as the intelligence drains from the narrative he drinks his way into the crowd. Williams – whose next novel was made into Sam Peckinpah's *Straw Dogs* – leaves him with his hapless peers on the terraces at Ibrox, roaring 'Kill they Fenian bastards'.

   Not surprisingly, a number of themes and motifs and types recur
in novels about the Glasgow experience: the ticket to New Zealand, the
slaughtered Clydesdale, socialist politics, the works hooter, the view from
the Necropolis, the insipid schoolmaster, the paralysed father; so that
their narratives can begin to resemble separate accounts of a shared mili-
tary campaign. Yet the two other fictions salvaged by *Growing Up in the
West* are much more than makeweights. *Fernie Brae*, the only novel by
J. F. Hendry, is the most clearly autobiographical book of the group, and
it unfolds with episodic leisure, setting its own resilient and humorous
character against 'the mechanical cackle called civilization' that threatens
to overwhelm it. David Macrae grows up in the real thick of things, on a
ridge in Springburn, surrounded on two sides by locomotive works and
on a third by Stobhill Cemetery. Like his creator, who became a Professor
at the University of Ontario, David does well enough to escape the city by
boat, along 'the river that ends in America'. More technically interesting,
though less evenly successful, is *Apprentice* (1983), the first in a trilogy of
novels by the playwright Tom Gallacher. The narrator is a sixteen-year-
old from a Sussex public school, Billy Thompson, who has come up in
the 1950s to serve his apprenticeship in marine engineering at a yard at
Greenock, as his 'successful' father had done before him. His experiences
there appear to him as 'a continuous roll of intermingled lives', and he has
sorted these for the telling into five loosely connected tales or character
studies. (Gallacher's method resembles that of Gaitens and Spence before
him, he also anticipates the classically Glaswegian feel of John MacGill's
That Rubens Guy, 1992, another recreation of Glasgow childhood that has
missed its due, where each of the 'houses' in a single tenement building
has its 'turn'.) *Apprentice* is also notable for its introduction of demoli-
tion, which has by now displaced the tenement at the architectural heart
of Glasgow fiction (as in Jeff Torrington's *Swing, Hammer, Swing*). At the
end of his five years, we understand, Billy becomes an 'Owner's Man', and
states again the insecurity of the artist approaching the Glasgow phenom-
enon even from within: the feeling that 'after all, I was really a dilettante
worker': 'And perhaps, a dilettante human being'.

DIGRESSIONS

Bottle Fatigue

To the 'Widget'

Drink: A Social History
Andrew Barr, Bantam

Alcohol makes history: empires have risen and fallen on its effects. Lloyd George, an abstainer, judged 'drink' to be a deadlier enemy to Britain than Germany, and that was in 1915. It had earlier threatened to obliterate the nation without the help of foreign arms. Henry Fielding, writing in 1751, tells of what 'that poison called gin' had done to London, in terms appropriate to the Great Plague of the century before: 'A new kind of drunkenness, unknown to our ancestors, is lately sprung upon us, which, if not put a stop to, will infallibly destroy a great part of the people of the metropolis.' At other times, alcohol has worked as an agent of the ruling class to keep the people in their place. According to Arthur Mee, a teetotal activist, it was Russia's prohibition of vodka in 1912 that made possible the revolution there: 'It was stopping drink that made 170 million people free.' These snippets from Andrew Barr's *Drink* address the same big subject: one in which lemonade is not a factor. Yet the book sets out to deal not only with alcoholic drinks, but also with mineral and tap waters, coffee, tea and milk. The histories of intoxication and refreshment are thus poured promiscuously together; inevitably, like oil and water, they separate, and several kinds of book, none complete, seem to contend.

The inclusion of non-alcoholic drinks may dilute the interest, because decaffeinated coffee, for instance, makes nothing happen (unless you drink 20 million cups a day, the fatal dose, apparently). It also dauntingly broadens the scope. Barr, more archivist than author, has unearthed a mass of interesting facts (his bibliography is prodigious); but his narrative is a blur of deferred connections ('This will be dealt with in chapter seven') and repetitions; the same information about the milk bars of the 1930s, for instance, is given in three different places. There is no binding argument, only flashes of opinion. But approached as the dispersed raw materials of an encyclopaedia, there is much in *Drink* that is instructive, amusing or provocative.

Barr is more interested in manufacture than consumption. There is all the technical information you could wish for: from the heretical practices of New World winemakers to the 'widget' that makes canned beer behave like draught. But, for a 'social history', the voice of the drinker is not much in evidence. It is intriguing that the pub 'bar' evolved to reflect the industrialization of the workforce: men took their stations at the counter for the more efficient achievement of drunkenness and to maximize the landlord's profits. But the lowlier consumer is not always as dumbly mechanical as Barr seems to assume: his opposition of today's 'lager drinkers' and 'bitter drinkers' takes no account of the fluid millions who prefer the cold, fizzy, refreshing, tasteless drink in summer and the warm, flat, sustaining, flavoursome one in winter. Still 'though it is not that kind of book' drink has its share of horror stories, of legendary performances, of incredible amounts.

In his memoirs, the old Welsh soldier Rees Howell Gronow, a veteran of the Battle of Waterloo, recalled that it had been standard practice for gentlemen to drink two or three bottles of port after dinner, that some men regularly drank four or five bottles, and that three lords of the realm, Lords Panmure, Dufferin and Blayney, 'wonderful to relate, were six-bottle men'. (Panmure, incidentally, lived past 80.) 'Wonder' in these matters is always relative. Benjamin Franklin could hardly believe what his companion at an English printing press put away: six pints of beer in the course of a day between breakfast and bed. But if, as we are told elsewhere, the body can break down one 'unit' of alcohol in about an hour, this is the equivalent, over a 12-hour day, of drinking nothing. Which, as recent research has established, was too little to be good for him. Barr makes pleasant fun of the notion of 'safe limits', mocking the British Medical Association's puny 1987 allowance of 21 units per week for men: a figure which, as an author of the report has admitted, was 'pulled out of the air'. Now we are told that 25–35 units per week 'that is, most of a bottle of wine per day' is healthier than no booze at all.

We might have worked that out for ourselves; as did the directors of the life insurance company which, in 1840, charged abstainers more. Medical science may soon have to swallow again, in Andrew Barr's words, 'the obvious fact that the ingestion of moderate quantities of alcohol improves the health of their patients for the simple reason that it gives them pleasure'.

In Praise of Ugly Bugs

Evolutionary Favour

The Beauty of the Beastly; Woman: An Intimate Geography
Natalie Angier, Little, Brown; Viking

Natalie Angier, a Pulitzer prizewinner though still only in her mid-thirties, is the sort of science writer who makes new nonsense of the old division between scientific inquiry and the humanities. The obscurer rituals and biological dances of the living world move her like art she writes of a 'lovely' series of experiments examining 'the impact of a male's coloration on female choice among the three-spined stickleback' and conveys the wonder of such things in prose of great charm and unpretentious artistry. The title of her second book of essays, originally written for the *New York Times* but smartened up for this occasion, proclaims a lighthearted 'mission' to redeem, by closer study, the reputation of organisms generally found repugnant: cockroaches, scorpions, worms, dung beetles, hyenas. (Only the malevolent aye-aye of Madagascar, the most endangered and least endearing primate in the world, with its long middle finger pointing like a curse, can teach us nothing but to dislike it.) Conversely, as she promises in her introduction, she exposes the baser qualities of her favourite species: 'Dolphins can behave like sailors at Tailhook; orchids advertise faux merchandise; the legendary workers of the field' the birds, the bees, the beavers 'spend more time at leisure than the average European.' As this suggests, a prime delight of Angier's writing is the colourful sort of human correspondence she finds for her creatures' behaviour even when it is the animal's absolute difference that is being expressed: 'Who but a snake could say, Look, Ma, no hands; look, Ma, no feet; look, Ma, no teeth, and say it with such feeling?' The richest field for such appropriation is sex and courtship.

The virilized genitalia of the female spotted hyena, 'an enlarged clitoris that resembles a penis and fused, protuberant vaginal labia that look like a plump pair of testicles,' are sportingly figured as her 'costume jewels'; at times the whole ark is comically saddled with the yearnings and neuroses of thirty-something New York. At the end of an essay on barn swallows, Angier has the writer's nerve to lapse out of science and back to the singles' bar: 'A female may pair up with an especially loud male ... just because he is the only one she hears or because he's the only one she's met who isn't gay, married or unemployed.' It has been said that to anthropomorphize the rest of creation is as absurd as making God in our own image: Angier has her own spin on this in an essay on cockroaches, warning us to consider, when praying for pesticides, 'whether the divinity we're beseeching has a wise old human face and a long white beard, or whether its head is tucked under and pointing towards the rear.' But the philosophical limitations of seeing things as us are unlikely to concern the general reader, especially when it renders so beautifully even the faceless factory work of molecular biology:

> A small chaperone called hsp70 drifts over and grips certain tender areas of the polypeptide ... Hundreds if not thousands of times each hour, they are alchemists, spinning dull chemical straw into the splash of protein gold.

There is much more anyway to this wonderful little book than its beastly vignettes. One fascinating piece examines how art criticism has been (generally) mucked about by retrospective diagnoses of eye disease in painters; another argues (with due compassion) that manic depression may be a mark of evolutionary favour. There is no piece among the 41 that does not deliver something memorable: whether a startling fact (half of all humans who ever lived have died of malaria); or a brilliant turn of phrase (since bees know the harder they work, the sooner they die, 'one can sympathize with a bee's desire to take a moment to stop and not sniff at the flowers'). Or take the choice bits of trivia: 'There are mites that can survive only in the rectum of a giant tortoise' (not much of a life, you'd think, though our own future king has aspired to something similar). And the variety of unexpected notes she finds to close her essays 'the broad joke, the warming pun, the flicker of poetry, the subtle diminuendo, the mortal full stop' puts you in mind of the shifts of another scientist and essayist, Francis Bacon, for whom, as it is for

Natalie Angier four centuries later, good writing was the best vehicle for all forms of knowledge.

In *Woman: An Intimate Geography*, Angier charts the marvels and miseries of half of our own species: the vastly more interesting half, in biological but also in poetical terms. The penis, for instance, wouldn't give her much to play with, metaphorically: 'a hose is a hose is a hose'. But the vagina:

> You can make it practically anything you want, need, or dread: an opening, an absence of form ... a pause between the declarative sentence of the outside world and the mutterings of the viscera ... a balloon, a turtleneck sweater, a model for the universe itself, which ... is expanding in all directions even as we sit here and weep.

As this extract suggests, her writing is itself an admirably flexible and expressive instrument, and she has great fun playing it, even while tackling issues as sombre as hysterectomy or clitoridectomy. She describes her book as a 'Fantasia', and in places the prose resembles a Disneyesque frolic. *Woman* may not be a radically original work either of biology or of sexual politics: though it draws on a number of fascinating 'personal histories', the bulk of it is a synthesis of what has been said or researched by others, from Hippocrates to the likes of Roy Baumeister of Case Western Reserve University, all decorously credited. But it is hugely instructive and deliciously readable.

The nineteen chapters compose a loose narrative, from the egg in the female foetus, ecstatically hymned as 'the true sun, the light of life', through to the thorny question of the biological usefulness of post-menopausal women. Considering the latter, Angier seems reluctantly compelled towards a sorry conclusion: 'the female chimpanzee breeds until she dies, around her fortieth year, and nature surely intended the same for woman, before civilization pointlessly protracted her lifespan.' But the scenario is transformed at the last minute by the greatest of all the unlikely heroines in these pages, a few dozen old ladies in Tanzania, the grandmothers of the Hadza tribe, whose foraging for fruits and tubers is the chief source of nutrition for Hadza babies. In Angier's delighted summation, this remote scraping and gathering confers residual purpose on the post-reproductive years of women everywhere. Not all the 'geography' surveyed is equally fruitful in the things that feed Angier's writing. She likes to anthropomorphize: 'Eggs must plan the party. Sperm only need to show up wearing top hat and tails, of course.' But when she comes to hormones, as she must, their lack of physical identity, and our imperfect knowledge of their operations, subdue her metaphorical method. It's hard to impart much character to serotonin, for instance, when it is necessary to report that 'the brains of successful suicide victims are in some cases low in serotonin and in other cases not'. Oestrogen is grease and won't solidify into a lively imaginative figure.

The clitoris, on the other hand, elicits a rapturous essay, entitled, by an analogy with the music of Bach that takes some following, 'The Well-Tempered Clavier' ('Can you expect women to play the fugue if their organ has no pipes?'). This has its boggling statistics (there are 8,000 nerve fibres hereabouts but how were they counted?) and some choice historical titbits (the eighteenth-century Dutch naturalist Johann Blumenbach wrote of a baleen whale clitoris measuring 52 feet, several feet longer than the baleen whale itself). It builds towards a glowing conceit, on the three architectural sections of the clitoris:

> Glans, shaft, crura: a tripartite Greek column whose order changes depending on mood, from the stately Doric of a working day through the volute, unwinding Ionic and cresting in the extravagant, midsummer foliage of Corinthian, when leaves and flowers are as fat as fists and life is drunk on its gorgeous, fleeting infinity calming to a commonsensical and irrefutable conclusion: 'The clitoris is designed to encourage its bearer to take control of her sexuality.'

The political Angier, 'the female chauvinist sow' as she calls that part of herself, comes to the fore in the later chapters of the book. There is nothing that will strike men as unreasonable or hostile; indeed, the most prominent ad hominem attack is directed at Camille Paglia. Yet she spends many pages in (for her) slightly ill-tempered engagement with the hoary formula that men are polygamous, women monogamous, as if it enjoyed more popular credit than is surely the case. When she hesitates, in resolution, to claim for her 'gals' the right to the very patterns of infidelity we deplore in President Clinton, the reader may imagine her husband looming over her shoulder.

And her own experiences naturally provide a part of her experience. Strictly where relevant, she shows us her types of orgasm, her fibroids (benign purple tumours that grow in the uterus), a diseased thyroid that left her looking, in her own words, 'like a tree-frog', her struggle to conceive, and the birth three years ago (when she was 38) of her daughter: at which the science and poetry of *Woman* pass happily into particular life. Indeed, she chooses to end this long, great-spirited and important book with a trope of outrageous silliness, a vision of her daughter as feminist mariner that leaves male cheerleaders (and that may be the intention) baffled on the beach:

> ... maybe she will trade up her mother's tatty bark canoe for a ship of gold and joy, with a mutinous crew of mad-haired Valkyries, cloven mermaids and chafing nymphs. My daughter will sing herself hoarse as she rows firmly through squalls and calm waters, now in tune with her mates, now roaring against them. She hasn't yet found the fabled free shore, but no matter. She is always at home in the sea.

Don't Fly Me

'Humanity too strapped in'

The Wild Blue Yonder: The Picador Book of Aviation
Edited by Graham Coster, Picador

Graham Coster launches his stimulating and informative introduction to *The Wild Blue Yonder* with a frank admission: that the aeroplane, though it has utterly transformed our notions of travel and the nature of warfare, has generally failed to interest our writers. His extreme cases are James Joyce, T. S. Eliot and D. H. Lawrence, in whose collected works, he tells us, there is not a single reference to powered flight. Even those writers with a practical passion for aviation have seemed inhibited from putting it into words; William Faulkner was keen enough to buy his own aircraft, but flying figures in only a couple of his short stories and the least of his novels (*Pylon*, 1935, about pilots at a Mardi Gras). There has been more flight in fiction since the 1940s, but its most conspicuous role has been to give certain novels (*Lord of the Flies*, *Alive!*, *The Satanic Verses*) a disastrous starting point; it remains Coster's case that 'flying has crept into modern literature at the margin, rather than been seized as a subject'. One explanation is that aviation has developed too quickly for it ever to have represented what Coster calls 'a stable fact of life'. Only a dozen years after Orville Wright first hopped off the tarmac, fighter planes were in combat over France; where 'bombing' once meant fleets of B52s remodelling the landscape of North Vietnam, twenty years later it means the laser-controlled zapping of individual offices in Baghdad. No sooner, it seems, has the imagination got flight in its sights than flight has moved on.

But what would a literature of aviation consist of? Almost all of that small number who flew before the Second World War were pilots. That one of these should have been a writer of the quality of Antoine de Saint-Exupéry was pure chance; and it is hard to see how one report of the pilot's solitary experience should differ significantly from another. Hardly more promising is the suffocatingly social experience of today's airline passenger, for whom, as Nicholson Baker observes, even to stow one's dinner-tray is to punch someone else in the back. Airliners are too big, their journeys too brief, their humanity too strapped in, to provide the stuff of fiction; or at least, anything more than what Coster calls the 'cliché' of arrival, the plane banking to deliver its 'pensive passenger' to 'the new country below, pregnant with destiny and secrets' – though he prints two superior examples of this, the emigrant in V. S. Naipaul's *A Bend in the River*, 'in Africa one day … in Europe the next', and Craig Raine dreaming of brides and boiling kettles while 'Flying to Belfast, 1977'.

In the circumstances he describes, Graham Coster has done well to assemble an anthology of this substance. There is at least no danger of his trying to squeeze too much in: there are a mere eight poems (Seamus Heaney's marvellous 'The Flight Path' is overlooked), and thirty-six prose pieces, many of these quite lengthy, with a preponderance of non-fiction, giving the book something of the balance of a special issue of *Granta*. (Coster has worked as an assistant editor on the magazine; and there is an extract from a book about football hooliganism by its founding editor, Bill Buford, which does not otherwise seem to belong here.) The book starts with H. G. Wells's *The War in the Air* (1908) and proceeds chronologically; its general trajectory is from the 'lonely impulse of delight' of the early aviators towards universal terror. The two most compelling items are pieces of reportage. G. L. Steer's account of the aftermath of the bombing of Guernica is like travel writing gone hellishly wrong:

> In the plaza, in the dark shadow of the Casa de Juntas … people sat upon broken chairs, lay on rough tables or mattresses wet with water … They were digging them out of ruined houses, families at a time, dead and blue-black with bruising … A fire brigade with a feeble jet was playing on the chapel of Andra Mari.

The pathos of Stanley Williamson's reconstruction of the Munich air disaster of 1957 derives from its minute reconstruction, drawing on every available eye-witness, of the movements of the doomed footballers through what seemed the minor frustrations of the hours before the crash (take-off was aborted twice, but not three times); it was a survivor, Harry Gregg, who joked, 'I don't want to die in Germany, I don't speak German'. Such ignorance is not bliss, according to Julian Barnes (digressing in *Staring at the Sun*), but the first of the 'most infernal conditions in which to die' created by the engineers who have 'elaborated' the aeroplane: 'If a wing fell off, the calm-voiced Scottish captain would tell you that the soft-drinks dispenser was malfunctioning.' These samples may misrepresent the tone of an anthology which is inclined towards celebration. Coster himself hymns the oddity or beauty of certain aircraft, finding in the bomber of the late 1950s, 'an eighth wonder of the world'; and one of the pleasures of his book is its gallery of types or characters, what the war artist Paul Nash calls, in a quirky essay, 'The Personality of Planes':

> … the short-nose Blenheim, is, naturally, enigmatical. You might say it has no face –… but I would prefer to say it wears a mask, or that behind a mask it is growing a face which, when at last it appears, may eclipse that of all others for its dire beauty.

Alas, the personality of aircraft has been displaced in our minds, as technology has advanced, by images of the destruction they bring; as Coster puts it, 'You cannot (now) see the aeroplane for the explosions'. He cites Thomas Pynchon's *Gravity's Rainbow* as the 'classic articulation' of our century's rediscovery of 'the biblical fear of destruction from the heavens'; what flies in that book are not men but missiles.

On Cricket

Vignettes

W. G.'s Birthday Party
David Kynaston, Night Watchman

W. G. Grace: A Life
Simon Rae, Faber and Faber

A hundred years ago this week, the first day of the annual match at Lord's between the Gentlemen and the Players was fixed to fall on the fiftieth birthday of W. G. Grace – the captain of the amateur XI, and by an innings the most important cricketer there had ever been. David Kynaston's elegant and evocative little book, *W. G.'s Birthday Party*, first published in 1990, and reissued now in a 'Centenary Edition', is centred on the events of this game. Its account of the play is marvellously vivid, but the special interest of the book lies in the extended postscript, 'After the Party', in which Kynaston follows the subsequent fortunes, not just of Grace, but of all the cricketers involved. There are some strange tales – Bobby Abel, Surrey's insatiable little opener, was forced to go into hiding because he so resembled Dr Crippen – and a surprising proportion of melancholy ones. Arthur Shrewsbury, the Players' captain and Grace's choice as the best opening partner, was tormented by his own baldness, and declined into hypochondria and suicide; Andrew Stoddart, Grace's sunny vice-captain, suffered latterly from poor nerves, financial problems and a loveless marriage, and shot himself in Maida Vale; 'Band-Box' Brockwell, the great dandy among the professionals, ended his days roaming Richmond Park for firewood, where a drenching thunderstorm brought on his final illness.

These affecting miniature biographies of Kynaston's are akin to the vignettes of three or four pages in which writers of an older school, like R. C. Robertson-Glasgow, would celebrate cricketing personalities. Such a treatment would do for most, but it can clearly not encompass Grace: who came, initially by his supremacy on the pitch (he had scored fifty hundreds before other batsmen of England had scored a hundred hundreds between them; and even in his second suit as a bowler, though he subsided from 'modest medium-pace' to gentle leg-breaks, he took more wickets than anyone else in the nineteenth century), then by the intimidating bulk of his person, and finally by the inexhaustible length of his career, to make the game in effect his own domain. There have, accordingly, been umpteen full-scale biographies, the most recent of them published only last year (Robert Low's *W. G.*); but in its scale and in the minute thoroughness of its research, as well as in the fittingness of its amiable, unpretentious prose, Simon Rae's monumental *W. G. Grace: A Life* outdoes them all. It may even be the biggest book ever written about anyone who was so exclusively a sportsman.

And readers will soon be clear, for all the social history it takes in on its way, that this is a cricket book. There are a great many scores and figures. Grace lived for sixty-seven years, but only in the last forty pages of this long *Life* is he not playing cricket (and then he is captaining England at bowls). Sir Colin Cowdrey has described the slightly chilly realization, which came to him towards the end of his career, that he had been 'standing at first slip for twenty-five years'. Grace stood at the (now rare) position of point through forty-two years of first-class cricket, and while he was there seems scarcely to have suffered an uncricketing thought. In Rae's account, everything else is marginal to the game. Grace's wife Agnes, for instance, is generally invisible: she only features – and then as part of a large group – in one of over thirty illustrations; and she looms no larger in the index than (say) Tom Richardson, the Surrey and England fast bowler. As for Grace's duties as a GP – and it took him twelve years to qualify: he seems to have honoured them during the off-season, but through the summer they were only another source of changing-room jokes, like the one about the difficult confinement ('it was fairly successful. The child died and the mother died, but I saved the father'). This makes Grace seem an uncomplicated, even a childish man; and the aptest introduction to his character is still the opening of Bernard Darwin's personal memoir of 1934:

'W. G.', said an old friend of his, 'was just a great big schoolboy in everything he did'... He had all the schoolboy's love for elementary and boisterous jokes: his distaste for learning; his desperate and undisguised keenness; his guilelessness and his guile; his occasional pettishness and pettiness; his endless power of recovering his good spirits.

Rae's volume illustrates this larky immaturity with a charming sequence of photographs from the Hastings festival of 1901: Grace, at fifty-three, is pretending to cry on the shoulder of the Kent captain, J. R. Mason, while Lord Hawke looks on with fine distaste.

Grace was born in Bristol in 1848, the fourth of the sons of a cricketing country doctor, three of whom – the others were E. M., 'The Coroner', himself one of the finest of mid-Victorian cricketers, and G. F., the unfortunate Fred, who died in 1880, aged twenty-nine, of pneumonia – went on to play Test cricket. But there was no such thing even as regular county cricket when their mother Martha taught the boys the rudiments of batsmanship in their orchard garden. Rae is an excellent guide to the raw state of the game – its dubious laws, coarse wickets, ill-assorted fixtures and commercial infancy – that prevailed before the Grace revolution. Overarm (rather than round-arm) bowling was only legalized in 1865, the year before W. G. made his first-class debut (for 'South Wales'). Demeaning mismatches and 'odds' matches were the norm, and betting was the motor. An essay 'On Cricket' published in 1868, which Rae attributes to Anthony Trollope, bemoans 'the so-called England Elevens, which go caravaning about the country playing against two bowlers and twenty duffers for the benefit of some enterprising publican'. That was the year Grace announced himself with 134 not out out of 201, and ten wickets for eighty-one, in the match at Lord's for the Gentlemen against the Players. A hero had arrived, and cricket had to reform itself if it was to support his exploits. The 'Golden Age' was thirty years away, but Grace was shortly presiding over an age of brass.

W. G., though not of the top order socially, was on the gentlemen's side of the fault that divided English cricket then and for many decades to follow. (Kynaston cites the famous entry from a fixture list of 1890, in which a Leicestershire professional found himself in exalted company: 'Cambridge University versus Gentlemen of England, with Pougher.') It was vital for the MCC, the game's governing body, that Grace, the nonpareil of cricketers, should stay under their aegis, rather than throwing in his lot with the (mostly Northern) professionals; and he exploited their

dependency by ignoring their posture on remuneration: 'that no gentle-
man ought to make a profit by his services in the cricket field'. Ostensibly
an amateur, Grace made between twice and ten times as much as his
professional team-mates through 'expenses' and 'appearance fees'; and if
he could simply bat through resentment of this at home, it made him –
coupled with an 'unfortunate infirmity of temper' – an unpopular tourist.

In fact, the first of Grace's four tours, to Canada and the United States
in 1872–3, was a happy affair, perhaps because this was an all-amateur
party, perhaps because someone else was captain. The King of Batting
was none the less in demand as a public speaker, despite his high, squeaky
voice (on account of which he once had a proposal of marriage rejected).
To meet this challenge, he patented an adaptable little speech: 'Gentlemen,
I beg to thank you for the honour you have done me; I never saw better
bowling than I have seen today, and I hope to see as good wherever I go.'
To the delight of his fellow tourists, Grace repeated this almost verbatim
at every venue, simply substituting for 'bowling' whichever noun was
appropriate (at Hoboken it was 'oysters'). But his tours to Australia, in
1873–4 and 1892–3, won him no friends. His own side were angered by the
terms struck by their captain; in the latter case, a fee of £3,000 (£140,000
in today's terms) plus expenses for his wife and two children, while his
professionals got £300 each. The colonials, for their part, disliked the way
Grace and his fellow amateurs shunned their team-mates socially, not
allowing them 'to come between the wind and their nobility'; they took
additional offence at several instances of 'sharp practice' on the pitch.

But the bitter (and ironic) predictions of Grace's Australian hosts that
'his name will become a synonym for mean cunning and fraud' did not affect
his reputation in England. Indeed, the longer he played, the more awe and
affection his name commanded. In 1895, at the age of forty-six, Grace should
have been in his sporting dotage: but now he became the first man ever to
score 1,000 runs in a month of May, passing, in the process, the once incon-
ceivable landmark: a hundred hundreds. He was still playing Test cricket in
his fifties (one of only four players to do so: the others are Wilfred Rhodes,
George Gunn and the Australian spinner Herbert Ironmonger) and had
the energy and influence to build and run a first-class club from scratch
(London County, at Crystal Palace, wound up in 1905). On his fifty-eighth
birthday (in 1906), in what was still the most prestigious domestic fixture,
he scored 74 for the Gentlemen against the Players, returned to the pavil-
ion, laid his bat on the table and proclaimed, 'There. I shan't play any more.'

And so to the golf course. Certain shocks had impinged on Grace's elephantine innocence: the deaths of his brother Fred (only a fortnight after his first Test match – 0, 0, and a brilliant catch); of his daughter Bessie, from typhoid, in 1899; and his son Bertie, after an appendix operation, in 1905. But games sustained him through all; and it was only with the onset of the First World War – and the image it gave him of young men lining up, in his own phrase, to be 'mowed down' – that his heart would begin to feel its age. 'The Champion', 'Leviathan', 'The Mammoth', 'The Beard', 'The Doctor', 'The Old Man': no one was so garlanded with epithets as Grace. In 1911, his name was on a list of putative peers drawn up by Prime Minister Asquith, in a move to challenge the Conservative majority in the House of Lords; but nothing came of it, and the honour might have seemed superfluous. As Neville Cardus commented: the very idea of 'Sir W. G. Grace' is comical '… He was an institution. As well might we think of Sir Albert Memorial, Sir National Debt, Sir Harvest Moon – or Sir Cricket!' Others have lodged Grace in English mythology or folklore by comparison to some other, fictional spirit. To G. K. Chesterton he was, as a creature of midsummer, a 'prodigious Puck'; to a later biographer, A. A. Thomson, he was like 'the jolly Ghost of Christmas Present … or the great Sir John Falstaff'. But every encounter with Grace was a strongly physical experience: Kynaston reports that he had the dirtiest neck to which one keeper ever kept ('We Graces ain't no bloody water spaniels'); and it is Rae's prime achievement, among many others, to have recovered the bounding human presence behind the bearded myth.

Every reader of his book will have felt what it was like to have been trapped before the wicket by Grace's lumbering leg-breaks, and dismissed with a threatening squeak, 'Pavilion, you!' Yet not even a *Life* as robust as this can take the sentimental, Falstaffian echo out of Grace's ending, his babbling of green fields while play was overtaken by deadly earnest. On October 9, 1915, W. G. suffered a stroke in the garden of his home in south-east London. He was thus bedbound when, four days later and ten days before he died, the first Zeppelin raids were launched on the city. These terrified him. A friend tried to cheer him by appealing to his cricketer's courage: 'How can you mind these, W. G., you who have played the fastest bowlers of your time (like the Australian Ernest Jones, who once fired a beamer through his beard)?' 'Ah, but I could see those beggars,' came the reply, 'I can't see these.'

*

Wally Hammond, The Reasons Why: A Biography
David Foot, Robson

From his Test debut in 1927 until the Second World War, that is, after Jack
Hobbs and before Len Hutton, Wally Hammond was the leading bats-
man in English cricket. In that time, only Don Bradman (to Hammond's
chagrin) in the world was a more prolific run-scorer; but non-Australian
connoisseurs would always prefer Hammond's 'majestic' bearing at the
crease and his classical strokeplay, especially his definitive cover-drive.
His character seems to have been less graceful. In 1938, he assumed
amateur status in order to captain England, an appointment made in
cheerless recognition of his formidable, even oppressive presence (sullen
to the point of silence, he was characterized by his successor as captain
of Gloucestershire as 'an absolute shit'). After a war spent drinking in
Torquay and South Africa, his career came to a melancholy end as the
overweight, fibrositic and unsuccessful captain of the 1946 MCC tour
team that was badly beaten in Australia. He retired to South Africa,
becoming a glorified groundsman for Natal University, and making model
ships in the evenings. He died with few honours, prematurely, in 1965.

Or so we glean from David Foot's biography – the fourth and most
excitable – of this apparently difficult, snobbish, promiscuous, miser-
able man, which he calls 'an affectionate portrait', though there is little
in it to suggest what to like beyond the glorious batting. And this isn't,
as Foot proclaims, 'predominantly a cricket book, so my painfully lim-
ited experience of Hammond's batting is not important'. (This doesn't
excuse cricketing howlers like the description of the Bill Bowes delivery
that bowled Bradman: 'It was a yorker on leg stump .... The ball seamed
away wickedly to take the middle stump out of the ground'; a yorker
pitches almost at the base of the stumps, and any movement off the seam
would be imperceptible as well as irrelevant. Neither does it exonerate the
prose, which is too florid for the purpose of making the cricket visible:
'His bat, as we have seen, was bejewelled with rare magic and touched
the soul with its poetic language and beauty.') What it is, predominantly,
is a syphilis book.

On his return from an MCC tour of the West Indies in April 1926,
the young Gloucestershire batsman, as yet uncapped, was seriously ill

with blood poisoning; amputation of a leg was considered, and 'only his exceptionally strong constitution pulled him through' (or was it the weakness of the disease?). Foot is definitive about the cause: 'He had contracted a form of syphilis or a related sexually-transmitted disease' (never mind that Hammond's symptoms as described do not resemble the secondary symptoms of syphilis; 'I base my findings on admittedly flimsy medical evidence'). His further contention is that not Hammond's disease, but the treatment of it – or what he supposes that treatment to have been, which is injections of mercury – quite deformed his character, making him moody and abrupt for the rest of his life. But do we need a chemical explanation for an unpleasant temperament? And if we do, is Hammond's daily heavy drinking not enough? But the principal weakness of Foot's hypothesis is that the illness and its treatment (whatever that was) both happened before Hammond's strength, concentration and self-confidence made him briefly the greatest cricketer in the world; and the brooding discontent of the decline is adequately (if not sensationally) explicable as a reaction to the loss of that stature. Foot is less indulgent of another vein of speculation – seemingly fantastical, though this at least has its source in the witness of Hammond's contemporaries: the late Joe Hardstaff noted, in the cricketing terminology of the time, 'a certain nigger-sweat' about Hammond in the field; the Somerset and England opener Charlie Barnett testifies that 'You only had to look at his fingernails. They were a dead giveaway.' But Hammond was not, if you can trust Foot's 'genealogical exploration' (and you might not, but the photographs tend to support him), the first black man to captain England.

*

Bill Edrich: A Biography
Alan Hill, Deutsch

Like many biographies of cricketers of the past, Alan Hill's life of Bill Edrich leaves a melancholy impression, another trace of what Gavin Ewart has described (in the title of a touching poem) as 'The Sadness of Cricket'. Not that one should be patronizing about a cricketer whose deeds in the field took him close to what is called greatness there, or about a man whose character was formed or deformed as much by his experiences as a bomber pilot. But for all Hill's cheering-on, his apparent assumption that, since cricket is for pleasure, cricketers' lives must be happy, and his concession therefore to Edrich's hectic idea of a good time, the minor hero who wanders from this book, in his dinner jacket, at the close of play, is one who had to beat off the spectre of loneliness with reckless drinking and compulsive marryings. The son of a Norfolk farmer, Edrich made his Test debut in 1938, soon after becoming, at the age of twenty-one, only the fourth player in history to score 1,000 runs in May. Yet within months his name was a byword for failure. In that summer's series against Australia, the selectors persevered with him as he scored 67 runs in six innings, including 12 out of a total of 903–7 at the Oval (when his opening partner managed 364). And in South Africa the following winter, his form actually declined: 21 runs in five innings, completing the worst eleven-innings run of any top-six batsman in Test history (a record suppressed by his biographer) before he made a double-century against lame bowlers on the seventh and eighth days of the 'Timeless' final Test at Durban.

Half of Edrich's (and Hutton's, and Compton's) cricketing prime was lost to the war, in which he won the DFC for piloting a Blenheim on daylight raids over Cologne; and his fame rests largely on his exploits in the golden summer of 1947, when both he and his Middlesex partner Denis Compton broke the record run aggregate for an English season; and when, in the series against South Africa, he at last proved himself a Test cricketer of spirit and power. His cricketing peers pay tribute here to Edrich's rare physical courage and 'magnificent defence'. But Trevor Bailey's comparison to 'an efficient plumber who knew his taps' is prosaic, and it was only in combination with the more dashing Compton that Edrich's play really caught the public imagination. And it was always Compton and Edrich, never the other way round; there is an Edrich Stand at Lord's, but only in the shadow of Compton's. In the record books, moreover, the family name has been usurped by a younger cousin, John, who played twice as many Tests, in the 1960s and 70s, with a higher batting average (44 to 40).

Bill Edrich would have played rather more international cricket himself had he not, in 1950 and this at the age of thirty-four, needed to be helped, 'paralytic', at 5am on the fourth morning of a Test, to his hotel room, the room next door to the Chairman of Selectors. He was subsequently banished (though not formally suspended) from Test matches for three years. This was not an isolated episode. 'Bill was in a terrible state, just about conscious really ... But he got himself better quickly and scored a century', etc: there are similar yams about Miller, Botham and a dozen others, but in this account of Edrich (who would get drunk very quickly) they become repetitive, though they are not perceived as a problem. Hill writes winkingly of an 'incorrigible rogue' (he married four times) and his 'exuberant lifestyle'; Trevor Bailey's verdict, not meant unkindly, is that 'He never grew up.' In 1986, twenty days after his seventieth birthday, he fell downstairs at home after a St George's Day Lunch, fractured his skull and died. If the book fails to convey a solid sense of its subject, part of the reason is Hill's omission of basic information, his perfunctory research. We are told that Edrich was 'short', but not his height; that in 1943, DFC or no, he was 'pronounced unfit' for flying duties, but not told why. And what, off the pitch, did Edrich do? When 'the newly turned amateur was barred by a new business venture' from the MCC tour of 1948–9, what was it? What did he earn? Where did he live?

Edrich wrote, or co-wrote, two books, but neither is mentioned, though one of them offers a livelier and more accurate account of the bombing raids than Hill can manage. The writing makes some mad dashes into the purple, such as the fantasia on Edrich's (brief) football career with Tottenham reserves: 'The nets, as he struck their inviting targets, billowed upwards like balloons caught on a sudden gust of wind ...' But it relies for the most part on the written (and uninterrogated) testimony of others. Few of these are inclined to look much deeper than the author ('everyone loved Bill'); but Edrich's younger son Justin gives us revealing glimpses of fallibility behind the runs and the rollicking: 'Dad got his pleasure from short-term highs rather than overall fulfilment or peace.' Otherwise, the most reliable part of the book is the statistical appendix, compiled, as if born to the job, by David Kendix.

*

C. B. Fry, An English Hero: A Biography
Ian Wilton, Cohen

The legend of C. B. Fry was made by exaggeration – with the complicity of such hero-worshippers as Denzil Bachelor and John Arlott. Fry did not get a First in Classics from Oxford (other than in his Mods, or first-year exams); in his Finals, in the wake of a nervous breakdown, he took a Fourth. Of his two international caps at football, the first was gained in an all-amateur selection against a side representing Canada that won only thirteen matches out of fifty-eight on tour. Fry equalled (but did not break) the world long-jump record in his second (not his first) year at Oxford; he did not put down his cigar to do so. And if, in later life, Fry ever believed himself to be a serious contender for the throne of Albania, then he was the victim of a practical joke against his vanity; it is more likely that he simply enjoyed the outlandishness of the claim. Iain Wilton's fine new biography – enlarging on Clive Ellis's *C. B.* (1985) – is concerned to restore the facts wherever possible; but he also considers the extreme private distress that underlay his subject's wary relations with the truth.

This said, Charles Fry's achievements were remarkable enough; though perversely the most enduring of them were his cricketing exploits. For several years he was the most prolific batsman in the world. His record of six successive first-class centuries, set in 1901, has twice been equalled but never surpassed; and his supremacy at the crease was complemented by his haughty good looks. For Neville Cardus, Fry was 'the handsomest sight seen on a cricket pitch by anybody', though his batting was more precision than flair, the prosaic element in the famous partnership for Sussex with his friend, the incomparably stylish Ranjitsinhji. Nerves affected his performance in Test matches, where his average of 31 did not reflect his abilities. But an amateur sportsman needs to be, or to go on to be, something else. The dispersed aspirations of the 'all-rounder' did not serve Fry so well in his maturity; as a result, he was still opening the batting for Hampshire in 1921, at the age of forty-nine. When he came, in 1939, to dictate his highly readable but unreliable memoir, *Life Worth Living*, it projected the fantasy of the wholly versatile man grown out of the champion youth. The subtitle was *Some phases of an Englishman*; and sport is only the earliest in a series of dazzling accomplishments: diplomacy, hunting, ballroom dancing, journalism, and so on. Yet one chapter or 'phase' of Fry's book had, in such a structure, the incongruous title 'A Life's Work'. It dealt with his role in running the Training Ship Mercury – a matter first explored by Ronald Morris in *The Captain's Lady* (1984), and one bound up with Fry's unlucky marriage.

Fry's son Stephen put it simply in 1984: 'My mother ruined my father's life.' When, in 1898, at the age of twenty-six, Fry married Beatie Sumner, she was ten years his senior, and mother of two illegitimate children by her scandalous union with Charles Hoare, the banker and founder of the Mercury. It was a disastrous choice. The arrangement initially allowed Fry the financial freedom to devote his summers to cricket; but, as Wilton reveals, Beatie remained devoted to Hoare after the marriage, and Hoare was almost certainly the father of the Fry's first child. Fry's role at the Mercury was likewise a sham; it was the bullying Beatie who ran the Mercury with sadistic harshness, while 'Commander' Fry twirled his bat in the school nets. Wilton's account of these humiliating circumstances scuppers the gentle justifications of *Life Worth Living*: "'fine show, C. B.. But for you it has been a backwater." "The question remains," I replied, "whether it is better to be successful or ... happy."' This Lord Birkenhead, the Lord Chancellor, is what had become of F. E. Smith, one of Fry's peers at Oxford. The jibe was made that of the two Varsity pals, Fry went on to make runs while Smith went on to make history.

Fry attempted belatedly to emulate Smith, standing and falling as a Liberal candidate in by-elections three times in the 1920s. Then, in 1929, he suffered complete mental breakdown, which his wife drily ascribed to 'thwarted genius'. It took five years, and electric shock treatment, before he was seen in public again. It is striking and impressive that when Fry did come back to life, at the age of sixty-two, his self-esteem was still, or was again, Olympian. Although he had completely missed out on concepts like Bodyline and Bradman, within months of his recovery he was the country's premier sports journalist (for the *Evening Standard*), in an impressionistic style he invented for the task. 'C. B.' as an old man was not to all tastes – revelling in his vitality, demonstrating the on-drive with umbrella, poker or assegai, hurdling gates, flirting till dawn, taking steps four at a time etc, garrulous, self-important, the definitive show-off. Even in the dilute traces of him which now come down to us, the flavour of the man is almost off-puttingly strong: hectic, condescending, but – as in this throwaway remark about Gloucestershire playing at the Oval – suddenly brilliant or charming: 'That's the trouble with these West Country teams. They bowl and field beautifully for an hour, and then – they begin to think of apples.'

On Rugby

Goodbye to All That Low Tackling

Muddied Oafs: The last days of rugger
Richard Beard, Yellow Jersey

Richard Beard is the author of four 'experimental' novels, each of which conveyed its story through some ingenious and demanding technical constraint. His first work of non-fiction, the direct, companionable *Muddied Oafs*, resembles these only if we think of it as a life revealed through its winter Saturday afternoons. Beard has been an enthusiastic amateur rugby player, a wandering, uninhibited fly-half. As his book closes, he is thirty-six years old: already qualified to play for Veteran XVs, and as far as competitive rugby is concerned, deep into time added on for injury. The farewell in his subtitle, *The last days of rugger*, is therefore addressed at least partly to his own participation.

But it also refers to the struggle of the better part of the game itself. Since rugby union finally sanctioned payment to players in the mid-1990s, it has split in two. The professionalized player now goes about his daily business, as Beard describes him, as if he had been 'kidnapped by a rather unimaginative cult at a tender age and returned to the field cyber-formed but empty-headed from some dim and religious full-time gym'. His alter ego, meanwhile, the devotee of what Beard calls (with some caution) 'rugger', meaning decent, modest club rugby, finds his stake in the game to be under threat. We're all supposed to buy into Team England now, the brand, the mitts, the Gatorade, the pointless substitutes, the painted turf, 'hopefully', 'the guys', 'the focus': 'The marketing of rugby needs spectators, not players'. Clubs are shrinking, others are folding, Barratt Homes have bought the pitches, etc, and fewer and fewer of us are getting a go at 'the greatest outdoor team sport in the world'. (Football is an acknowledged blind spot.)

But the spirit of rugger still animates Richard Beard, who is sane, curious and healthy, as he says, and he does not dwell long on this gloomy prognosis. His book takes its admirably neat structure from visits to each of the seven clubs or institutions where he has played his rugby, and his attempts to get a final game in their colours. They are, in chronological order: Radley College (First XV, 1983–4); Pembroke College, Cambridge; Mid-Argyll, Lochgilphead; SCUF, Paris (where he is registered as Yves Maréchal); Norwich RUFC; Sporting Club, Geneva; and Midsomer Norton, in the Mendips, from 1998 until 2003. Each chapter vividly evokes a distinct rugby milieu, and affords the opportunity besides to probe, with a redeeming sense of humour, a relevant rugby issue. At Cambridge, where college rugby is now a laboratory for RFU experiments, we consider the laws. At Lochgilphead, we observe the British game's battle for survival at its geographical limits. At Radley, Beard examines origins. The game took root in certain isolated schools: the absence of outside opposition required, so the Radley archivist reveals, the construction of teams on arbitrary lines, Light Hair v Dark Hair, A to G against H to Z, or (Beard's favourite) Disyllables v The Rest of the World: the 'Disyllables proved much the stronger, with Pearson, Deacon, Edgell and Mitchell conspicuous, and Cholmondeley for the Rest' – which raises the usual question about Cholmondeley.

Readers of the *TLS* might be most interested in the chapter on Norwich RUFC. Since Beard played for this club while he was enrolled on Malcolm Bradbury's Creative Writing course at the University of East Anglia, his return prompts a consideration of the links between rugby and literature. On the way in, he takes a poke at Bradbury's successor as Professor there, the unsporting Andrew Motion, who as a fellow Radleian must have enjoyed compulsory rugby: 'All I wanted was ten minutes of his time to compare his opinion of rugby with his views on writing': but the Poet Laureate – for reasons we can only surmise – declines the request for an interview.

And connections between writing and playing rugby are generally hard to prove. Beard tries to assemble a fifteen, a seven, of those who have done both. He pencils in Robert Graves, quoting with relish the lines

> In Rugby Football I have killed more men,
> Playing full-back and tackling with ill-will,
> Killed them, I mean, in murderous intention,
> Than ever I killed at Loos or Passchendaele …

as evidence that Graves was a 'combative full back'. But these words are taken from a dialogue, in the poem 'At the Games', between a personification of England and his French counterpart, and are not about Graves at all. ('At the Games' was itself competitive, however, and won the gold medal for poetry at the 1924 Olympics). Beard might rather have cited 'The Face in the Mirror' (1957), where the ageing poet examines his 'Crookedly broken nose – low tackling caused it'. Again, though, Graves's own account of his first thirty-three years, *Good-bye to All That* (1928), barely refers to the game: he complains of his first preparatory school in Wimbledon, where he was sent at the age of seven, that 'I was oppressed by compulsory Rugby football, of which nobody taught me the rules'; it was only at the fifth of his six prep schools that he 'learned rugger', and it was the round-ball game that was compulsory at Graves's public school, Charterhouse, from where he went to war. After that, at Oxford, he was 'unfit for games'. It would be interesting to know of any fixture after his fourteenth birthday in 1909 in which the poet's nose could have suffered lasting damage.

Beard's one really solid pick is the Australian novelist Thomas Keneally, though even he seems more attached to the old professional game of rugby league which he played as a youth in Sydney. Keneally has rugby on the brain, giving his novels titles like *The Playmaker* or *Season in Purgatory*; but asked if he knows of other contemporary writers who might have the 'faintest idea' about the game, he concedes, 'You don't meet too many'. One was the late Gavin Ewart, a champion of light verse, whose most treasured possession was a Scotland cap won by his grandfather (E. N. Ewart of Glasgow Academicals) in 1879, and who wrote with affection of Bill Beaumont (a 'walrus') and Gavin Hastings ('stronger / than the whole of Tonga'). But Welsh pub bards aside, there aren't that many others to meet.

How few, we can confirm by looking at *A Rugby Compendium: An authoritative guide to the literature of Rugby Union*, compiled by John M. Jenkins, whose first edition appeared in 1998. A lot of rugby literature falls into one of three categories: club histories, tour books and season summaries, or (since the relaxation of amateur regulations) player biographies and ghosted memoirs, some of them, like *Midfield Liaison: The Frank Bunce/Walter Little story*, pungently ephemeral. But Jenkins also conducts a trawl through the sport's appearances in imaginative literature. Rugby was first read about in stories of the public schools where it was born, and first of all in *Tom Brown's Schooldays* (1857), set at Rugby herself, where W. W. Ellis is said to have launched the game in the 1820s; Kipling (in *Stalky and Co.*), Hugh Walpole and Wodehouse were later exponents. Going up to the Varsity, it figures tangentially in the novels and Oxbridge stories of John Buchan (*Castle Gay*), Conan Doyle and E. F. Benson, and in J. C. Squire's popular poem, 'The Rugger Match'. But as a definitively amateur pursuit, Rugby Union has never won the grown-up novelistic treatment enjoyed, for instance, by Rugby League in David Storey's *This Sporting Life* (1960); though its identity in South Wales or Gloucester was no less fruitfully 'working-class'.

It may be that the lack of good literature about rugby is mere chance: but as the field is so empty, *Muddied Oafs* is all the more welcome. Yet like the game he celebrates, Richard Beard might himself be accused of giving way to commercial inducements. The book follows his 'career' up to the early months of 2003; his publishers were clearly resolved to get it out in time for the World Cup in the autumn; and his last chapter, the twilit, Somerset chapter, seems rushed in the delivery, spun out with platitudes: 'I'm reminded that it's a hard game' etc. The set piece here is a 'composite game' of all those Beard has played for Midsomer Norton. It involves, as it must, injury, concussion, some petulant behaviour: but also credits him with both his team's tries, both perfectly executed, the second the match-winning score in the last minute. This is pretty fiction, no subtler than our own, and it inclines the reader in the corner to tackle him. 'A bit of proofreading', Beard suggests of some hapless souvenir pamphlet, 'wouldn't have hurt.' In which case, 'Corryvrecken' (p.10), 'Cromerty' (40), Brian 'Liebenburg' (62 and *passim*), Fabien 'Gaulthier' (63), 'The Ball of Kerrymuir' (164) and 'Hicka' Reid (211) are mis-spellings.

The Road from Marrakesh*

A Journey

Hassan II of Morocco likes to compare his kingdom to the desert palm: rooted in Africa, watered by Islam and rustled by the winds of Europe. Anyone travelling south through the country will experience each of these elements in reverse order: from the cosmopolitan French-built port of Casablanca, through Fès, the world's largest medieval Islamic city to Marrakesh, which is unmistakeably African – almost parodically African – Marrakesh is a place where the clichés come true, where the beggars are blind and the dancing is lewd, where the smells of the spices assail you, where the eyes of the children are almonds, where the legs of the Berber women bow beneath their loads: Marrakesh, in a way, is Timbuktu. There is nowhere so close to London – the flight takes less than four hours – that will give you such a strong sense of foreignness and mystery as this: a sense that neither 44 years of French occupation (which ended in 1956), nor the subsequent influx of tourism, has managed to erode. Marrakesh is as alien, exciting and slightly scary today as it was when Edwardian travellers joined caravans to blanch as its slave market. The special intensity of the place resides not so much in its physical appearance, though the sun-baked red mud of which the old town is built and the snow-capped blue of the Atlas mountains to the south, are an unforgettable visual combination; nor in its monuments, though the minaret of the Koutoubia mosque is one of the great buildings of the Muslim world; nor in our sense of its history, which, as a sometime capital of the vast Moorish empire, is long, curious and bloody. It is to be found instead in the strange activity and high colouring and exotic aromas of

*   Mick Imlah / Traveller © The Condé Nast Publications Ltd.

its daily life: specifically in its famous souks, and in the constant carnival that fills its central square, the Djemaa El Fna.

Variously translated as 'the place of the dead' and 'the mosque that came to nothing', the Djemaa El Fna will indeed not seem much in the empty hours of the morning: an irregular field or Tarmac like a municipal car park, surrounded by undistinguished low buildings erected in the 1960s. The day's first arrivals are boys serving nuts and orange juice from barrows, and by noon the square is swarming with activity. There are two distinct turns of duty. Through the afternoon, snake-charmers, water-carriers, monkey-trainers, fortune-tellers and dentists with piles of pulled teeth play on the fears and fascinations of the tourist. After dusk, rows of kitchens appear, with tables and benches, under the hiss of gas lamps, to serve visiting Berber farmers, while storytellers and comics and musicians strike up to entertain them. You can watch it all from one of a dozen cafes that overlook the square, or you can plunge in with certainty of memorable sights and encounters. In his book *The Voices of Marrakesh*, Elias Canetti describes one such: watching a young Berber flay and abuse his famished old donkey for the amusement of a hard-hearted gathering, Canetti is certain that the poor beast will not last the night. But the next evening, the pair of them are back in the square again, with the same cruel act, the donkey looking, if anything, even more haggard and defeated, but turning to reveal suddenly a huge and defiant erection. Marrakeshis still have a robust sense of humour.

The great labyrinth of the souk extends from the northern range of the square. Though it is smaller and more noisome than the souks of Fès, and the quality of the goods is generally inferior, there is something archetypal about the souk of Marrakesh; you might believe all other markets were derived or refined from it, as if the market and Marrakesh were the same word. Enticing and intimidating in equal measure, it thrills the senses and jangles the nerves. Certain sectors are as tranquil as nineteenth-century prints; in others the vendors are aggressive to the brink of assault. Even when you know your own way, you may not be left alone. If you're not in the mood to make friends, be positive in the exchange. Don't mutter – say you're from the Outer, not the Inner Hebrides, or smilingly insist that you're mad. They will soon tire and fall off if you dominate the conversation.

Whether alone or accompanied, avoid carpet shops unless you really want to buy a carpet (and Moroccan carpets are generally inferior to Persian): you will find it very hard to leave without a spat or a token camel rug once the staff start going to such obvious pains to show you everything. Instead, your first objective on a tour of the souk might be the open courtyard of the Rahba Kédima, with its innumerable spice and jewellery stores, and its hanging screens of dried eagles and snakes and porcupine used in the preparation of so-called aphrodisiacs; there are also the raw materials of Moroccan cosmetics: henna leaves, cochineal and blocks of antimony (to be ground into kohl). On no account should you miss the Souk des Teinturiers – the dyers' quarter – where brilliantly coloured cloths are hung above the alley to dry against the deep blue of the sky; nearby are the Souk des Babouches, full of curly slippers in many shades of leather, and the intriguing Souk Haddadin – the blacksmith's souk – surrounded by charcoal sellers.

For all its marvels, Marrakesh is undeniably noisy, dusty, jostling and demanding. Half of you wants to engage with it, half to escape. And anyone with more than a couple of days to spare will want to hire a car and explore the contrasting attractions of the surrounding area. The most popular picnic excursion, especially in the parching heat of the summer, is to the Ourika Valley, where the river sparkles among boulders and the terraced gardens are in bloom all year. Two hours' driving will get you to Essaouira, formerly the Portuguese port of Mogador, on the Atlantic – by general consent the nicest town in the country, with impressive fortifications, a friendly souk, active craftsmen, broad beaches, sea breezes and sardines grilled by the harbour. But if you can uproot and spend a night or two away from Marrakesh, two great roads take you south through the mountains of the High Atlas: the Tizi-n-Tichka, which connects Marrakesh with Ouarzazate and the blazing skies of the sub-Saharan oases; and the Tizi-n-Test pass, which connects Marrakesh with Taroudannt, with its smaller, golden version of Marrakesh's red ramparts.

One of the most spectacular half-day drives in the world, the Tizi-n-Test begins in earnest an hour south of Marrakesh around the hamlet of Ouirgane (where there is a luxurious staging post in the hotel La Roseraie). From here the road climbs into the delightful pastoral scenery of the high valley of Nfiss – like a Scottish salmon river on a rocky bed, lined by pretty terraced gardens and sculpted *pisé* (sun-baked clay) Berber villages, with a backdrop of increasingly tremendous mountains (Jbel Toubkal, the highest in North Africa at 13,500ft, is one). Set on the opposite bank of the river is the fortress-like mosque of Tin-Mal, recently restored. (It was in the citadel of Tin-Mal in the twelfth century that a puritanical Berber religious reformer called Ibn Tumert trained the mountains tribes to wage war against his enemies. Ibn Tumert's successors were to found the Almohad empire, which extended over Spain and as far east as western Libya: their capital was Marrakesh.) Tin-Mal is one of only two mosques in Morocco that non-Muslims may enter: the roof has gone, and the heavy brick pillars cast deep shadows in the otherwise glowing interior; a pair of owls nests in one of the domes.

The higher reaches of the pass are not for the nervous. The road narrows to the width of about one-and-a-half cars, and there begins a sequence of twisting hairpin bends which you have to negotiate with no fence or barrier between you and a vertical fall of half a mile. More giddying still are the glimpses of the road ahead: it looks like a mere fault or pencil line on the surface of the mountainside ahead and above. The French were rightly proud of their engineers who completed the pass in 1928: even today, the road can be made impassable by snow or rockfall, by meltwater or by sudden treacherous ice, at any time between December and March. The summit of the pass – at 6,800ft – is reached with relief and exhilaration, a fact not lost on the suave Berber who waits there to sell you his things. The altitude must affect the wits, for when he produced his various trinkets from a holdall, describing their provenance in the remotest Saharan villages, they looked to my friend and me like a treasure. At once, we threw away our few haggling skills and simply gave him all our dirhams, £30, a disposable camera and a Gap T-shirt for however much of the loot he would allow us to take. It was only as we began the descent to Taroudant – and this was coming down to earth with a vengeance, 5,000ft in 12 miles – that we began to doubt our wares. The coral beads seemed too massy and coarse for Western wear. And the amber ashtray – hadn't we read after all, that Moroccan 'amber' was often synthetic? Wouldn't we see dozens of the same in the airport souvenir shop? Then a twist in the road suddenly revealed the end of the journey, the vast open plain of the Sous, shimmering and green, and we felt that Morocco routinely makes you feel awed, child-like, as if at the start of a new adventure.

The Legend of Iron Joss

Against the Gravity of Sickness

Wasdale has the hardest, most masculine profile of any valley in the Lake District. At the head of it, a wet little hamlet with an inn and a field for climbers' tents shivers beneath a horseshoe of big, bare mountains, Yewbarrow, Kirk Fell, Great Gable, Lingmell and Scafell Pike, the highest in England; 'Oh my God,' gasped Coleridge, the first recreational fell-walker, pausing here in the summer of 1802, 'what enormous mountains these are behind me!' Its lake, Wast Water, though only four miles long, has the depth and gloom of Loch Ness. One bank of it is formed by the Screes, a rampart of rock half a mile high, in which broad red streaks are folded through the grey stone, the whole plunging and crumbling to the water's edge. On the opposite bank, with more fells massing behind, there is a solitary farmhouse, the home of Joss Naylor, sheep farmer, fell-runner and modern Lakeland hero: a man whose work and play is so bound up with the landscape he inhabits, you might compare him to Wordsworth's Lucy, 'Rolled round … with rocks and stones and trees', if only there were more trees; if only he were not so unrestingly alive, and so much less of a girl. Joss Naylor gets stuck in.

This midsummer weekend, for instance, 22–23 June, he will run up and down sixty peaks over 2,500ft, one for each of his sixty years, in thirty-six hours; leaving the gate on Walna Scar near Coniston at 3am on the Saturday and finishing in the car park at Glenridding on Ullswater at 3pm on Sunday; over 100 miles in distance, and over 40,000 feet of ascent, the equivalent of climbing and descending Everest, from sea level, one-and-a-half times. Not exactly a stroll in the country; but nothing out of the ordinary either for a man whose notion of pushing himself has shifted mountains for decades. The special toughness of the Wasdale character may come partly from its being cut off by its mountains from the softer lakes of Westmorland to the east, the cream teas and choking tourist traffic

of Ambleside, Grasmere, Hawkshead. You approach Wasdale instead
from the West Cumbrian coast, south from Workington or north from
Barrow-in-Furness, through grey towns and villages – Flimby, Frizington,
Drigg – of rusting rugby posts, abandoned workings and shops for sale.
I found this out, anyway, one autumn afternoon, by trying to take a cab
across the Lakes from Kendal station to Wasdale. Not twenty miles, as
the buzzard flies; but two hours later, the driver, who had never been to
Wasdale before, had a £50 fare and a double puncture. Joss Naylor could
have run it quicker.

Neither is there anything false or pretty or self-conscious about the
traditional sports and contests that go on at the Wasdale Show. This hap-
pens each year on the second Saturday in October, the last show in the
Lakeland calendar, the chilliest, drizzliest and heaviest-drinking. To lay
a hound trail, two runners head off in opposite directions, each dragging
'a sock full of other socks' soaked in aniseed, to meet somewhere half-
way round the course as the owners let their foxhounds off the leash. A
pair of Cumberland wrestlers, in their daft flowery knickers, lock to in a
mismatch: the grinning old hand upends the plump teenage apprentice
with friendly restraint. Prize sheep, big muttony Herdwicks, their coarse
grey fleeces dyed rosy red for the show, are bundled roughly back in the
wagon with the losers. And as the farmers disperse from the beer tent,
over the wavery PA a little girl sings a song, written by a local teacher, in
honour and praise of 'our Joss'.

And 'their Joss' is how they see him; everyone here is pleased to tell
you how they know him; proud, too, of his being not quite like them or
ourselves, invariably reaching for extra-human terms – a 'whippet', a
'cougar', a 'man of steel', a 'bionic shepherd' – to describe him. Arriving
at the show, I meant to ask where I could find him, but knew him as soon
as I saw him: the tall spare figure in the tracksuit, leaning in, sipping a
Mackeson and nodding in conversation but strikingly more alert and
intense than those around him, as if on the look-out for something in the
field to herd or hurdle. Fell-running projects the ordinary animal urge, to
go farther and faster, into territory that obstructs it: where tussocks and
peaty holes and sudden stones keep up a constant uneven percussion on
the knees and ankle-joints; through pathless tracts of boulders covered
with bracken and heather; and up on to sharp rocks that blister and bruise
the feet and cramp and shred toes. The weather, too, will attack you. Joss
Naylor describes running on consecutive days: one in dry mountain heat,

'like trying to stand close against a bonfire', when 'there was no sound but the rasping of air in your throat'; the next, of such pummelling horizontal rain that it made of his face a featureless balloon. There are extra surprises – clouds of midges, minutes-long, that invade the mouth, the nose, the ears; and the black joke of the summits, the oatmeal scatterings of old fell-walkers' ashes underfoot. And the best endure these not for hours but for days, pressing past exhaustion until, sleepless and swollen-jointed, the stumbler loses his appetite for food, his ability to swallow, and can only report, as Naylor did of one escapade with his blood-coughing support team, 'I do not have the words ... to describe the discomfort, the physical pain, the frustration, and worry we all had to suffer.'

Joss Naylor is famous because for a period of nearly twenty years he could absorb this suffering at a pace and for a duration that no one else could match; and because in the course of this supremacy, he performed new acts of resilience that demanded more than local astonishment, and so singlehandedly put fell-running on the national map. The strange explanation for Joss Naylor's unique capabilities is that for large parts of his early life he was literally immobile. Hampered from his childhood by a serious back condition, he took little part in sports as a boy. He left school at fifteen to help on his father's farm; he was deemed unfit for National Service. In 1954, when he was eighteen, he had an operation to remove the cartilage from his right knee. They made a mess of it, so that, ever since, this legendary runner has had a knee joint which doesn't work, which won't lock out straight, hence the peculiar pattering gait which has been his hallmark. (At sixty, he's just started a course of physiotherapy: 'It's much easier, like, I can stride out now.') In 1958, two discs were removed from his back at hospital in Manchester; he was six weeks encased there, and it was many months before he could usefully work again. Even after, he was in continual pain, and occasionally in a surgical jacket, until he was about forty: but by then he had become one of the outstanding long-distance athletes – if it is possible to compare fell with Alp or bush or track – in the world.

Since this medical history didn't deter him from endurance racing, it must instead have helped him to withstand its ordinary aches and pains. It certainly helps, on runs of twenty-four hours or more, to be able to do without sleep, as Joss Naylor's back forced him to learn to do. On runs of more than two days, he will take three hours' sleep a night on his mattress in the back of a van. Neither, by the way, is he too careful about his diet. 'I'll eat owt,' he says, meaning not that he prefers restaurants but that anything will do. In fact nothing will do him most of the working day – just water and a chocolate bar; on big runs, he will take mouthfuls of sweet rubbish, macaroni pudding, trifle, weak tea; and a few cans of stout at night. He doesn't, in a phrase, look after himself, but leaping bogs and crashing down scree requires its own kind of fitness. What he recognizes in himself is that he 'carries no weight' (at about 6ft and nine-and-a-bit stone, he is indeed 'as thin as that', as an admirer says, holding up a single finger) and that he has 'a tremendous amount of power': a power which is not built up in a gym or fuelled by food or rest, but seems in some slightly disquieting way to generate itself.

Joss Naylor first raced in the summer of 1961, when he saw a trial beginning near his father's farm at Wasdale Head. On impulse, he joined in in his work boots, led for eight miles until he got cramp, and had found what he wanted to do. By the time he was thirty, he was best on the circuit. In those days, fell-running was really only a local curiosity; but soon he began the sequence of record-breaking exploits that have helped the sport transcend its seemingly natural limitations. (In the Nineties, Lake District runners travelled to world championships in Italy and Switzerland.) He won the classic Mountain Trial, run annually round a different course, ten times ('It should have been more, but my navigation let me down'). Among his records are his coverage, in 1986 at the age of fifty, of all 214 of the summits listed in Alfred Wainwright's Lake District guides, in seven days, one hour and twenty-five minutes, clipping half a week off the existing record (it took Wainwright himself thirteen years). He says: 'I would have done it in six days, but I had trouble with my feet' – that is, the flesh on both ankles was cut through to the nerve. Asked which single run has given him the most pleasure, he chooses his Lakes, Meres and Waters record run of 1983: 'It was one of the most beautiful things I ever did, seeing every drop of water in the Lake District, twenty-seven of them in nineteen hours, just over. When we finished at Derwentwater, it was becoming dark, but we saw everything else in a single day's daylight – a beautiful clear June day it was, only a little bit of mist early on. That was something.' But ever since Bob Graham did his celebrated 'round' of forty-two peaks on 13 June 1932, the most coveted fell-running record has been for the number of peaks scaled inside twenty-four hours.

In July 1975, Joss Naylor ran through a heatwave Sunday to raise his own record by nine to a total of seventy-two peaks, an achievement that amazed the pacers melting in his wake ('He's just not human,' they said again), won him the MBE and seemed to set a record that would last forever. Now fell-runners generally support one another; much of Joss Naylor's running is done as back-up or as a guide for younger runners, literally as a shepherd to men. Neither would he be so popular in Cumbria if he were thought to be jealous of his achievements. But he knows his own strengths and how to measure others against them. When, in 1988, a young man called Mark McDermott took the 24-hour record, with a run of seventy-six peaks – when a lifetime's endurance was effaced by someone who seemed to have poured all his ability into a single day – it rankled. And it still rankles today. 'He's hardly won a race in his life, before or since – you'd think if he was capable of doing that, he'd be winning every big race in the country. And his training, two hours a night round a blooming football pitch, and coming out and doing a bit here at week-ends ...' Which are the sort of dark thoughts that will simmer away in a sport whose ground is determined by the participant, whose regulation is voluntary, sketchy, a matter in the end of good will. Was Joss Naylor never tempted then to test his mettle instead on the track or on the roads? 'Well, I could have done. I had the pace. But there was no sponsorship in athletics until I was about forty-three or forty-four, though I was running well then. And I couldn't have left the farm on a regular basis without sponsorship.'

So he has remained what he had always, as a boy, expected to be, a sheep farmer. As I arrived at his farm one Sunday afternoon in the lambing season – he'd been working a couple of hours since a five-hour run earlier – he was up to his elbows in blood performing the old trick to attach an orphaned lamb to a bereaved ewe; cutting the fleece from the dead lamb – 'nipped' by a fox, its stomach eaten out by crows – and fitting it over the other as a jacket. But it seems that the new generation of young dalesmen, even without many alternatives, are put off by the physical hardness and financial leanness of such a working life – that Joss Naylor may be one of the last of his kind. It's part of the aim of the National Trust – which 'protects' the whole of the Lake District, and which now owns, for instance, most of Wasdale – to maintain traditional land use where possible. But Joss is scornful of the Trust management. 'The footpath on Black Sail there, it was kept right by the council until 1970 – they used to go up twice a year, just, and there was no erosion at all. Now it's eroded to nothing. The Trust leave things too late. And you can't tell 'em. Sixteen or seventeen years ago, I went specially to see the man in charge of the area and told him exactly what was wrong – that when it comes quite a lot of rain, water washes over the footpath from this point to that point. I said "I'm sure one of your workers could put it right in a couple of hours." "Oh," he said, "you couldn't take a spade with you when you go out on one of your runs, could you?" Nothing was ever done, and it's meant thousands and thousands of pounds' worth of damage to a good bridleway.'

Joss and his wife, Mary, agree that things are improving, but only by dint of short-term measures. The Trust have their own maintenance teams of wallers – 'good wallers, some of them' – who go into farms and repair the dry-stone walls. 'So the farmers won't keep up that skill, and they won't be able to pass it on.' And as the trickle of trippers and climbers swells down the slopes, so the habit of labour in solitude that was the sheep farmer's exacting inheritance seems another thing that must erode away. For local people not involved in farming, employment choices boil down to tourism – if they have a property, for instance, to take advantage of the sporadic B&B trade hereabouts – or Sellafield, on the coast twelve miles to the west of Wasdale – again, if they're lucky. Joss Naylor himself, true to his place even in this, worked shifts for several years as a fitter's mate at Sellafield, enabled by his need for only a little sleep and enjoying the companionship (after sheep) of what his wife called the 'idiots' there – 'good lads, would do anything for you.'

British Nuclear Fuel's Sellafield site is a complex of 600 buildings over 480 acres, including the old atomic power station, Calder Hall, and the plutonium factory, formerly called Windscale. For fifty years, the nuclear industry has shielded the Cumbrian coast, whose coal and iron and shipbuilding industries petered out in the Thirties, from outright employment failure. There was even something of a boom time during the construction of the THORP reprocessing plant. At its height, there were 7,500 people at work there, half of them local. But since the plant became operational in 1992 only 2,000 are employed there. Sellafield itself, once known locally as the Holiday Camp on account of the light demands made of employees, is reducing its workforce from a peak of 8,000 to a projected 4,600 by the end of the century. Month by month, the fabric of the local towns registers the decline. So the attitude to Sellafield prevailing here is a grudging, provisional gratitude. Safety seems not to concern too many; perhaps because of the hundreds who lost their lives over the years in the old coal mines; perhaps again, as Mary points out, because 'we're sitting a few miles from Sellafield, and the only time there's been any fall-out here it's come from the Ukraine.'

Yet, despite the brave-new-world ambitions embodied in the visitors' centre at Sellafield, the nuclear and tourist industries are hard to reconcile. The little Victorian resort of Seascale, a couple of miles to the south, was a thriving place, with bathing and golf and a sizeable hotel, the Sca Fell. Then, in 1983, in the so-called Beach Incident, radioactive discharge was washed back from the Irish Sea in a crud. The beach at Seascale was closed to the public for six months and beachcombing went out of fashion for good. In the same year, a Yorkshire TV investigation found an incidence of leukaemia and other cancers ten times the normal. The subsequent Gardner report, published in 1990, established a link between men working at Sellafield and cancers in their children. Vivien Hope, the daughter of a Sellafield fitter and a resident of Seascale, fell ill in 1988 with Hodgkin's lymphoma; surviving her illness, she has since sued BNFL, unsuccessfully, for damages for personal injury. Yet she has now returned to work at Sellafield as a clerical assistant. As she says: 'There's nowhere else to work round here.' The Sca Fell Hotel, which had been shutting down room by room, pipes bursting everywhere, closed completely over last winter.

The new hope for the area, if hope is the term, is the NIREX project of a dump for the dry storage of spent nuclear fuel, to be bored 650 metres beneath sea level, somewhere near Sellafield; there because, as an adjunct to Vivien Hope's resignation about her job opportunities, 'no other part of the country will accept it'. The first site to be explored lies between Sellafield and the village of Gosforth on the very edge of the Lake District National Park. But should the geology here prove unsatisfactory, NIREX will seek permission to drill in the National Park itself, 'beneath the fells to the east of Gosforth'; that is, under Joss Naylor's 140 rocky acres. Joss's announcement of his sixty-peak marathon represents a comeback not much less dramatic than Vivien Hope's. Four years ago, spraying sheep after shearing them, he inhaled sheep-dip, whose toxic effects on humans have been highlighted in other recent cases:

> I had a dust mask there, but I got careless and didn't put it on, and I was breathing these particles in, for about three weeks. And I just gradually got that way that I could hardly catch sheep, and all the power had gone from my body. I was still running a bit, but just going through the motions, and

I got real low, like. It's taken about three year to get it all out of my system but I was lucky to get away with it, lucky I didn't get enough in my system to drag me right down, like …

When Joss Naylor did his Wainwright round in 1986, the money raised went to fight arthritis; for his new sixty-peak attempt, it's Multiple Sclerosis: another aspect of his cussed, on-going crusade against paralysis and decay. And when this champion, his energies restored and harnessed for charity, steps out and up from Walna Scar in the dark that early morning, the lights of Sellafield a faint glow to the west, he scores one more outrageous victory in the battle we're all involved in: to set our power, while we've still got it, against the gravity of sickness.

Away From It All

A Modern Hardyesque

Tamara Drewe
Posy Simmonds, Jonathan Cape

There is a revealing if not quite romantic story about the illustration of Thomas Hardy's *Far from the Madding Crowd* – his tale of contending suits and the wrong marriage. The novel first appeared as a serial in the *Cornhill* magazine, running in twelve monthly instalments from January 1874. The magazine's editor, Leslie Stephen, adorned the text with a series of woodcuts he had commissioned from Helen Paterson, a highly regarded former pupil of Frederic Leighton's. When novelist and illustrator met in person for the first and (as far as we know) only time, at the Pall Mall Cafe in May 1874, she was twenty-six, and he thirty-four; each was engaged to be married that August, Helen to the Irish poet William Allingham, a man of fifty, Hardy to his long-term fiancée Emma Gifford. Whatever was said at the dinner, she subsequently declined his invitation to further work – on *A Laodicean* – claiming she had given up book illustration for good.

As late as 1906, however, when the widow Helen Paterson Allingham was a well-known watercolourist, Hardy described her ruefully in a letter to Edmund Gosse as 'the best illustrator I ever had'; the letter goes on to surmise, with a huff of profanity, that 'these two simultaneous weddings would have been one but for a stupid blunder of God Almighty'. And it is to Mrs Allingham – or 'H. P.', as she is designated there – that Hardy dedicates a poem of 1914, called 'The Opportunity', where she is cast as one of those missed chances on which he liked to dwell. The third stanza runs,

Had we but mused a little space
At that critical date in the Maytime,
One life had been ours, one space,
Perhaps, till our long cold claytime.

Tamara Drewe is the second of Posy Simmonds's graphic novels, after *Gemma Bovery* (1999), to base itself on a classic work of fiction; and it is tempting to propose it as the perfect match between text and picture. Simmonds first came to fame as a cartoonist for the *Guardian*, where *Tamara* appeared last year as a weekly feature; and her visual invention, enhanced here by a step from monochrome into colour, may still take the lead: her shrewdest characterization is done in clothes. But the book will take as long to 'read' as many an ordinary novel, and its single most impressive attribute is the brilliant management of what would be termed, in a purely literary context, the plot.

The first page of artwork presents an advertisement, torn from the classified section of a literary journal, which at once points to the source: 'Far from the Madding Crowd. Working retreat for writers. Easy access M96'. (Readers can adjust to the sharpness of the detailing ahead by discovering that the 'M96' is a crash-test site in the Cotswolds.) The village is Ewedown, the postal district (as glimpsed on a letterhead) is Bournemouth: we might call the setting Wessex. The retreat is run by Beth Hardiman (there is plenty of gentle wordplay), a good, busy, unglamorous woman of fifty, who is also required to manage the life of her husband Nicholas, creator of the lucrative series of 'Doctor Inchcombe' detective novels. (Nicholas 'likes to show off to women', and as the book opens he is guiding his wife through the ruins of his latest affair in publishing, with Nadia from foreign rights – 'I won't lie. She was important to me'.)

In this nest of authors, Beth is one of four characters whose informal diaries and scrapbook recollections are the means through which the story emerges. The others are Glen Larson, an American academic in semi-permanent residence, an inert, spongey presence and mild opportunist; Casey, a teenage girl from the council houses with no expectations, who reports the incursions into the plot of her more adventurous friend, Jody; and Tamara Drewe herself – the counterpart of Hardy's Bathsheba Everdene – who has returned to the village on the death of her mother to take over the farmhouse they bought there, and to write an undemanding column about it for the *Monitor*. (Her own urban 'improvement', in Hardy's term, is symbolized by the surgeon's reduction of her rustic 'hooter' to a neat little modern nose.)

Like Bathsheba, Tamara has her affections pulled three ways. The flashy, irresponsible Sergeant Troy is refigured as Ben, the former drummer of the band Swipe, the connection picked out in a scarlet jacket worn on the band's promotional photos. Ben is an unshaven layabout with a rank philosophy ('Life's a shit sandwich sometimes') and a yellow Porsche; like Troy, he becomes involved with the heroine while sulkily fixed on an old flame. Alone of the characters here, he is shown to make nothing: not literature of any kind; not Beth's cakes and dinners; not Jody's fantasies of love beyond her station; not even the songs he once wrote for his band; only money. Yet Ben is no Victorian villain either, for he deals clumsily but decently with the overflow of Jody's infatuation. And as he withdraws from Tamara's bed, Nicholas Hardiman moves in, with squirearchical certainty. Waiting by various gates and cabbage patches, meanwhile, is the uprooted Gabriel Oak figure of Andy Cobb, with his bouquet of 'earth, dog, tobacco, engine oil', gardener to the incomers and conscience of the village, ready to rake up the pieces.

But to approach this book through reference to Hardy's novel risks neglecting its richness, its originality, its very particular imaginative coherence. For one thing, the plot is propelled by modern gadgetry. Liaisons are 'papped' on 'mobies'. Young Jody sets the whole thing racing by breaking into Tamara's house and computer to send her potent version of Bathsheba's valentine: an email to Ben, subject 'Love', cc'd to Nicholas and Andy, reproduced here in Arial 10pt, reading 'I want to give you the biggest shagging of your life'. And a consumer product new to the market proves a fatal instrument.

If there was a time when what Posy Simmonds seemed to offer was an 'entertaining satire on the middle classes', that limitation no longer applies. There is nothing in Hardy, you might say, which more grimly conveys the paralysis of lesser rural life than her pictures of Casey and Jody at the old bus shelter. Andy Cobb laments that Ewedown now has 'no shop, no bus, no post office', but it is the teenage population who have to act out the consequences: 'We were going to get a lift into Hadditon with Jody's mum, but decide not to – we're skint, it's freezing, and getting back means staying there bloody hours till her mum finishes her shift at Tesco'. On the verbal side, Posy Simmonds has the knack of rendering particular idioms, such as the vinegary flavour of the kids' 'sex' talk, without overdoing it: 'Furthest she's ever gone was with Sam. Clothes on, zip stuff. Patted the dog through the letterbox'; 'Ryan's been standing there porking out on Quavers'. There is real punch, too, in Jody's burst of anger at Nicholas because 'he's a cheater, like my dad'. Then, just as Casey has amazed herself by stumbling on a modest romance of her own – 'When Ryan throws his ciggie down I throw mine down too' – their first kiss is illuminated by the arrival of an ambulance in Aspen Close.

When, on stage at the Monksted Literary Festival, rattled by the presence in the audience of both wife and girlfriend, Nicholas announces the death of his detective Inchcombe, 'a gust of dismay' blows through the gathering, 'as though a real death's been announced'. Readers may feel a similar jolt as this book reaches its double climax. But it is now part of Posy Simmonds's repertoire as a storyteller to shock and disturb. That said, one of the book's fatalities is treated, rather charmingly, in the spirit of its victim, as a murder mystery. The autopsy reveals death by 'multiple injuries inflicted by the cows' – a spooked herd of Belted Galloways – 'and a collision with the water trough'. But the quiet American – cake-eating, feet-up Glen – has secrets of his own.

INTERVIEW

With *Oxford Poetry*

The following is an interview Mick Imlah (MI) gave with Nicholas Jenkins (NJ) which appeared in a 1983 edition of *Oxford Poetry*.

NJ: *Many poets questioned about their 'influences' tend to name only twentieth-century predecessors. Why is that?*

MI: 'Influence' is a word poets tend to apply to something they've grown out of; Larkin's *North Ship* is a classic case of influence. I don't think it's a very fruitful way of approaching a writer. It suggests that their main inspiration is a literary one. Critics will often try to find your poems like someone else's because it makes their job easier – that's lazy and frequently false. They make similarity sound like plagiarism. You can borrow someone else's style to get your poem written, and yet it can be quite individual. I've always liked Tennyson more than most people seem to. I don't think I write like him. I don't know why, or if, people cite their twentieth-century favourites – I suppose to claim Shakespeare as an influence is redundant or facetious.

NJ: *But has there been, do you think, a break with traditional techniques?*

MI: What, since I was born? The reaction to modernism was well entrenched by then. Free verse is just another option. Today's poet is a bit like a Victorian architect; there's no single staple native style available (as, say, the heroic couplet was for Pope) so he has to choose a model for each piece of work: Middle Pointed Gothic, neo-Egyptian, blank verse, this or that kind of stanza, silly one-word lines, whatever. Everyone knows it isn't the real thing, that there's an element of exercise about it, but it's better than rubble. I don't like poems which look like rubble. And I think this self-consciousness and versatility is a good thing in poetry; unlike a town, a book of poems looks better for a mixture of styles.

NJ: *Do you not then feel part of any general poetic, or social, movement? Or part of a particular tradition?*

MI: No. I don't think many writers enjoy being labelled in that way, and they certainly don't do it to themselves.

NJ: *I know you think of yourself as a Scot. Does the fact of being Scots, or British, or English mean anything to you, or your poems?*

MI: My family moved south from Glasgow when I was ten, so the most important part of my upbringing was English; I developed an inconspicuous accent quite quickly, though I still have the other one up my sleeve like a dirk for tight comers. I suppose I only feel Scots on major sporting occasions now. It's not something I'd write about.

    I also have a gimmicky nostalgia for England as I imagine it was between the wars, or before concrete buildings, or whenever. One of my favourite books is a 1949 Batsford Book called *The Counties of England*, full of the charm of Rutland etc. I found the idea of a recent TV programme called 'The Beauties of Northamptonshire' appealing, though I couldn't watch it. Such things are good showoff material. Quite often I lament the felling of the elms in the Suffolk village of Long Melford, which I learn from the Batsford Book were very fine, thought I don't know whether the elms have been felled or not, and I haven't been to Long Melford. I suppose if I had I wouldn't feel so warmly about it; a church and a bunch of trees. Not travelling has its own glamour; if I could drive, for example, I could knock off the beauties of Northamptonshire in a weekend. It's the places I haven't been that are interesting to me.

    There's something of this in the imaginary travel poems that I write, which recount variously plausible adventures in places which may or may not exist: 'Brawl in Co. Kerry', 'Visiting St. Anthony', 'At the Grave of Michael Hofmann' and others. The pleasure is in the pretending. I spent a month in America recently, and enjoyed it, but I didn't want to write about it. In this respect experience can be confining, almost a handicap.

NJ: *To what extent do you think the monologue relies on the common nature of intimate experiences? Or would you call the dreamy world of your poems a new one?*

MI: I suppose 'dreamy', taken literally, is the right word. I don't think I approve of using dreams in poems, but I do it. About half the poems refer to them, or at least to that grey area between waking and sleeping. The narrators are often in and out of bed because that's where I get the ideas for their poems. Sometimes I try to bring them on; in the past, if I've had a free weekend, I've eaten lumps of cheese before sleeping because that's meant to stir up vivid dreams. A well-judged hangover can be equally fruitful. 'Abortion' suggests that the process of recovery or resurrection is only a delusion, and that you really are doomed by having drunk so much. (Of course it's also about abortion; not in any League Against Cruel Sports way, just an effort to imagine what it feels like, the would-be-sinister point being that it isn't felt, though they say now the embryo can tingle at four weeks.) Another longer sequence, 'The Drinking Race', stems from my waking up once, after a drink or two, having dreamt vividly the taste of human blood. It stayed with me for days; very rich. It could have been the taste of rusty tap-water, but it was called blood in the dream. That's the kind of productively unpleasant state you have to bring on.

NJ: *Your poems, in their energy and sonorousness, seem to relish the frail and misconstruing characteristics of the narrators. Why is that?*

MI: I'm not so interested in my narrators, theoretically, as you suggest. I write in the first person because I find I like to consider a poem as a statement made by someone, whether in a speech to someone else, or in a written narrative. There are different degrees of characterization. 'Quasimodo' and 'The Zoologist's Bath' are dramatic speeches, happening in a specified time and place; the hunchback speaks to the sleeping girl until she wakes up, the Zoologist soliloquizes for the duration of his bath. The interest isn't really in the characterization. The hunchback's mind is a fairly obvious place to set a meditation on beauty, and his body is a physical representation of the kind of self-doubt or disqualification everyone feels in certain relationships. The Zoologist is an exceptional case – his mind is the object of the parody – but there's more than one voice even so; a comic anachronistic register ('You're in the Deluge, right?') offsets a more serious attempt to mimic the happy mania of religious argument.

My narrators are becoming more thinly drawn, since I've moved away from dramatic speech towards fictional narrative. The narrators of 'St. Anthony' and 'Doing It' are meant to be thirty years apart in age, but there's only a slight difference in tone – a certain worn-out cynicism in the one, an overreacting priggishness in the other.

NJ: *You tend to write relatively slowly. Has this anything to do with a problem in accommodating private experience into a fictional context?*

MI: Why's that a problem? Do you think my poetry is especially defensive of its origins?

NJ: *Perhaps.*

MI: But what are the origins? No-one's interested in a student not being able to get to sleep. You're protecting the reader as much as yourself by working your insomnia into a myth. And poems soon detach themselves from whatever provoked them; they're not a secret therapy, and they're not a coded version of the poet's life. Still, even if they only reveal themselves, it's a worry when they're nearly finished, because they're what you do, and you want to be thought good at it. I don't like sending things out for public display with holes or patches. So I revise, much too much. In the quest for polish or evenness you can rewrite the life out of a thing. Revision – mine, anyway – tends to substitute the elaborate for the simple; trying to turn everything into a flashy 'good bit'. In 'Quasimodo', for example, I replaced the hunchback's desire for a simple exchange of affection with the girl ('To greet you with a smile, and get a smile') with a reference to his role as a scorned provider of food ('To greet you with a face, and not a plate') – because I thought the latter was smarter, funnier. I can see now that the first version was truer to the character's situation and idiom, and that the second interrupts the momentum of his fantasy. I suppose this connects back to your question, if it's a case of allowing the way I wanted to appear personally (i.e. not soft or naive) to interfere with a sentimental poem. So you may be right after all.

NJ: *What sort of poems do you want to write now?*

MI: I don't know that many poets have that much control. You might as well ask me to design my children – not that I think of my poems as children. I don't much like the 'sort of poem' I've been writing lately; they're nasty, lurid, not colourful. They take place in alleys and toilets in places like Norwood. I yearn for the open air.

NJ: *Your personae often seem motivated by a need to relate an experience they cannot define. It's noticeable that many poems evade a clinching final statement. How do you think this relates to the tensions between poet and fictional character?*

MI: Evasion seems the natural way to do it – I don't know what I'd want to clinch. Maybe the end of 'Abortion' is an example of what you mean. There's meant to be a tension between what the reader understands to be happening, and what the hero thinks:

> I was doubled-up in air, but couldn't breathe,
> And dizzy I saw an experiment
> With magnets, me the broken one,
> A horseshoe facing down,
> Sucked up. I passed clean out
> And was lucky to survive: the boat
> Melted in blood, but I stiffened safely,
> A rabbit's foot, gristly
> In someone's cabinet.

We think the hero misjudges his fate to see it in terms of good luck charms, and to call it survival. But his thumbs-up is also meant reciprocally to alter our view. The cabinet can be the mind of the parent, a display case, the place where people shut away secret medications, or the loo where things get flushed away. 'Brawl in Co. Kerry' is an anecdote about a bar brawl with a spooky pretentious ending. The narrator and his girlfriend have escaped a clumsy assault feeling very English:

> She and the moon
>
> Blinked at each other through the mottled speed
> Of fugitive clouds; and from the walled-up fields
> There came a sound like a host's embarrassed cough,
> The formal tick tick of the tongueless cricket.

This tries to present the complexity of Ireland's attitude to its guests, and of the visitors' view of the hospitality they receive, without saying anything about either.

The avoidance of simplification or judgement may be criticized in a poem called 'Justice' which is an extreme case of relativism. It deals with the most unpleasant assault I could imagine, which was actually a real one, and proceeds through a series of legal clichés to blame the five-year-old victim for what happens to him. 'Justice' hates all the protagonists. The force of the poem may therefore be that we need more authority, more 'clinching statement' – but I don't think it reads that way.

NJ: *What do you feel about James Fenton's idea of a poem that has an intrinsically interesting subject?*

MI: I think it's an excellent idea.

NJ: *Your work seems to raise that possibility and then deny it.*

MI: You mean that you find my titles more interesting than my poems? Fair enough. Titles are pure suggestion. I'd like to write a book of them. 'War: A Comic History.' 'Love On All Fours.' 'Heaven.' I like big, bold titles to go with oblique poems that don't do the discursive work you've been led to expect. I've learned the importance of titles from reading manuscripts at *Poetry Review*: 'Fantasy.' 'Waiting For The Bus.' 'The Old Man.' Then you get the ones that think they're punchy – 'Socks.' 'Sex.' 'Implosion.' 'Brixton 1981.' – Or sophisticated: 'Play of Light in New Hampshire (for Harriet).' You have to read them through, of course, but a poem never recovers from a bad title. Look at 'The Zoologist's Bath.' A poet like Dick Davis, a good poet, is more or less unreadable because of his titles. You have to be careful; very careful.

Acknowledgments

The editors would like to express their gratitude to Alan Hollinghurst and Mark Ford, the co-executors of Mick Imlah's literary estate, for their kindness and confidence; as well as to Maren Meinhardt, Jane Wellesley, John Fuller, Bernard O'Donoghue, Alan Jenkins and Christabel Scaife, our editor at Peter Lang.

Acknowledgment is gratefully made to the editors of the following periodicals and publications in which these pieces have appeared.

ON WRITERS

Blind Harry and Robert Baston	'A Burel Broth', *TLS* 20 August 2004; Issue No: 5290
Walter Scott	'This Right Hand'; *TLS* 12 August 2005; Issue No: 5341
Alfred, Lord Tennyson	Introduction to *Alfred, Lord Tennyson: Poet to Poet* Faber and Faber (2004)
Anthony Trollope	Introduction to *Dr Wortle's School* Penguin Classics (1999)
Matthew Arnold	'A Poet Aged Before his Time'; *TLS* 4 September 1998; Issue No: 4979
James Thomson ('B. V.')	'Sad Days in the City of Dreadful Night'; *Independent on Sunday*, 13 February 1993
A. C. Swinburne	'Swallowed by the Sea'; *TLS* 27 February 1998; Issue No: 4952
Robert Bridges	'You are Old, Doctor Bridges' *Independent on Sunday*, 9 August 1992
S. R. Crockett	'Where the Whaups are Crying'; *TLS* 18 October 2002; Issue No: 5194

J. M. Barrie	'Lost Boys, Lost Plays'; *TLS* 11 August 2000; Issue No: 5080
W. B. Yeats	'A Genius, A Fool'; *TLS* 11 April 1997; Issue No: 4906
Laurence Binyon	'In his Master's Moonlight'; *TLS* 05 July 1996; Issue No: 4866
G. K. Chesterton	Review of *Poems for all Purposes*; *TLS* 10 March 1995; Issue No: 4797
John Buchan	'A Pretty Turn of Speed'; *TLS* 10 August 2001; Issue No: 5132
Edwin Muir	Introduction to *Edwin Muir, Selected Poems* Faber and Faber (2008)
'In the Dorian Mood'	*TLS*, 16 June 1995; Issue No: 4811
Robert Graves	'Unrest Cure'; *Guardian* 17 December 1995
Graham Greene	'The Chap Who Told Tales in his Sleep' *Independent on Sunday*, 15 November 1992
Henry Green	'Dash and Melancholy'; *TLS* 13 October 2000; Issue No: 5089 Review of Doting; *TLS* 25 December 1998; Issue No: 4995
Gavin Ewart	Review of *Selected Poems 1933–93*; *Observer*, 7 July 1996
Philip Larkin	'Selfishly yours, Philip'; *TLS* 23 October 1992; Issue No: 4673
Christopher Logue	Review / Profile; *Punch* 22–28 March 1997
Harold Pinter	'The Chaotic Energies of Youth'; *TLS* 5 October 1990; Issue No: 4566
Alasdair Gray	'Autumn Leaves'; *TLS* 28 November 2003; Issue No: 5252
Tony Harrison	'Dead Men's Mouths'; *TLS* 11 August 1995; Issue No: 4819
Ian Hamilton	'Other Men's Glowers'; *TLS* 19 April 2002; Issue No: 5168

Seamus Heaney	'Nostalgia for World Culture'; *Independent on Sunday*, 10 September 1995
Douglas Dunn	'Grave and Muffled Beats'; *Independent on Sunday*, 16 January 1994
Julian Barnes	'Revenge of a Tortoise'; *TLS* 28 July 2000; Issue No: 5078
James Kelman	'After Closing Time'; *TLS* 14 August 1998; Issue No: 4974
Peter Reading	'Thanoptic Designs'; *TLS* 4 January 1985; Issue No: 4266
Christopher Reid	'Modest Metaphors and Tiddly Riddles' *Independent on Sunday*, 8 September 1991
Martin Amis	'Return Ticket to Auschwitz' *Independent on Sunday*, 22 September 1991
Paul Muldoon	'Abandoned Origins'; *TLS* 4 September 1987; Issue No: 4405
John Burnside	'A Connoisseur of Rain'; *TLS* 7 May 1999; Issue No: 5014
Michael Hofmann	'No Pop, Still Fizzy'; *Independent on Sunday*, 3 October 1993
Irvine Welsh	'In a Chemical World'; *TLS* 7 June 1996; Issue No: 4862
Douglas Galbraith	'Taking tincture with "Claret Colquhoun"' *Observer*, 10 September 2000
'Auld Acquaintances'	*Guardian*, 23 January, 1997
'I Belong to Glasgow'	*TLS*, 15 August 2003; Issue No: 5237

DIGRESSIONS

'Bottle Fatigue'	*Observer*, 24 December 1995
'In Praise of Ugly Bugs'	*Observer*, 24 September 1995

'Don't Fly Me'   *TLS*, 21 November 1997; Issue No: 4938
On Cricket   'Sir Cricket's Long Innings'; *TLS*
                                        24 July 1998; Issue No: 4973
                                        'Captain Cheerless'; *TLS*
                                        6 December 1996; Issue No: 4888
                                        'At Close of Play'; *TLS*
                                        14 July 1995; Issue No: 4815
                                        'A Mercurial Life'; *TLS*
                                        23 July 1999; Issue No: 5025
On Rugby   'Goodbye to all that low tackling'; *TLS*
                                        6 February 2004; Issue No: 5262
'The Road from Marrakesh'   *Condé Nast Traveller*; April 1998
'The Legend of Iron Joss'   *Independent on Sunday*
                                        9 June 1996
'Away from it All'   *TLS*, 16 November 2007; Issue No:
                                        5459

INTERVIEW

with Nicholas Jenkins   *Oxford Poetry*; Vol. I; Issue 2, 1983

Index